LIKE A MIGHTY ARMY

A HISTORY OF THE CHURCH OF GOD

BOOKS BY CHARLES W. CONN

Like a Mighty Army (1955)

Pillars of Pentecost (1956)

The Evangel Reader (1958)

Where the Saints Have Trod (1959)

The Rudder and the Rock (1960)

The Bible: Book of Books (1961)

A Guide to the Pentateuch (1963)

Christ and the Gospels (1964)

A Certain Journey (1965)

Acts of the Apostles (1965)

Why Men Go Back (1966)

A Survey of the Epistles (1969)

The Pointed Pen (1973)

Highlights of Hebrew History (1975)

A Balanced Church (1975)

LIKE A

Charles W. Conn

MIGHTY ARMY

Revised Edition

A HISTORY OF THE CHURCH OF GOD

1886-1976

PATHWAY PRESS
CLEVELAND, TENNESSEE 1977

289.94

LIKE A MIGHTY ARMY
Copyright, 1977, by Pathway Press
All rights reserved

REVISED EDITION
First Printing

Library of Congress Catalog Card Number: 77-82067
ISBN: 0-87148-510-9

Set in Fairfield Medium type and printed by
Pathway Press, Cleveland, Tennessee

*In gratitude that early in life she chose to lay aside her
private ambitions to share those of her husband, and
because she has by her quiet, calm confidence
in God been a fountain of inspiration and
pillar of strength to him, this book
is affectionately dedicated to*

MY   BELOVED   EDNA,

*whose   delight   in   life   is   to
bear   up   in   prayer   the   members   of
her household, and in whom are embodied
the Christian graces of a virtuous woman, the
heart of whose husband doth safely trust in her, and
whose twelve adoring children rise up and call her blessed.*

CITATION

In recognition of his contributions to the heritage and lore of the Church of God, the Executive Council named Dr. Charles W. Conn the first official Church Historian in January 1977.

Whereas Dr. Charles W. Conn has made significant contributions to the body of Pentecostal literature; and

Whereas thousands of hours have been dedicated to historical research with the objective of preserving the rich and illustrious history of the Church of God and to give direction to its future; and

Whereas he has received worldwide acclaim for ability in this field; and

Whereas he has authored three books of Church of God history, namely, *Like a Mighty Army,* the history of the Church of God; *Where the Saints Have Trod,* the history of Church of God World Missions; and *The Evangel Reader,* a history of the editorial and publishing ministry of the Church of God; and

Whereas, Like a Mighty Army has now been revised and updated by him after three years of intensive research,

Therefore Be It Resolved That this General Executive Council, in session on the twelfth day of January, 1977, designate Charles W. Conn as Historian of the Church of God.

THE EXECUTIVE COUNCIL

January 12, 1977

FOREWORD

Writing history with a heart is something of an achievement, and in this Historian Charles W. Conn has achieved remarkably well. In *Like a Mighty Army* he has traced the history of the Church of God from its obscure origins to its present place of far-reaching influence in the Christian world. Since the turn of the century the Church has been in the vanguard of the Pentecostal Revival, one of the most significant spiritual renewals in Christian history.

The Church of God began with the conviction of a number of people in the mountains of Tennessee and North Carolina that the existing denominations had become spiritually decadent and were in need of reformation and revival. The fruit of this conviction was a fresh outpouring of the scriptural baptism of the Holy Spirit. The historian's assignment was to examine the record of that conviction and follow its course from its beginning to the present time. The result is an absorbing account of how God gave life and hope and growth to men of faith in this century. From its stark and tenuous roots the Church of God has experienced ninety years of phenomenal growth; it is in fact a phenomenon of growth, and its history is the story of a miracle.

To give cohesion and perspective to his comprehensive study, the author traces the aspiration of the Pentecostal followers backward into a renewal of The Upper Room experience and forward into an application of that experience in modern life. Under the author's persuasive style it is seen how the primal faith of the Church of God has been kept singularly stable and effective through the pressures of unrelenting conflict and trial.

We regard *Like a Mighty Army* to be a classic of historical writing, a work of art. It is easy to imagine what persistent labors the author poured into its research and transmission to written form. One can easily see the exhausting hours of interviews with people with hazy memories, of poring over faded and fragile records, of sifting the significant from the trivial and redundant, and of organizing the whole into a flowing, readable account. The author's success in such an undertaking suggests that he was spiritually anointed for his task. Those who worked closest with him during the research and writing hold a conviction that the author was often guided by what writers call inspiration and preachers call anointing.

If Dr. Conn has written a history with a heart, perhaps it is because his heart is so much a part of what he has written. He has been no mere observer of the events he has described but rather a deep and vital part of them. He has done more than record history; he has helped to make it.

We, the Executive Council of the Church of God, present this monumental historical work to the public with gratitude to God for His blessings and guidance which are so much a part of our heritage. We commend this revised edition of a much-acclaimed work to all who would know more about the ways of God in the affairs of men.

THE EXECUTIVE COUNCIL

March 1977

§ 6. AFRICA

It was not until 1938 that Church of God missionaries entered "The Dark Continent."* At the Assembly of 1937 (Thirty-second) Edmond and Pearl Stark offered their services to the Missions Board for Angola, Portuguese West Africa. Stark, a native of Oklahoma, had been a member of the Church of God for many years, but his wife, formerly Miss Pearl M. Pickel, had served previously as a missionary to Africa for the Assemblies of God. Back in America, while teaching in a Bible school of that denomination, her health became very bad. She believed that her illness was caused by her being out of God's will and was convinced that she should return to Africa. Edmond Stark also felt a divine call to Africa, so when they were married, she joined the Church of God and they presented themselves to the Missions Board.

On April 7, 1938, the Starks sailed for Angola, a humid land south of the equator. Waiting to hear the gospel in this Portuguese colony were three and a half-million souls. The young missionary couple entered their work with great energy and within a short time had a mission station well organized. Stark taught the natives handcraft along with the primary spiritual truths. The Angolan work was a success from the outset.

After nine months' ministry among the natives, Stark was stricken with a tropical fever. Days of mental anguish followed. Day and night for over two weeks Pearl Stark nursed her de-

---

months before December, I tried to persuade Brother Pitt to take a furlough and come back to America for a rest and change. Somehow, he didn't feel led to do it."

With that, a shroud of silence fell, as all communication was cut off. The Church tried in vain to get communication and finance to Pitt, pursuing every likelihood and failing in each. When the war was over, the Church learned that the brave and selfless man, whom they had never seen but dearly loved, had died during the Japanese occupation. The "Bamboo Curtain" that came with post-World War II Communism to China prohibited the Bethany Mission from further direct communication with the Church of God.

*There seems to have been an abortive and premature attempt to establish a work there in 1926-1927. A party of eight assayed to reach Ougadougou, French West Africa, but sickness and insufficient funds brought the attempt to an end. (Conn, *Where the Saints Have Trod*, pp. 24, 25.)

lirious husband all alone.[17] With their black friends to assist her in her struggle to save his life, this brave lady prayed and hoped until the last wisp of hope was snuffed out. On March 22, 1939, Stark died and was buried on the field for which he held such compassion. Mrs. Stark poignantly related to the *Evangel* at the time: "Just two days before he passed away he had been asleep for a few minutes and awoke suddenly with such a worried look on his face, then said, 'Oh, I am so glad we are still here in Africa. I dreamed I was on a steamer going home and we were almost there. It made me feel so sad to think I had started back home, but I am so glad it was not true. We did not come out here to go home, did we? We are here for Jesus' sake and I am glad.' "[*] His wife returned to the United States because the Missions Board was reluctant at that time to permit a woman to remain alone in Africa.[†] With such heroic self-sacrifice to inspire it, the Church of God became more and more conscious of other nations around the world and of its commission to teach them. The obsession of the Church became one of planting the Pentecostal message in all the world.

---

17. Simmons, *op. cit.,* p. 138.

*A missionary of another denomination in Angola wrote to the Church of God concerning Stark: "His short nine months in Angola were not in vain; his zeal for God and his work was a rebuke to us all . . . he was a ripe Christian, one who loved God, His Word, and His people, and I feel that we are all the better Christians through getting to know him closely." *Church of God Evangel,* May 6, 1939, p. 6.

† Until 1948, Pearl M. Stark traveled in behalf of world missions, longing to return to her Angola. She was finally permitted to return in February, 1948.

Chapter 23
THE PERSISTENT VISION

§ 1. THE INCONVENIENCE OF PROGRESS

While the Church was extending its ministry into distant parts of the world, it also strengthened its bases in the homeland. Improvement always brings its inconvenience, when usual procedures must be amended and deterring sentiment must be swept from the path of progress. The Church of God entered its metamorphic period of change and experimentation gradually as its growth and perspectives demanded it. The period dates roughly from the time the Assemblies moved from Cleveland to Chattanooga, and has continued to the present day; it represents a constant effort to keep pace with the growth God has given the organization. Physical assets of the Church become quickly outgrown or outdated. An organizational structure well-balanced one year may be inadequate for smoothest operation a few years later. Progress is disturbing to sentimentalists and romanticists, but it is the inevitable fruit of people with a vision. The Church of God was driven by a vision—a vision to reach the lost in all the world, to learn of Him whose burden is light, to become fathers and mothers to the fatherless, and to fulfill all the Word of God.

§ 2. A PLACE FOR WOMEN

At the Assembly of 1936 (Thirty-first) the national ladies' auxiliary of the Church came into being. From the earliest days of the Church women were used freely as evangelists and church workers; numerous local churches came into being through the tears and labors of consecrated handmaidens of the Lord. Regarded as co-workers in the evangelization of the unconverted, women were permitted a restricted ministry which did not include ordination.* Even though there were numerous women preachers, there was no official organization for the women laity. Several states sponsored statewide ladies' societies under such names as "Ladies' Prayer Band," "Women's Circle," and "Dorcas Circle."[1] Mrs. S. J. Wood, wife of the overseer of Oklahoma, is regarded as the chief organizer of these local societies and the principal proponent of a national ladies' organization.

The national women's auxiliary formulated by the 1936 Assembly was named "Ladies' Willing Workers' Band." Each local band was to

> . . . meet each week, or as often as convenient, to engage in such legitimate pursuits as may seem profitable to raise funds to be disbursed in behalf of the local church needs. [2]

This did not restrict other local ladies' societies, in lieu of or in addition to the national society. The work of the women in the Church of God has made an incalculable contribution to its material expansion. Through the Ladies' Auxiliary, as it was renamed in 1972, impoverished pastors have been financially supplemented, parsonages have been built, bought, or furnished, missions have been supported, churches have been redecorated or remodeled, church extension work has been sponsored, and other projects wrought or made possible. The work has not been altogether material and physical, for many local women's groups meet for devotions, for sessions of prayer, for distribution of tracts and other literature, for home and hospital visitation, or for other charitable and benevolent purposes.

By virtue of her position, the wife of each state overseer

---

1. Simmons, *op. cit.*, p. 71.
2. *Minutes of the Thirty-first Annual Assembly,* 1936, p. 35.
*Women preachers may not perform marriages, baptize, conduct business conferences, administer the sacrament, or "usurp authority over the man." They may not be ordained and have no voice in the General Assembly business sessions.

has generally served as president of the Ladies' Auxiliary in her state. Similarly, the wife of the General Overseer serves as national president. [3]

§ 3. EMPHASIS ON EDUCATION

The academic advancement of the Bible Training School under J. H. Walker was paralleled by financial success under Zeno C. Tharp.[4] This does not mean that there was no academic advancement. During the nine years of Tharp's presidency, outstanding academic progress was made and the enrollment reached an all-time peak. In 1937 the vacant Assembly auditorium was turned over to the Bible School. [5] Still the school's need of space was not met, even though a new women's dormitory had been built in the winter of 1936-1937, at a cost of more than $12,000.[6]

The school was moved to Sevierville, Tennessee, for the 1938-1939 term. The Church purchased the entire school plant of Murphy Collegiate Institute in the picturesque town nestled in a verdant valley of meadowland between Knoxville and the Smoky Mountains. The property featured a large central two-story administration building which housed an auditorium, study hall, classrooms, offices, laboratories, library, and with dining halls and kitchen in the basement. Flanking the large building were a men's dormitory and a women's dormitory.

Under Tharp's guidance the school grew from 157 students the last term in Cleveland to 216 in 1939-1940. All available space in the newly purchased plant was filled.[7] Tharp urged upon the Assembly of 1941 the erection of a new $40,000 building on the Sevierville property. [8] This project was financed by the Publishing House. [9] The five-story building

---

3. *Minutes of the Forty-third General Assembly,* 1950, p. 73.
4. *Minutes of the Thirty-second Annual Assembly,* 1937, p. 34.
5. *Ibid.,* p. 35.
6. Simmons, *op. cit.,* p. 96.
7. *Minutes of the Thirty-fifth Annual Assembly,* 1940, p. 21.
8. *Minutes of the Thirty-sixth Annual Assembly,* 1941, p. 48.
9. *Minutes of the Thirty-seventh Annual Assembly,* 1942, p. 33.

held an eight-hundred-seat auditorium, kitchen, dining rooms, storerooms, classrooms, and twenty music studios.

Simultaneous with the acquisition of these facilities arose thoughts of accreditation, a junior college division, and other academic improvements. The first step toward these goals was a change from a six-month term to a standard nine-month term. In 1941 the Bible Training School established a junior college division, and its high school division was accredited by the State of Tennessee.* Its name was changed to Bible Training School and College—and the enrollment was increased to six hundred.

§ 4. Fathers for More Fatherless

When the Bible School moved to Sevierville, the Orphanage and Children's Home purchased the new women's dormitory in Cleveland. The Orphanage had since its beginning in 1920 added several new homes to its property, including a 119-acre farm eight miles from Cleveland.† Purchase of the school dormitory in 1938 provided quarters large enough for all fifty-six girls in the home. The forty-nine boys remained in the smaller houses, an arrangement that became increasingly unsatisfactory.

The Assembly of 1940 (Thirty-fifth) approved the erection of a new building for the boys. A large three-story boys' home was erected on a large tract of land five miles south of Cleveland. E. L. Simmons, chairman of the Orphanage Board, was instrumental in this project; he stimulated interest and support among the business people of Cleveland, who contributed funds for the building. It was dedicated on September 2,

---

*The Board of Directors was to ". . . negotiate, consummate, and execute plans for the establishment . . . of a junior college in compliance with the requirements of the Southern Association of Colleges, beginning with the 1941-1942 term, if it can be done without adversely affecting the Bible Training School" (*Minutes of the Thirty-fifth Annual Assembly,* 1940, p. 31).

†One home had been built in 1921 largely with funds raised in Cleveland, and appropriately named City of Cleveland Orphanage; being the second building, it was also called Number Two. A third was built in 1922 with funds raised among the Kentucky churches, and named Kentucky Home, or Number Three. The farm was purchased in 1928. (*Ibid.,* p. 114.)

1941, at the time of the General Assembly. Because of a polio epidemic in Chattanooga, the Assembly was not as well-attended as others;[10] yet, a long motorcade of delegates drove to the new home, where they were met by a motorcade of businessmen from Cleveland.[11] The home was impressive, with an imposing facade of modified Ionic columns centered between symmetrical concave wings. Built behind the building were completely modern stock and dairy barns. Understandably, the Orphanage became the pride and joy of the Church of God.

The well-being of the home thereafter is reflected in the report given at the Assembly of 1943:

> We have built a new potato house that will take care of both Irish and sweet potatoes for both Homes, a new milk house that will make our dairy Grade A, a new silo, a new well house, and new poultry house that will take care of about 1,500 hens. We have put in concrete walks from the Home to the barn and installed a walk-in cooler that enables us to do our own butchering and furnish fresh meat for both Homes. [12]

Up until this Assembly of 1943 (Thirty-eighth) the Orphanage had no general superintendent, but each home was cared for by its own matron or manager, with the chairman of the Orphanage Board serving as superintendent *de facto.* F. R. Harrawood was selected during the 1943 Assembly to serve as the first full-time superintendent.[13] After two years, Harrawood was succeeded by J. A. Muncy. During Muncy's tenure the new boys' dormitory became overcrowded and a second farm was purchased. In 1947, a combination office building and girls' home was erected on the site of the old Assembly auditorium. Applications for admission to the home came from across the nation on behalf of orphans and homeless children of many denominations and backgrounds. Not

---

10. *Church of God Evangel,* August 23, 1941, p. 4.

11. *Ibid.,* p. 3.

12. *Minutes of the Thirty-eighth Annual Assembly,* 1943, p. 50.

13. *Ibid.,* p. 31.

all could be cared for, not because of their religious—or non-religious—training, but because of lack of space. Needy children, tender hearts, and generous contributors kept the Church of God Orphanage in an expansion program which has not ceased today.

§ 5. EDITORIAL EMPHASIS

The three years between 1939 and 1942 brought great advancement in the publication field. At the Assembly of 1939, S. W. Latimer was succeeded by E. L. Simmons as editor and publisher. The new editor was a discerning savant in the Scriptures and church history. He brought fresh readability to the Church publication by the employment of up-to-date editorial techniques. Previous to his editorship, Simmons had written *A History of the Church of God,* which was, in reality, a brief pictorial resume of the Church.

§ 6. INTO SOUTH AMERICA

In 1940 J. H. Ingram planned a third world mission tour, but the lowering clouds of war made it inadvisable. The countries whence came calls for help could not be reached until the world's nightmare ended. Thwarted in his third tour around the world, Ingram turned southward and followed the east coast of South America to Buenos Aires, Argentina.[14] On previous tours Ingram had become greatly concerned about Argentina and hoped to establish the Church of God there. The Church had previously sent missionaries to Argentina, but their efforts had come to naught.*

In Buenos Aires Ingram visited an organization called the Pentecostal Evangelical Church, of which Marcos Mazzucco, of Italian background, was founder and leader. Ingram was impressed with this organization of eleven churches and mis-

---

14. McCracken, *op. cit.,* p. 106.
15. Vessie D. Hargrave, *South of the Rio Bravo* (Cleveland, Tenn.: Church of God Missions Board, 1952), p. 34 ff.
*Especially F. L. Ryder, whose work is mentioned briefly on page 144. See also, *Where the Saints Have Trod,* p. 157.

sions in Buenos Aires and its suburbs. The largest church had about 430 members. On June 30, 1940, all of the churches by unanimous vote came into the Church of God.

Ingram reported home concerning his visit with Marcos Mazzucco:

> Brother Mazzucco is a real missionary, and we have been putting our theory into practice, going from house to house. He does not go about talking over weather conditions, but storming the homes with songs, prayers, and the Word of God. The Lord has blessed wonderfully in the last few weeks, with whole families turning to God. Forty have received the Holy Ghost in the meantime. [16]

Mazzucco indeed seemed indefatigable, driven with a passion for Christ. After twelve years, Vessie D. Hargrave would call him "the most active pastor in the Church of God." Under Mazzucco's supervision, the work in Argentina has prospered, and the Church of God is today the strongest Pentecostal denomination in the South American country. The central church alone has more than 3,000 members, which is the largest congregation anywhere in the Church of God.

Also reached by the Church in 1940 were Southern Mexico and El Salvador. J. W. Archer and his wife went to Mexico from their home in Colorado and did a creditable work in strengthening a mission recently organized by the Church. El Salvador, where Ingram had opened a work earlier in the year, became the field of H. S. Syverson, who had once been associated with Paul C. Pitt of China. Syverson was at the Northwest Bible and Music Academy in Lemmon, South Dakota, at the time he felt the call of God to El Salvador.

§ 7. THE HAITIAN AFFAIR

It was in February, 1938, that John P. Kluzit and his wife replaced J. Vital Herne in Haiti. Kluzit was a science teacher in Croton-Harmon High School, Croton-on-Hudson, New

---

16. J. H. Ingram, *Church of God Evangel,* September 14, 1940, p. 7.

York, and his French wife taught French in high school and
college. They received the Holy Ghost baptism in 1937 and
were separately, but simultaneously, called to the Haitian mission field. They went to the island without the backing of a
mission board. In Port-au-Prince, they were providentially
brought together with J. H. Walker and J. H. Ingram, who
were in the city to settle a problem with Vital Herne. The
outcome was that the Kluzits found a mission board, and the
Church of God found capable missionaries. The work in
Haiti so thrived under the new leadership that its success in
little more than three years brought the Church of God to
the unfavorable attention of the Haitian Government.

While attending the Assembly of 1941 (Thirty-sixth), Kluzit received the news that every church and mission of the
Church of God in Haiti had been closed by order of the Government, and the people were being subjected to severe persecution. The missionary flew posthaste to Port-au-Prince to
investigate the situation. It was a discouraging picture. Kluzit
saw that there would be no immediate softening of the Government's attitude, which was borne of prejudice and ill-ad-
vice. Ten converts had been arrested for merely singing and
praying in their homes. Eight of these were sentenced to six
months' imprisonment and fined the equivalent of eighty
dollars.* It appeared to Kluzit, from the attitude of the local
priests, that the persecution was fomented by the Catholics,
aroused because the Church of God was gaining too much
strength and popularity.† Kluzit made immediate and persis-

---

*The per capita Haitian income at that time was about one American dollar
a year, which meant the people were fined the equivalent of a lifetime wages.

† *Church of God Evangel,* October 11, 1941, p. 7. ". . . a priest was passing
by the home of one of our former native workers. The priest saw him reading his
Bible just outside his home, and said, 'What are you reading that for? Don't
you know your churches are closed?' Brother Christophe replied, 'Yes, our
churches are all closed up, but my heart is still opened up toward heaven. I
am reading God's Holy Word for comfort.' The priest returned with a soldier
and ordered the arrest of Christophe. But the soldier would not arrest him, as
there was no evidence of breaking the law. The priest told him to hide until he
heard them singing Pentecostal songs. That night, before retiring . . . Brother
Christophe and Brother Weiner were praying in the house and singing. The

tent appeals to the American legation in Haiti. In correspondence dated September 4, 1941, he pointed out that within three and one-half years

> . . . over 300,000 people have heard the gospel, at least 15,000 definitely converted, and 3,200 brought into membership in our Church; 145 missions established, also two Bible training schools organized; and a little orphanage supported, caring for fifty-three little children . . . picked off the streets in a starving or dying condition and nursed back to normal health. In the interior where there are no schools for teaching the natives and where . . . our work [is] established, we have opened up simple rural schools for teaching the children the rudiments of reading and the Bible. [17]

The missionary appealed to the President of Haiti, Elie Lescot, who had served as Haitian Ambassador to the United States for four years before becoming President. Lescot was impervious to any entreaty, and the churches remained closed for two years, even though no legitimate reasons were ever given for closing them. The only consolation for the Church during the period was that it had become large enough and influential enough for a national government to attack it. The President had personally ordered the churches closed, without notice or formal process. It seems that he became incensed when a visiting minister made statements while preaching that were considered derogatory toward the Haitian Government.[18] Regardless of what the missionaries did, the churches remained closed, but not the hearts of the people.

The persecution ultimately helped the Church in Haiti rather than hurt it. It also aroused the people in the United States. Petitions were signed by 36,500 people requesting the State Department to intervene. Most of the signers were Church

soldier knocked at the door and said they were under arrest . . . They were sent to Cayes to be tried in the Correctional Court . . ." (Correspondence from John P. Kluzit to J. H. Walker dated September 27, 1941.)

17. McCracken, *op. cit.*, pp. 49, 50.

18. J. Herbert Walker, Jr., and Lucille Walker, *Haiti* (Cleveland, Tenn.: Church of God Publishing House, 1950), p. 33.

of God members, but about 2,000 were congressmen, senators, governors, mayors, and other officials across the nation who were well aware of the good being done in their areas by the Church of God. On October 22, 1941, J. H. Walker, with two congressmen* presented the petition to Secretary of State Cordell Hull, who gave assurance of intervention by the State Department.[19] But the wheels of diplomacy, turned by hands in doeskin gloves, move softly, silently—and slowly.

While the Church of God waited for the State Department to effect relief, the African Methodist Church in Haiti befriended the harassed churches in a brotherly and unexpected way. The Church of God was granted the use of their churches, which enabled the Pentecostal people to continue their worship almost without interruption under the name of the African Methodist Church. The Church grew miraculously under this arrangement, learned much about self-reliance, and lived closer to God. In due time the work of the diplomatic machinery became evident, and the barred doors were opened on August 13, 1943.

> After spending two years of activities behind closed doors, the work reappeared in broad daylight. A great revival broke out in the south and many people were converted. By the aid of the United States brethren much property was purchased. Schools were reopened. [20]

The vision of the Lord's work is a persistent vision. It survives prosperity, or change, or persecution. The vision goads, pricks, and exerts itself; once suppressed, it springs back with greater force than ever; hidden for a moment, it shines all the brighter when seen anew. The Haitian affair gave strong indication that the Church of God was thus envisioned on foreign soil as well as in the homeland.

---

19. *Church of God Evangel,* November 1, 1941, p. 3.

20. Walker, *op. cit.,* p. 33.

*Congressman Joseph Bryson of South Carolina, and Congressman (later Senator) Estes Kefauver, of Tennessee.

Chapter 24
NEW HORIZONS

§ 1. ANOTHER ASSISTANT GENERAL OVERSEER

No man ever poured his energies more copiously into his labors than did J. H. Walker as General Overseer of the Church of God. A typical year's travel took him to six state ministers' meetings, twenty-seven state conventions, five foreign conventions, then to the Negro National Assembly, climaxed by the Bishops' Council and General Assembly.[1] Not only did Walker travel widely in his leadership of the Church, but he was also an exceptional administrator in the office. A man of natural poise and precision, he made an exceptional moderator of the Assemblies and chairman of the Supreme Council.

R. P. Johnson, the Assistant General Overseer, was ideal as a co-worker with Walker; he supplied pulpit brilliance as Walker supplied executive direction. By 1941, however, it was decided that the General Overseer really needed another assistant if the many state conventions were to be visited from headquarters each year. Earl P. Paulk, overseer of North Carolina and member of the Council of Twelve, was elected to the office of Second Assistant General Overseer at the Assembly of 1941 (Thirty-sixth).[2] Paulk was eloquent enough to rank with Johnson as a preacher and aggressive and dynamic enough to rank with Walker as a leader, so he became

---

1. *Minutes of the Thirty-second Annual Assembly,* 1937, pp. 14, 15.
2. *Minutes of the Thirty-sixth Annual Assembly,* 1941, p. 18.

a valuable representative of the Church. His sound judgment and progressive thinking helped steer the Church into fields of greater service for God.*

§ 2. EXECUTIVE MISSIONS SECRETARY

Another new office was created a year later, at the Assembly of 1942 (Thirty-seventh), an executive missions secretary.[3] Previously, a member of the Missions Board served as part-time secretary, but constantly expanding missionary interests brought about the need of an executive secretary who would give full time to the work. M. P. Cross was appointed to the new position. Cross was a veteran state overseer, a prominent member of the Missions Board, and had been a member of the Council of Seventy when it existed. He was also one of the greatest enthusiasts of world missions in the Church of God, an important factor in his selection. And so it was that increasing areas of activity brought greater demands for additional administrative personnel.

§ 3. NAE: NEW-FOUND BROTHERHOOD

A group of evangelical churchmen of various denominations met in St. Louis on April 7, 1942, to explore the possibilities of a National Association of Evangelicals. The Church of God sent four delegates to this conference.† This exploratory conference concluded that such an association was feasible, and certainly desirable, so a Constitution Convention was scheduled to meet in Chicago in the spring of 1943. Even though most of the men who met in St. Louis were non-Pentecostal, they cherished a deep appreciation for the Pentecostal people.

---

3. *Ibid.,* pp. 37, 38.

*One of Paulk's chief responsibilities was to head the embryonic youth work, then recognized as an important element in the Church, but not yet a separate department. *Minutes of the Thirty-seventh Annual Assembly,* 1942, p. 42.

†Church of God delegates to the National Conference of United Action Among Evangelicals were E. C. Clark, M. P. Cross, E. L. Simmons, and J. H. Walker. *Evangelical Action!* (Boston: United Action Press, 1942), pp. 92-100. By virtue of his position as overseer of Missouri, Houston R. Morehead represented the Church as an unregistered delegate.

Significantly, the Church of God and other Pentecostal groups were also invited to attend the Constitution Convention in Chicago. Before this invitation could be accepted, the matter of participation had to be favored by the Council of Ordained Ministers in Birmingham. This was done at the Assembly of 1942 (Thirty-seventh).

The proposed association was a brave venture and reflected mature thinking among evangelical leaders—and among the Pentecostal brethren.* As was to be expected, a few of the Church of God preachers questioned the propriety of such close association with non-Pentecostals. Nevertheless, a vast majority of the delegates realized that there is but a hair's-breadth between the current of conviction and the shoals of bigotry. Many a church has begun with the simple faith that its organization is divinely ordained, only to end behind solid walls of ecclesiolatry. It is easy to confuse separation from the world with aloofness toward all that is unlike oneself—and then regard the misunderstanding as a virtue. An aggressive, vital, evangelistic church is in danger of such absorption in its own affairs that it loses its outside perspective and looks askance at all others than itself. Sometimes this is done to the point of doubting the sincerity, fitness, or divine acceptance of others. The proposed association was a great step toward breaking down such barriers of distrust and misunderstanding.

---

*Indirectly the Pentecostal churches played a great role in the formation of the Association. Another association of similar objectives (the American Council of Christian Churches) had preceded the NAE in the field of evangelical cooperation. This earlier group proposed an amalgamation of the two groups even before the NAE was officially organized. The American Council urged the younger association to join ranks with it, maintaining that it had priority in the field. For a while it looked as if the two groups would come together, but for various reasons the efforts failed. As late as 1944 a serious attempt was made to combine the two bodies. The American Council, by whom the Pentecostal people were particularly disliked, did not want an outright merger of the two groups with all their members. Instead, the various members of the NAE were to apply to the consolidated association for membership. The American Council demanded this in order to bar the Pentecostal churches from membership in the combined body. The founders of NAE refused to forsake their friends and brethren, so the union was never effected. And the NAE continues as a vital organization of evangelical cooperation today. Harold Lindsell, *Park Street Prophet* (Wheaton, Illinois: Van Kampen Press, 1951), pp. 118-120.

The principle of NAE has always been "cooperation without compromise."

The Church of God readily accepted the invitation.[4] Among most of the ministers there was an eagerness to join forces with other fundamentalists in the protection and promulgation of the evangelical precepts. General Overseer J. H. Walker led a progressive committee of Church of God delegates to the Constitutional Convention: Earl P. Paulk, E. L. Simmons, M. P. Cross, and E. C. Clark.[5]

The historic and present objectives of the National Association of Evangelicals are stated as follows:

1. To encourage evangelism in all its forms and assist in the promotion of evangelistic effort.
2. To provide a service to mission boards in securing passports, visas, the rapid transmission of funds and supplies to the fields, and the extension of missionary interest. To protect the missionary enterprise from undue restriction and regulation.
3. To act as a clearing house in chaplaincy matters for denominations and groups not now represented by other organizations at Washington.
4. To protect the freedom of gospel broadcasting.
5. To maintain and defend the American doctrine of the separation of the church and state.
6. To assist in the correlation of the work of the churches: promoting understanding and cooperation among its organizations.
7. To encourage and promote Christian education in all its fields.
8. To provide information, leadership, and assistance in every way to all organizations engaged in propagating the gospel message.
9. To provide an interdenominational medium of spiritual fellowship and inspiration for Bible-believing Christians. [6]

---

4. *Minutes of the Thirty-seventh Annual Assembly,* 1942, p. 36.
5. E. C. Clark, *Church of God Evangel,* May 29, 1943, p. 3.
May 29, 1943, p. 3.
6. Lindsell, *op. cit.,* pp. 117, 118.

Church of God men have served on important commissions and boards of the NAE since its beginning. Stemming from the parent association are several related but indigenous associations of which various departments of the Church are members. The *Evangel* and *The Lighted Pathway* are members of the Evangelical Press Association; the Department of Youth and Christian Education, the Editorial Department, and the Publishing House are members of the National Sunday School Association; and the Missions Department is a member of the Evangelical Foreign Missions Association.

§ 4. ADMINISTRATIVE SHAKE-UP

Restrictions on travel during World War II made a General Assembly in 1944 very difficult, but a limited delegation completely filled the Memorial Hall in Columbus, Ohio. The sun shone as brightly as before, the closing days of summer were just as balmy, and the delegates were perhaps more excited as they approached the Ohio capital. Everything was too normal for them to know that it would be an Assembly of drastic changes. But it was.

It was a great Assembly. An eventful one. Although the revolutionary measures were not planned, once begun they swept throughout the Church like a mental chain reaction. Some of the changes were permanent; some were regretted before a year had passed; others were only openings for greater changes in the future. But—good, bad, or indifferent—changes were made.

The nine-year tenure of J. H. Walker came to an end in 1944. Even though he had been an outstanding leader, he was the victim of a growing sentiment that no man should be retained as General Overseer too long. Walker received a majority of the ministers' votes, but he regarded the minority too influential for him to accept the nomination. The circumstances were very much as they had been nine years earlier. Only, then it was S. W. Latimer who stepped down from the office and Walker who was elected to it. Now Walker stepped down and made way for another.

John C. Jernigan was elected General Overseer when Walker declined the narrow nomination. Jernigan had been a state overseer for many years, having served in Virginia, Kentucky, Georgia, Florida, and Tennessee. His sound ministry in those states made him a logical choice for the General Overseership. The new Overseer was a strong leader, a deliberate, yet jovial man who had for many years been a favorite among the ministers of the Church of God. Jernigan would be a popular and folksy Overseer.

At this same Assembly Zeno C. Tharp resigned as president of the Bible Training School and College. This resignation did not come as a surprise since there had been indications for a year or so that it would come. J. H. Walker was appointed to the vacant position, from which he had been elected General Overseer nine years earlier. Tharp was appointed overseer of South Carolina, where nine years earlier he had pastored the Greenville church.

§ 5. THE GREAT EXPERIMENT

The tenures of Johnson and Paulk as Assistant General Overseers were abruptly ended. For some time there had been a general feeling that the Church was stronger in the Southeast than in other sections of the nation because its General Offices are there. Recurrent through the years had been debates on whether or not to move the General Offices to a city more nationally central than Cleveland. This idea could never gain sufficient support to be enacted. As a compromise of sorts, it was decided by the Assembly of 1944 (Thirty-ninth) to elect six Assistant General Overseers, each of whom would reside in a different section of the United States. Each of the men would have the general oversight of the states in his region.[7] Each man would live in his geographical area and thereby create six foci of Church operation. The Supreme Council then divided the nation into six districts and appointed the six Assistants over the districts. Neither Johnson

---

7. *Minutes of the Thirty-ninth Annual Assembly,* 1944, pp. 22, 23.

nor Paulk was among the six men chosen. H. L. Chesser, the first man elected, was sent to the Northwestern district; Paul H. Walker was appointed to the Northeastern; A. V. Beaube to the South Central; E. L. Simmons to the Southeastern; E. W. Williams to the North Central; and J. D. Bright to the Western.*

It was a great experiment. But an experiment that hinted of fragmentation. And it didn't work.

§ 6. LIMITED TENURES

The administration shake-up was not yet over. It is a truism that perpetuated authority often tends to become autocratic, or to draw a privileged clique around itself. The Church of God was anxious lest it should someday face such an eventuality, so this revolutionary Assembly decreed that all general officials of the Church, plus the Council of Twelve, should be limited to four-year tenures. Election would occur biennially, with no official permitted to succeed himself more than once. State overseers should also be limited to four consecutive years in any state or group of states.[8] Reported abuses of authority in a few states led to this uprising. The ministers of the Church were determined on the idea of limited tenures for those whose authority was administrative, or who possessed powers of appointment. At first the limitation rule provided that an eighty percent vote could reelect the General Overseer or his Assistants after four years, but the temper of this Assembly continued, and even that possibility was removed at the Assembly of 1946 (Forty-first).

---

8. *Minutes of the Thirty-ninth Annual Assembly,* 1944, p. 23.

*The six districts were as follows: *Northeastern*—Maine, New Hampshire, Vermont, Massachusetts, Connecticut, Rhode Island, New York, New Jersey, Pennsylvania, Delaware, Maryland, Virginia, West Virginia, North Carolina, and the District of Columbia. *North Central*—Wisconsin, Michigan, Illinois, Indiana, Ohio, Kentucky, and Tennessee. *Southeastern*—South Carolina, Georgia, Florida, Alabama, and Mississippi. *South Central*—Missouri, Arkansas, Louisiana, Kansas, Colorado, Oklahoma, Texas, and New Mexico. *Northwestern*—North Dakota, South Dakota, Minnesota, Iowa, Nebraska, Montana, and Wyoming. *Western*—Idaho, Washington, Oregon, California, Arizona, Utah, Nevada.

§ 7. A Nascent Youth Organization

It was at this Assembly that natal urgings for Sunday school and youth entity began to be felt. A Sunday School and Youth Literature Board was appointed, whose duties were "to supervise the editing, and publishing of Sunday school, YPE, daily vacation Bible school, and other youth literature and tracts."[9] The chairman of the board was to be editor in chief of Sunday school and youth publications. Except for the one previous year when there was an editor of Sunday school literature, the General Overseer had edited the material for the Sunday school. A scholarly and talented man, Frank W. Lemons, was appointed chairman of the new board.[*] Lemons, the son of pioneer preacher M. S. Lemons, was himself one of the earliest Church of God preachers.[†]

§ 8. North Carolina Home for Children

A. V. Childers, the personable young pastor of the Kannapolis, North Carolina, church, founded a new children's home when he responded to a plea to assist a family of small children who had been abandoned by their parents.[10] This was in January, 1944. Childers sheltered the two deserted children in his home while he made appeals over his radio program for their assistance. Within a short time over $7,000 was contributed. This resulted in the opening of a new orphanage, which was adopted as part of the general orphanage program in 1944.[11] In 1945, the orphanage purchased 193 acres of land and a twelve-room house halfway between Kannapolis and Concord. Soon two large brick homes were added, and the

---

9. *Minutes of the Thirty-ninth Annual Assembly,* 1944, pp. 29, 30.

10. From correspondence from Mrs. A. V. Childers, dated October 4, 1954, and an article by Mrs. Childers in *North Carolina Echoes,* February, 1944, p. 5.

11. *Minutes of the Thirty-ninth Annual Assembly,* 1944, p. 29.

*The entire Sunday School and Youth Literature Board was: Frank W. Lemons, D. C. Boatwright, Harry Kutz, James L. Slay, H. D. Williams.

†Two sons of M. S. Lemons became prominent preachers in the Church of God, the other being David, a leading pastor, Bible teacher, state overseer and member of the Council of Twelve.

Home for Children steadily became a prominent part of the Church's ministry of benevolence.

H. D. Williams was appointed superintendent of the orphanage in 1946, the first full-time superintendent of the institution. C. H. Rochester served as superintendent from 1947 to 1952, during which time good progress was made. In 1949, the Duke Foundation granted the home an endowment, from which it received increased allotments each year. This was the first of several homes for children the Church of God would open in different states.

§ 9. STILL ONWARD WITH MISSIONS

Amid the critical changes at home, the Church of God still pressed onward into other lands with the full gospel. Cuba was reached in 1943.[12] Hoyle and Mildred Case, recently returned from India where they had labored for four years with Robert F. Cook, were put in charge of the Cuban work. One main church and two smaller mission stations were reported at the Assembly of 1943.

Alaska became a Church of God mission field when a young Dakotan, George Savchenko, and his Scandinavian wife went there in July, 1944. Together this brave couple toiled to gain a foothold in the northern territory—and succeeded with one church in Matenuska Valley.*

In 1944 other countries were reached by the Church: Nicaragua, Honduras, British Honduras, and Costa Rica in Central America; Bermuda, Puerto Rico, the Dominican Republic, and various smaller islands of the Caribbean.[13] These were not simply names on a roster. They were accessions to the message of the Holy Ghost, labored for, wept for, prayed for by those in whose bosoms still flamed the fire of pioneer full-gospel work.

---

12. *Minutes of the Thirty-eighth Annual Assembly,* 1943, p. 50.

13. *Minutes of the Thirty-ninth Annual Assembly,* 1944, pp. 49, 50.

*Savchenko has related in a letter dated September 30, 1954, that his first winter in Alaska was spent in a chicken house rented for $15 a month. This, in a land of astronomical prices, reveals the bad condition of their quarters.

§ 10. AFTER TWELVE MONTHS

The six Assistant General Overseers went to their territories with great ambitions. Some succeeded in organizing their regions for greater evangelistic efforts and sound plans for church expansion were laid in same regions. It was an imaginative experiment—but it failed. Loud protests were raised by some of the state overseers, who felt that there was too much overlapping of responsibilities and too much unavoidable interference with their work. The ministers came to the Assembly of 1945 (Fortieth) determined to revert to the former administrative structure. Dissatisfaction was so keen that the whole idea of multiple assistants was cast aside, and only one was retained.

The Assembly of 1945 was a limited but eventful one. It convened in Sevierville, Tennessee, in the auditorium of the newly erected addition to the Bible School. The small attendance was due to congested wartime travel. The two-day meeting was announced for ordained ministers only, but the end of World War II on August 14, 1945, relieved the restrictions on travel in time for about two thousand delegates to be present. The year since the Columbus convention had been a good year, especially in numerical growth. The Church had grown wonderfully—173 new churches and 11,363 new members; the membership now surpassed a hundred thousand —to 101,441.[14] Besides these gains, there was a property increase of more than two million dollars. The dissatisfaction with the regional Assistant General Overseers was not the result of an unfruitful year.

H. L. Chesser, first of the six men elected in 1944, was chosen to continue as the one Assistant to the General Overseer in 1945.[15] Chesser, a native of Florida, had served as state overseer in Alabama and North Carolina. A forthright man and a wise councilor, he carried a great portion of the burden of administration as Jernigan's assistant.

---

14. *Minutes of the Fortieth Annual Assembly,* 1945, pp. 27, 28.
15. *Ibid.,* pp. 28, 29.

§ 11. A Better College

E. L. Simmons succeeded J. H. Walker as president of Bible Training School and College in 1945. Walker, who had returned to the college only the previous year, now retired to a local pastorate, where he was able to relax somewhat from the tremendous pressures to which he had been subjected since he was elected General Overseer in 1935. Things had not gone too well with the school during the year of his presidency. E. L. Simmons, the new president, later explained,

> The [Board of Education] had hired a business manager, and for some reason the financial status began to drop. The business manager resigned, but too late to save the financial status of the school . . . [16]

During his first year with the school, Simmons completed a $200,000 dormitory, begun while Tharp was president, and made extensive improvements on the property. During Simmons' presidency Earl M. Tapley was added to the faculty and appointed Dean of the School. Tapley was academically trained in the field of education, holding degrees from Vanderbilt University and Peabody College. With Simmons as president and Tapley as dean, the college division improved sufficiently to merit the approval of leading universities and colleges in the nation. Graduates were soon able to transfer to major schools for the completion of their education.

What was widely considered to be a golden opportunity for the Church presented itself in 1946. Bob Jones College, in Cleveland, planned to relocate in another city and offered to sell its Cleveland property to the Church of God for one and a half million dollars. The ministers of the Church voted by mail to accept the proposition, and now the school again would be in the same town with the general headquarters. The move was made in time for the 1947-1948 term, and the prospects were rosy for the educational program of the Church. The name of the school was changed to Lee College

---

16. From the manuscript of the unpublished revision of Simmons' *History of the Church of God.*

at the time of the move, in honor to the great leader F. J. Lee, second president of the institution.

§ 12. Shaping of the Youth Program

Another step was taken toward the formation of a separate youth department at the Sevierville Assembly. A Youth Program Committee was appointed to serve the needs of young people concerning education, recreation, and spirituality. Two men mature in years but young in heart and three young men with mature minds were named to the committee. They were E. L. Simmons and R. R. Walker, the elders; and Ralph E. Williams, Paul Stallings, and Robert Johnson, the young members.[17] The committee was responsible to assimilate and disperse helpful information, suggestions, and other material to the state youth leaders. Perhaps the greatest task of the new and ambitious committee was to arrange for a National Youth Congress. This was a real challenge since it was a completely new area for the Church; yet such a Congress was scheduled to precede the Assembly of 1946.[18]

The Church of God entered these new areas of Christian service with a sense of responsibility. It was a period of trial and effort; the Church's growth and ambition demanded new and better ways of serving the spiritual, social, and intellectual needs of the people.

§ 13. Middle East

The first interest the Church of God had in the Middle East was the meager support it sent to Lillian Thrasher during the first years of her activity in Egypt.[19] Much later, contact was made with an Egyptian Pentecostal minister named Boutros Labib, who was tentatively accepted into the Church, and given modest financial support. Final arrangements were

---

17. *Minutes of the Fortieth Annual Assembly,* 1945, p. 30.
18. Cecil M. Truesdell, "National YPE and Sunday School News," *The Lighted Pathway,* January, 1946, p. 20. Et scq.
19. See pp. 143, 144.

to be made when J. H. Ingram visited Egypt during his proposed third world mission tour.[20]

Ingram reached Egypt in the spring of 1946, stopping first in Palestine. Because of an Egyptian law restricting foreign missionaries, he had to wait six weeks in Palestine before he could get a visa to Egypt.* During his wait in the Holy Land, the missionary met an Arab family of Bethlehem—living in Jerusalem at the time—who were Christians of the Pentecostal faith. Hanna K. Suleiman, with his wife and two children became interested in the Church of God during Ingram's visit, but they did not join at that time. A short time later they became members, and a promising Pentecostal work was begun in Palestine.

When Ingram finally entered Egypt, he found Boutros Labib's work in good order. Labib had already registered his sixteen churches with the authorities in Cairo, asserting that his work was affiliated with the Church of God in the United States. Ingram formally accepted the organization into the Church of God, then spent six weeks touring the country, visiting the churches, and ministering to the natives of the ancient land.

Ingram's report to the Missions Board upon his return was happily received. It was also felt that an American missionary was needed in the Middle East as soon as possible. At the Assembly of 1946 (Forty-first) D. B. Hatfield, a successful and popular pastor in West Virginia, was appointed to the Holy Land. He and his wife had felt the call of God to the Middle East for more than ten years, so they accepted the appointment as an act of God. The first superintendent of

---

20. Information for this section was obtained largely from interviews with D. B. Hatfield, and from an unpublished manuscript, *History of the Church of God in the Middle East,* by Hatfield.

*"In 1936, the Egyptian government passed the Montraux Convention Law restricting new missionaries from coming into Egypt. Only the foreign religious organizations that had been established in Egypt prior to 1936 could send new missionaries into that country and they could only be replacements." (D. B. Hatfield, *History of the Church of God in the Middle East,* unpublished manuscript.)

Palestine and Egypt sailed from New York with his family on April 23, 1947 and landed in Haifa, Palestine, on May 8. Palestine was in a state of civil upheaval at the time because of the Israeli demand for independence from England. Armed conflict resulted.

> The number of Arabs being double that of the Jews made it a problem for Britain to consider the Jews' wishes for independence. Because of the British refusal, the Jews formed hard-hitting, fearless and determined groups of terrorists. . . . Attacks were made at all times without previous warning, and this made the country an extremely troubled place with a lot of tension and insecurity rising daily. [21]

Amid the strife the Hatfields conducted services in the Suleiman home, where a hopeful mission was begun. Suleiman, an employee in the registration department of the Palestinian government and part-time preacher, became a minister in the Church of God.

From the beginning, Hatfield managed to visit Egypt with some frequency. Because of the troubled conditions in Palestine, he was reluctantly permitted to remain in Egypt—with little welcome, but with timely tolerance. He described the tenuous, uncertain time:

> . . . on the 28th day of November, 1947, the United Nations ruled on the partitioning of Palestine. This act brought seven Arab countries in battle against Israel. Egypt marched her troops up through the Sinai desert . . . and declared Egypt to be a country at war. They announced martial law in effect and no exit visas (were) to be granted anyone in Egypt. [22]

Hatfield remained in the land until the spring of 1949. The missionary and his family turned to Cyprus in May, and established headquarters there. The Church in the Middle East has not enjoyed tremendous gains, but the work has been fruitful, the gospel has been preached in the lands where it was first heard.

---

21. Hatfield, *op. cit.*
22. Hatfield, *op. cit.*

§ 14. THE PHILIPPINE ISLANDS

In 1947 the Church of God extended its missionary efforts to the Philippine Islands. For about thirty years the tropical, rain-swept archipelago had attracted the attention and burden of the Church. Jennie B. Rushin, pioneer missionary to China, visited the Philippines in 1918 and reported that there was no Pentecostal work on the island.[23] J. H. Ingram also went to the Islands in 1936 and was deeply impressed with the spiritual needs of the land.[24] Several Church of God servicemen who were stationed in the Philippines following World War II were also impressed with the missionary possibilities and needs of the Islands. At least two of these, J. C. Williams and Elmer T. Odom, wrote home encouraging the Church to send missionaries to the war-torn land.[25]

The first Church of God missionary to the Philippines was Frank Parado, of Pittsburgh, Pennsylvania, who had earlier been a missionary to the Philippines for another denomination. While in the United States, he joined the Church of God and in February 1947 returned to Manila as a Church of God missionary. Eventually he settled in Ilocos Norte, a province in the extreme northwestern corner of the island of Luzon. Fluent in the Ilocano dialect, Parado won numerous converts among the Filipinos. The work grew so rapidly that by May 1947 the six ministers and 280 members of the Church of God came together for a convention.

When Parado returned to the United States after eighteen months, he appointed Fulgencio R. Cortez, an Ilocano Christian, to supervise the young churches in his absence. He did not return, and the missionary work remained under Cortez and other Filipino workers for almost a decade. Rapidly the Philippine Islands became one of the foremost missionary fields of the Church of God. The record of the Filipino workers is one of courage in the face of opposition and hardship. They

23. *Church of God Evangel,* June 1, 1918, p. 3.
24. Ingram, *Around the World With the Gospel Light,* p. 81.
25. *The Macedonian Call,* Second Quarter, 1946, pp. 4-28.

went into remote villages of the northern provinces of Luzon and preached the Word of God. Hundreds of souls were won to Christ.[26]

Of a total of seven thousand islands, there are four principal islands in the Philippines; the largest is Luzon in the north, and the second largest is Mindanao far to the south. After a decade in Luzon the work was extended to Mindanao where the native missionaries experienced great evangelistic success among the Morros. The wild and lonely mountains on the lush tropical islands constituted a mission field within a mission field. Successful Bible institutes were organized on both Luzon and Mindanao to train native missionaries for the prodigious work of evangelizing the backward, primitive people of the hinterland.

---

26. F. R. Cortez, an unpublished history of the Church of God in the Philippine Islands.

Chapter 25
BROADENED
HORIZONS

§ 1. ANOTHER REVOLUTIONARY ASSEMBLY

Only two years following the sweeping changes of 1944, there came another Assembly equally as revolutionary in its changes. In 1946 the metamorphic period of the Church of God was in full swing. World War II was over, and new fields of opportunity and outreach lay open to the Church of God. The new college plant purchased in Cleveland was ready to become the home of Lee College; during the twelve months preceding the 1946 Assembly, the Church had gained more than 14,000 members and three million dollars in church property. Such gains were encouraging to the eight thousand delegates who gathered in Birmingham, Alabama. The wonderful growth was taken to be a manifestation of God's blessings upon the people who had toiled, fasted and sacrificed for His cause.

§ 2. DOCTRINAL SOLIDARITY

Any fear that the Church might be de-emphasizing its holiness tenets was effectively dispelled at the Ordained Ministers Council. One of the stormiest sessions ever held by the Council developed out of the feeling that some of the ministers might hold views contrary to the historic doctrine of sanctification. The debate centered not so much around the reality of sanctification as around the time and process of its inception in the human heart. Some held vigorously that it is an instantaneous or "definite" work of grace, and others held it to be progressive rather than instantaneous. The dramatic controversy served mainly as a manifestation of the Church's complete adherence to the doctrine and experience of sanctification itself. Even though no dictum was handed down by the Assembly, no room was left to doubt that the Church of God is solidly, basically, and determinedly a fundamental, holiness, Pentecostal Church. It has frequently changed its administrative structure and its practical teachings, but not once has it changed a single doctrine.

§ 3. THE LAST ANNUAL ASSEMBLY

One of the cohesive forces of the Church of God since 1906 had been its annual Assemblies. Since the initial gathering, with the exception of 1918 when a nationwide influenza epidemic prohibited such a gathering, there had been an Assembly every year. For several years prior to 1946 there was considerable agitation for biennial rather than annual meetings, but the idea was discarded until it ripened sufficiently to be adopted in 1946. Because of its tradition there was general reluctance to bring an end to the annual Assembly. Indisputable logic, however, could not be overruled by sentiment. Annual meetings meant an annual appointment of pastors and overseers, with the resultant loss of time in the process of the frequent changes; and forced on each preacher the inertia of indecision concerning his appointment preceding each Assembly. Also, the heart of the revival season was taken away each year. The cost of the annual gatherings had become very great —the cost of the actual meetings, plus travel, meals, and lodging for the thousands of delegates. The combined expense and loss of evangelistic time would be cut in half by the change. This was the principal argument for the biennial Assembly.

There had been a time when frequent general meetings were highly beneficial and actually necessary. But with annual state camp meetings, many of which were much larger than the earlier Assemblies, annual district conventions, annual ministers' meetings and prayer conferences, the need of annual Assemblies decreased. Pastors and overseers could work two years without being interrupted by a long trip or by uncertainty of appointment. This lengthened period would permit better planning of local and state work.

And so the annual Assembly was changed in 1946 to a biennial General Assembly.[1] Paradoxically, this break with tradition was done in order to conserve the traditional objectives of the Church of God. The next two years were so satisfactory and filled with activity that there were no evident regrets that there was no Assembly in the middle of the period. Within a short time the majority of opinion swelled into unanimity of approval.

§ 4. ADMINISTRATIVE CHANGES

From the beginning of the Church's publishing efforts in 1910, the editorial and business departments were combined under one head, called editor and publisher. While the publications program was small, this arrangement was sufficient; but, as the number of periodicals increased and the sales of literature mounted, the responsibility became too great for adequate supervision by one man. It was felt that there should be a director of publications, with a second person in charge of production and sales. This overdue step was made at the Assembly of 1946, with J. H. Walker named editor in chief and E. C. Clark, who had filled the combined post prior to the division, named business manager.[2] This latter office is now called publisher.

The Assembly of 1946 marked the end of E. J. Boehmer's distinguished career as General Secretary-Treasurer. Upon the resignation of the magnanimous minister of Christ, the General Overseer paid him great tribute:

> No man in the history of the Church of God has ever retired with greater honors than E. J. Boehmer. No man has ever held the confidence of the Church in general to a greater degree than he . . . His honesty has never been

---

1. *Minutes of the Forty-first Annual Assembly,* 1946, p. 22.
2. *Ibid.,* pp. 22, 26, 32.

questioned and his character has ever been above reproach, without a stain upon it.[3]

R. R. Walker, former principal of the Bible Training School, was the Assembly's choice to succeed Boehmer.

Another resignation was made at the 1946 Assembly, that of M. P. Cross as executive missions secretary. His missionary zeal had not waned, but Cross intensely desired to be freed from the routine of executive work. Appointed to the office was a young man from Maryland, J. Stewart Brinsfield, who had distinguished himself as state overseer of Pennsylvania.

§ 5. YOUTH IDENTITY AND IMPACT

Probably the greatest innovation of this Assembly was the National Youth Congress which was conducted during the first three days of the meeting, August 27-29, 1946. The three days were filled with study sessions, workshops, and devotional periods. It was the true beginning of a work that had been slowly gathering strength for several years.

The Sunday School and Youth Literature Board was merged with the Publishing Interest Committee into a General Editorial and Publications Board,[4] and the Youth Program Committee was reformed into a National Youth Committee. A national youth director was appointed to head a National Youth Department and pioneer the youth ministries of the Church of God. Ralph E. Williams, who had a solid background of state youth work was appointed to this important work. At last the young people of the Church of God had identity, and, in the manner of youth, they would rapidly become one of the most efficient and productive departments of the Church.*

---

3. *Ibid.,* p. 25.

4. *Ibid.,* pp. 22, 23.

*It was not until the Assembly of 1948 (Forty-second) that the Sunday school was formally placed under the supervision of the National Youth Director (*Minutes,* p. 33). In 1952 his title was changed to General (or, National) Sunday School and Youth Director, and he was directed to "devote his full time to the promotion of the Church of God Sunday school and young people's work." (*Minutes of the Forty-fourth General Assembly,* 1952, p. 30.) In 1970 the name Department of Youth and Christian Education was adopted.

Under the leadership of Ralph E. Williams, the Sunday School and Youth Department, or Youth and Christian Education Department, as it is presently known, made an immediate contribution to the forward motion of the Church of God. In lieu of a second national youth congress, regional congresses were conducted in 1948 in numerous areas of the United States. The meetings consisted of lectures, workshops and displays of materials beneficial to local youth and Sunday school workers. The regional congress program was so successful that it was continued for a decade, with six such meetings conducted biennially in the years when there was no General Assembly. It was with these meetings that the Church of God began in earnest its demand for, and development of, teaching skills and methods on the local level.

§ 6. PFNA: COMBINED FORCES OF PENTECOST

Another area of interdenominational fellowship was explored in 1948 when eight Pentecostal groups attending the NAE Convention in Chicago discussed the formation of a Pentecostal fellowship.* These groups met on May 7, 1948, and found the proposition of a Pentecostal association much desired by all of those present. Plans were made for a second meeting on August 3, 4, "for the purpose of exploring the possibilities of interdenominational Pentecostal cooperation and fellowship and to formulate bylaws for such a fellowship . . ."[5] The bylaws were to be presented to each denomination for its study and acceptance.

When this second meeting convened, several new groups were also represented; the news of a Pentecostal fellowship had been heard widely, and the response was enthusiastic. Various committees were appointed, especially a constitution

---

5. *Minutes of the Conference of Pentecostal Leaders,* Chicago, Illinois, May 7, 1948.

*Besides the Church of God, which was represented by John C. Jernigan, H. L. Chesser, and J. Stewart Brinsfield, were the Assemblies of God, Pentecostal Holiness Church, Pentecostal Assemblies of Canada, Church of the Foursquare Gospel, International Pentecostal Assemblies, Elim Missionary Assemblies, and Open Bible Standard Churches.

committee which met in Des Moines, Iowa, on October 26-28, 1948.[6] The Pentecostal Fellowship of North America has done much in the cause of unity, fellowship, and cooperation among the member denominations.

It is a dynamic fellowship with no purposes to be more than that. Objectives of the PFNA include:

1. To provide a vehicle of expression and coordination of effort in matters common to all member bodies, including missionary and evangelistic effort throughout the world.

2. To demonstrate to the world the essential unity of Spirit-baptized believers, fulfilling the prayer of the Lord Jesus "that they may be one," John 17:21.

3. To provide services to all its constituents which will enable them to accomplish more quickly and efficiently their responsibility for the speedy evangelization of the world.

4. To encourage the principles of comity for the nurture of the Lody of Christ, endeavoring to keep the unity of the Spirit until we all come to the unity of the faith.[7]

§ 7. PENTECOSTAL WORLD CONFERENCE

In 1947 the Pentecostal world became fully aware of itself. In Europe, Asia and other parts of the world there were bodies of Pentecostal believers much like the PFNA in North America. A strong desire for international fellowship grew to be more than a wistful impulse, and a Pentecostal World Conference was scheduled to meet in Zurich, Switzerland, during the summer of 1947. Among the conveners of the conference were Donald Gee of England, Lewi Pethrus of Sweden and Leonard Steiner of Switzerland.

The Church of God has been a participant in the triennial meetings from their inception. The conferences have no business to transact, only ministry of the Word and Spirit, inspiration and worship, and a happy fellowship in Christ. As

---

6. *Loc. cit.*
7. *Constitution and By-laws of the Pentecostal Fellowship of North America.*

many as twenty-five and thirty thousand believers from all over the world gather at these meetings to share their common faith.*

§ 8. First Fruits of Limitation

The limitation set on executive tenures was felt for the first time at the Assembly of 1948 (Forty-second), when John C. Jernigan, who had earnestly promoted the limitation during his four years in office, was replaced by his Assistant General Overseer, H. L. Chesser.[8] Jernigan had been an exceptionally popular overseer, which gave rise to some misgiving that he must retire from the overseership. Still, the limitation was held to be a good thing. Jernigan was appointed state overseer of Virginia, where he had served when he was a young man.

Zeno C. Tharp, overseer of South Carolina, was elected Assistant General Overseer. Tharp's previous experience on the Appointing Board, or Executive Committee, when he was president of BTS made him a logical choice for the position. At fifty-one years of age, Tharp was widely regarded as a shrewd man of business and conservative leader in the Church.

E. L. Simmons resigned as president of Lee College at the Assembly of 1948, which began a concatenation of personnel changes that were to affect several offices. J. Stewart Brinsfield was selected as Simmons' successor at the college, which left the office of executive missions secretary vacant. J. H. Walker resigned as editor in chief to accept the missions post, whereupon J. D. Bright, pastor in Alabama City, Alabama, was elected to the editorial position.

Other changes were also made. E. C. Clark resigned as business manager of the Publishing House, being replaced by

---

8. *Minutes of the Forty-second General Assembly,* 1948, p. 25.

*Sites of the conferences have been: Zurich, Switzerland (1947); Paris, France (1949); London, England (1952); Stockholm, Sweden (1955); Toronto, Canada (1958); Jerusalem, Israel (1961); Helsinki, Finland (1964); Rio de Janeiro, Brazil (1967); Dallas, Texas (1970); Seoul, Korea (1973); London, England (1976).

A. M. Phillips, pastor in Atlanta, Georgia. J. A. Muncy was succeeded by William F. Dych as superintendent of the Orphanage. Amid all these changes, perhaps the most noticeable change of all was in the editor of *The Lighted Pathway*. The change of editors evoked much attention because of Alda B. Harrison's long service with the magazine. Mrs. Harrison had founded the publication in 1929, since which time she had served as its only editor. When failing health necessitated her resignation in 1948, she was succeeded by Charles W. Conn, pastor in Leadwood, Missouri. Mrs. Harrison was named editor emeritus. She had become a tradition among her readers and a symbol of warm personal friendship. Despite their disappointment concerning her retirement, the readers accepted the new editor kindly.

§ 9. RAPID SUCCESSION

Even though the presidents of Lee College are not limited in their tenures, the changes in that office actually have been more frequent than those subject to limitation. Brinsfield served only two terms and one semester. During the second semester of the 1950-1951 term, E. M. Tapley served as acting president. In an effort to stabilize the presidency of the school, the Board of Directors appointed John C. Jernigan in 1951,[9] but he remained for only one term. R. Leonard Carroll, pastor in Anderson, South Carolina, was appointed president in 1952, and remained until 1957. The rapid turnover affected the progress of the school both scholastically and in enrollment. In 1944-1945, while the school was still in Sevierville, there were 630 students; yet only 530 students registered for the fall semester of 1954-1955, and 496 for the spring semester.

The college endeavored to compensate for its structural weaknesses by having a sound academic program. However, there was a strong feeling among some influential alumni and

---

9. F. Gene Horton, *A History of Lee Junior College* (unpublished Master of Education thesis, University of South Dakota, 1953), p. 38.

leaders that the quest for liberal arts accreditation would side-track the original impulse behind the school—that of being a thorough and efficient Bible college.* Accordingly, a Bible College curriculum was initiated in the 1953-1954 term. The full four-year curriculum was put into effect for the 1954-1955 term, with the first Bible College class graduating in the spring commencement.†

§ 10. CAMPUS FOR THE HOMELESS

The campus in Sevierville, left vacant when the college returned to Cleveland, was turned over to the Orphanage and Children's Home at the 1949 spring session of the Executive Council.[10] The commodious quarters easily housed all the children—both boys and girls, thus putting brothers and sisters together again—and provided them with a spacious campus and ample recreation space. The classrooms were a great benefit, when an elementary school was begun for the children. The little town of Sevierville was unable to provide enough school space for the influx of pupils, so the State of Tennessee endorsed and agreed to support the Orphanage school. In this way, the children were taught on their own campus with complete public school regulations and advantages.

All of the Orphanage property in Cleveland was sold except the new girls' dormitory and administration building. This, being adjacent to the Publishing House and General Offices, was converted into executive offices for the denomination.

---

10. *Minutes of the Executive Council,* September 7, 1949, p. 179.

*Even though the liberal arts program was never severed entirely from the Bible department, there was a temporary decrease in Bible requirements for college students. "During the terms of 1941-1942 and 1942-1943, ten semester hours in Bible and Religious Education were required. In 1944-1945 the requirement was lowered to six hours of course work in Bible. For the 1946-1947 term four hours of Bible were required for graduation, and in 1948-1949 the requirement was lowered to three hours of Bible Study. In 1951-1952 the amount of Bible study required was raised to six semester hours." (Horton, *op. cit.,* pp. 23, 24.) The liberal arts program in 1955 required six semester hours of Bible study, called Bible Introduction.

† In 1950, General Overseer Chesser said: "The objectives looked forward to in this institution are a four-year, fully accredited college and a fully accredited Bible College." *Minutes of the Forty-third General Assembly,* 1950, p. 12.

When this move was made, it somewhat relieved the congestion of the overcrowded Publishing House—but not for long.

§ 11. A DECLARATION OF FAITH

At the 1948 Assembly, the title of ordained ministers was changed from bishop to ordained minister, and the title of licensed ministers was changed from evangelist to licensed minister. The Council of Ordained Ministers has since been called the General Council.

During this meeting of the General Council, the need of a Declaration of Faith was discussed, and a committee was appointed to begin work on such an article.* So manifest and unified was the faith of the Church of God that the committee was able to draft a brief statement of faith and report to the same meeting. The proposed Declaration was incomplete, and the committee was urged to continue its work and draft an exhaustive statement of faith. The committee remained intact for several years and endeavored to expand the doctrinal instrument, but there has been neither addition nor expansion to it. The short Declaration has become the official expression of Church of God belief:

We believe:

1. In the verbal inspiration of the Bible.

2. In one God eternally existing in three persons; namely, the Father, Son, and Holy Ghost.

3. That Jesus Christ is the only begotten Son of the Father, conceived of the Holy Ghost, and born of the Virgin Mary. That Jesus was crucified, buried, and raised from the dead. That He ascended to heaven and is today at the right hand of the Father as the Intercessor.

4. That all have sinned and come short of the glory of God and that repentance is commanded of God for all and necessary for forgiveness of sins.

---

*The committeemen were James L. Slay, Earl P. Paulk, Glenn C. Pettyjohn, J. L. Goins, J. A. Cross, Paul H. Walker, R. P. Johnson, E. M. Ellis, and R. C. Muncy.

5. That justification, regeneration, and the new birth are wrought by faith in the blood of Jesus Christ.

6. In sanctification subsequent to the new birth, through faith in the blood of Christ; through the Word, and by the Holy Ghost.

7. Holiness to be God's standard of living for His people.

8. In the baptism with the Holy Ghost subsequent to a clean heart.

9. In speaking with other tongues as the Spirit gives utterance and that it is the initial evidence of the baptism of the Holy Ghost.

10. In water baptism by immersion and all who repent should be baptized in the name of the Father, and of the Son, and of the Holy Ghost.

11. Divine healing is provided for all in the atonement.

12. In the Lord's Supper and washing of the saints' feet.

13. In the premillennial second coming of Jesus. First, to resurrect the righteous dead and to catch away the living saints to Him in the air. Second, to reign on the earth a thousand years.

14. In the bodily resurrection; eternal life for the righteous, and eternal punishment for the wicked.[11]

This Declaration of Faith was written forty-two years after the first General Assembly. It was a manifestation that in those forty-two years of change and expansion there had been no change in the faith of the Church. The truths that possessed the hearts of the twenty-one Pentecostal believers at the 1906 Assembly also possessed the hearts of the eight thousand delegates in 1948.

§ 12. School for the West Coast

Another regional Bible school was established by the Church of God in 1949. On February 16, the West Coast Bible College was begun in the church at Pasadena, California, under the

---

11. *Minutes of the Forty-second General Assembly,* 1948, p. 188.

direction of J. H. Hughes, overseer of California.* There was
sufficient interest in the project for a high school department
to be added for the term of 1949-1950, during which the
school also enjoyed an almost continuous revival in its classrooms and dormitories.

> It was then decided that a more central location in the
> state was needed. Property was secured in Fresno, Califor-
> nia, and the 1950-51 term opened (on) September 5 in
> the Church of God Temple. During this term the school
> was firmly established.[12]

As with the Northwest Bible College in Minot, North Dakota,† the California school operated for several years under
the *ex officio* presidency of the state overseer. Lemuel E. Johnson, who had formerly been connected with the Pacific Northwest Bible School in Spokane, Washington, was principal during the formative terms. Growth of WCBC has been modest,
but the college provides a great service for the Church of God
on the Pacific Coast.

---

12. *Sentinel,* Annual of West Coast Bible School, Fresno, Calif., 1953, p. 7.

*Several years earlier a school known as the Pacific Northwest Bible School
had existed in the far West. C. C. Rains, Overseer of Washington and Oregon,
was founder and superintendent of the school, and E. E. Coleman was principal.
A nine weeks' term began in Yakima, Washington, on January 17, 1944. A six
months' term began in October, 1944. The third term was begun in newly
purchased quarters in Spokane with Lemuel E. Johnson, the new overseer of
Washington and Oregon, as superintendent. Despite the good hopes of the
Church in that area, the school was discontinued after only three years because
the constituency of the Church there was too small to continue its operation
and support. However, the California school is regarded as a reorganization
of the Washington school. (*The Harbinger,* Annual of the Pacific Northwest
Bible School, Spokane, Wash., pp. 4, 5.)

†The name of Northwest Bible and Music Academy was changed to Northwest Bible College in 1958.

Chapter 26
A GLOBAL
PERSPECTIVE

§ 1. FULL GOSPEL AMALGAMATION

Conditions in several foreign territories in 1949 prompted the new General Overseer, H. L. Chesser, and the executive missions secretary, J. H. Walker, to visit these lands. Their trip literally took them around the world—with stops in North Africa, Palestine, India, the Philippines, and Hawaii. The first-hand knowledge gained by this trip helped Chesser in his work as head of the Church. Both he and Walker were progressive-minded leaders who readily made friends for the Church and welcomed every opportunity for the advancement of its testimony.

In the spring of 1949, Chesser, Walker, and several other Church of God preachers attended the second Pentecostal World Conference in Paris. The secretary of the conference was David J. duPlessis of the Union of South Africa, who had become a close friend of the Church of God and its leaders during a visit to this country preceding the Paris meeting.* DuPlessis introduced Chesser and Walker to J. H. Saayman, assistant general moderator of the Full Gospel Church of South Africa, who was on his way to the United States to study the organization of the Pentecostal churches in this country. Chesser invited Saayman to visit the Church of God. An itinerary was scheduled for the Afrikaaner that took him into many local churches, both large and small. Saayman immediately ap-

---

*Lee College employed duPlessis as Bible instructor for the 1949-1950 term, during which time he resided in Cleveland.

preciated the Church—its organization, fellowship, zeal, and
vision. He wrote to the Full Gospel Church for permission to
join the Church of God. Permission granted, Saayman united
with the Church and attended the 1950 Assembly in Birmingham. When he spoke in one of the sessions, considerable interest was aroused concerning South Africa, as was
demonstrated by an offering given by the delegates for the
building of churches there.[1]

The affinity between the Church of God in America and
the Full Gospel Church in South Africa increased until correspondence was begun concerning an amalgamation of the
two groups. Arrangements were made for Chesser and Walker
to visit the South African Church in the spring of 1951. Plans
for this meeting went along smoothly in America, but in South
Africa there was considerable misgiving and reluctance concerning amalgamation with the Church of God. On January 6,
1951, the Executive Council of the Full Gospel Church
adopted a resolution that discouraged the merger, but did not
entirely close the door to negotiations.[2] Notwithstanding this
discouragement, Chesser, Walker, and Saayman flew to Johannesburg in February as planned.

Their reception in South Africa was cordial but doubtful. In
many ways the two groups were identical, but in a few matters of organization there was severe divergence.* The obsta-
cles did not prove insurmountable, however, and the amalgamation was effected on March 28, 1951. The Full Gospel
Church lengthened its name to Full Gospel Church of God;
a complete change of name would have forfeited recognition
and privileges gained during the thirty years the Church had
been established in the Union of South Africa. In America
the Church would continue to be simply the Church of God.

The Full Gospel Church was the second largest Pentecostal

---

1. *Minutes of the Forty-third General Assembly,* 1950, p. 77.
2. Correspondence from H. R. Carter to H. L. Chesser, January 10, 1951.
*For instance, the Church of God is stern in its centralized form of govern-
ment, whereas the Full Gospel Church "strongly favored decentralization."
(*Minutes of the Executive Council of the Full Gospel Church,* January 6, 1951.)

work in South Africa. Its earliest pioneer, Archibald H. Cooper, first went to South Africa from England during the Anglo-Boer War in 1902. In 1904 Cooper came under the influence of Evangelist Gypsy Smith and was converted during a revival in the city of Capetown. Soon afterward he went to Johannesburg, where, in 1907, he received the baptism of the Holy Spirit under the ministry of John G. Lake and Thomas Hezmalhalch, evangelists from the United States. Cooper then felt the call of God upon his heart and began a church in Middleburg, Transvaal.

From that beginning the Full Gospel work grew, not dramatically but consistently. It gained greater strength in 1921 when Cooper's Pentecostal mission and a small group known as the Churches of God united under the name Full Gospel Church. The first constitution of the organization was signed on April 19, 1922.[3]

It was in 1910 that the Full Gospel Church initiated a missionary outreach among the natives of Africa, with W. A. duPlooy as its first missionary. Pastor duPlooy eventually established a mission station at Levubye in the Northern Transvaal.[4] While the leadership of the denomination consisted altogether of Europeans—those of British or Dutch descent—its principal evangelistic success was among the Africans: the "Bantus," the pure blacks of Africa; the "Coloreds," those who were racially mixed; and the "Asiatics," those who had earlier migrated from India. Most of the Asiatic work was the fruit of two men's labor, J. F. Rowlands and his brother Alex.

As a condition of the amalgamation:

> It is agreed that the Moderator of the Full Gospel Church of God in Southern Africa shall by virtue of his office be a member of the Supreme Council of the Church of God of the United States of America. . . .

---

3. *Constitution of the Full Gospel Church of God.*

4. Information for this section has been drawn from Alex Thompson, *Church of God Evangel,* April 13, 1970, p. 20; H. G. Jenkins, *Sow,* Winter, 1976, p. 13, plus interviews with Mrs. Dorothy Wooderson, daughter of A. H. Cooper.

> . . . The General Overseer of the Church of God of the United States of America shall by virtue of his office be a member of the Executive Council of the Full Gospel Church of God in Southern Africa.
>
> Voting rights in each respective General Council are granted to Ordained male ministers of both churches and it is agreed to afford equal recognition of the ministers of the Full Gospel Church of God in Southern Africa and the Church of God in the United States of America when visiting the respective churches.

The agreement was signed by H. L. Chesser and J. H. Walker for the Church of God; and by F. J. M. Beetge, General Moderator, and H. R. Carter, Secretary General of the Full Gospel Church.* Upon consummation of the amalgamation, J. H. Saayman was elected General Moderator, largely in recognition of the work he had done to effect the merger.

The amalgamation opened a wide field for the Church of God on the continent of Africa. The Full Gospel Church had about thirty thousand members, an excellent school in Kroonstad—Berea Bible College—and numerous well-established mission compounds in many parts of the African interior. With the added strength from the United States there was such immediate expansion in South Africa that it approached the phenomenal. From thirty thousand in 1951, the Full Gospel Church of God grew to 39,257 in 1952; to 49,257 in 1953; and to 56,839 in 1954.

Even though the two groups are totally indigenous, with the exception of the reciprocal seats in the Church councils, there has been a steady stream of American preachers to South Africa and South African preachers to the United States. This free interchange has cemented fellowship and understanding between the two bodies. M. G. McLuhan, former president of Northwest Bible College in Minot, North Dakota, went to South Africa as president of Berea Bible College, Kroonstad, in 1953. James L. Slay assisted in evangelistic work in the

---

*Witnesses whose signatures appear on the document were A. H. Cooper, W. A. duPlooy, W. D. Badeshesste, and J. F. Rowlands.

Union 1952 to 1953. Ray H. Hughes spent two months there in 1954, in interest of the Sunday School and Youth Department of the Church.

§ 2. THE ADMINISTRATIVE PATTERN

While these strides were being made abroad, the Church in the United States was satisfactorily following the self-decreed course of administrative limitation. R. R. Walker was succeeded as General Secretary-Treasurer by Houston R. Morehead at the Assembly of 1950 (Forty-third).[5] Morehead had served as overseer in Missouri, Michigan, and South Carolina prior to his election to this general office. Even though he was a young man, his evident consecration and consistent sense of equity retained the confidence of ministers everywhere who had grown accustomed to such unassuming and deeply spiritual men as Boehmer and Walker. Morehead's ability as a preacher became a great asset to the Church, for he was instantly in demand as the official representative at state conventions and ministers' meetings across the nation. He was not only an eminent preacher, but a lucid thinker as well. Under him the office of General Secretary-Treasurer became vital in its administrative function, in addition to its wonted efficiency as custodian of the Church's finance and business.

At the Publishing House in 1950, A. M. Phillips resigned after only two years as business manager to accept a local pastorate. Appointed to replace him was Cecil Bridges, who had been business manager of Lee College for two years.

Ralph E. Williams' tenure as national Sunday school and youth director expired at the 1950 Assembly, also. He was succeeded by Lewis J. Willis, who had brought himself to the attention of the Supreme Council by his distinguished service as Sunday school and youth director of Florida. Willis was a member of the National Sunday School and Youth Board, which experience contributed very much to his success as national director.

---

5. *Minutes of the Forty-third General Assembly,* 1950, p. 21.

Two years later, at the Assembly of 1952 (Forty-fourth), there was a change in every general office of the Church, precipitated by the four-year limitation on most offices. Two offices were added to the Executive Committee—a second Assistant General Overseer and the editor in chief.[6] Zeno C. Tharp was elevated from Assistant General Overseer to General Overseer. His astuteness in the affairs of the Church and his long service as a minister and administrator made him a natural choice. Houston R. Morehead and John C. Jernigan became his Assistants; H. L. Chesser was retained on the Committee as General Secretary-Treasurer; and Charles W. Conn was added to the Committee as editor in chief.

Ray H. Hughes was elected to replace Lewis J. Willis in the Sunday School and Youth Department. Although Hughes was a pastor in Chattanooga, his greatest prominence came from his evangelistic work. Whereas Williams and Willis had been outstanding organizers and administrators of the department, Hughes was exceptional as a promoter and speaker. His contagious ebullience was a perfect capstone for the solid organization that had been welded by his predecessors.

Willis was appointed editor of *The Lighted Pathway* where he soon demonstrated a distinctive editorial ability and wielded a ready pen. In the Music Department, Otis L. McCoy, who had edited more than fifty songbooks during his sixteen years in office, was succeeded by V. B. (Vep) Ellis, son of E. M. Ellis and grandson of pioneer J. B. Ellis. For years Ellis had been hailed as one of America's most talented composers of gospel music. Through the years the Church of God used this revivalistic type music, but with appreciation for, and use of, the traditional hymns. Ellis's occasional venture into the field of hymn composition produced creditable music of stately and traditional quality.

To round out the personnel changes, Paul H. Walker replaced J. H. Walker as executive missions secretary when the latter was appointed overseer of Ohio. The new secretary came

---

6. *Minutes of the Forty-fourth General Assembly,* 1952, pp. 31, 36.

into the office with wide experience as state overseer, member of the Supreme Council, and the Missions Board. By starting at a young age and accepting difficult assignments, Walker became a man of great experience while still comparatively young.

In October following the Assembly of 1952, the Missions Board appointed Wade H. Horton foreign missions field representative. This was not a new office, for J. H. Ingram had been popularly regarded as field representative during his years of missions travel and activity. In 1938-1939 Paul H. Walker had served as field representative for one year,[7] and when his appointment expired, the office was left vacant but was not abolished. Horton was an outstanding pastor before his appointment to the post. He had gained wide attention as pastor in Washington, D. C., but was pastor in Charlotte, North Carolina at the time of his appointment as field representative.

In the spring of 1953, William F. Dych resigned as superintendent of the Orphanage and Children's Home. His successor was R. R. Walker, overseer of Kentucky, whose kind, fatherly spirit made his choice for the Home a happy one. Earlier, in 1952, George W. Ayers, pastor in Cawood, Kentucky, had come to the Home as an assistant superintendent. Together, Walker and Ayers succeeded in providing the Home an atmosphere of benevolence and orderliness.

§ 3. Latin American Center

What J. H. Ingram did for the initial missions endeavor of the Church, Vessie D. Hargrave did for Latin America. Hargrave, a member of the Church of God since his childhood and a preacher since his eighteenth year, was pastor of several churches in his native Texas, and state youth director there before his assignment to Mexico as social and moral director.[8] This was in 1944. After one year he was appointed superintendent of the Latin-American Department of the

---

7. *Minutes of the Thirty-fourth Annual Assembly,* 1939, p 24.
8. Vessie D. Hargrave, *Evangelical Social Work in Latin America* (unpublished Master of Science degree, Trinity University, San Antonio, 1951) pp. 190, 191.

Church of God. Under his guidance the Latin-American Department made commendable progress. Its growth created the need of a Spanish literature and a distribution center. San Antonio, Texas, became a virtual headquarters for this Latin work in 1947 when Hargrave established administrative and editorial offices there. A Spanish edition of the *Evangel, El Evangelio de la Iglesia de Dios,* and other periodicals were distributed widely throughout Hispanic America.*

§ 4. PERU

Organization of the Church of God in Peru was a result of this Spanish publishing effort. Readers of *El Evangelio* began to inquire about the Church, so Hargrave visited Peru in 1947, and succeeded in planting the Church there. For two years only native workers were used, but in 1949, A. S. Erickson was appointed missionary to the South American country. Erickson and his wife had formerly served as missionaries to Peru for another denomination, but at the time of the 1949 appointment he was employed at the Publishing House and Lee College. Under the leadership of this couple the work prospered, and the Church of God was well established in several sections of the country.

§ 5. BRAZIL

In 1948 Hargrave went into the interior of Brazil, where he contacted Albert J. Widmer, who had first learned about the Church of God in 1944. In March of that year Widmer was present at the dedication of the large Church of God Temple in Buenos Aires and was impressed by the wonderful work of Pastor Marcos Mazzucco. At the time of the meeting of Hargrave and Widmer in 1948, arrangements were made for Widmer to work with the Church of God. In 1951 Widmer was recognized as a missionary of the Church of God and centered his ministry in the State of Parana.

---

*The *Church of God Evangel* was published in Mexico for about three years before being published in San Antonio. Now *The Lighted Pathway,* Sunday school literature, and other periodicals are published in Spanish editions.

Another missionary was received into the Church in 1954—Mathilda Paulsen—who had for a number of years labored in the Amazon nation under the auspices of a small organization on the West Coast of the United States. When this group was no longer able to sponsor her work, she was left free to unite with someone able to support her and her South American project. She chose to bring her Brazilian mission into the Church of God. On Júly 7, 1954, Miss Paulsen returned to Brazil and the work she had founded, which was composed of about twenty workers and several hundred members. The leaders of her organization voted unanimously to follow her into the Church of God.

§ 6. CHILE

Chile was another field reached by the Church of God through *El Evangelio.* After reading the Spanish edition of the *Evangel,* Enrique Chavez, a Chilean pastor, wrote to Hargrave asking about the Church of God, which led to correspondence between the two men. Hargrave paid Chavez and his church an annual visit until 1949, at which time a young lady of the Chilean church was sent to International Preparatory Institute.* She was Rosa Vega, who became the first Church of God member in Chile.

In 1953, Edmund F. Outhouse visited Hargrave and the Institute in San Antonio. Outhouse for ten years had been a missionary to Colombia, but was forced out of that country because of severe persecution there. He was not affiliated with any particular group but was supported by friends throughout the United States. He knew a great deal about the Church of God, having had some correspondence with the superinten-

---

*International Preparatory Institute in San Antonio was one of the most colorful of all Church of God schools. It was begun in 1947 as a training center for Latin-American missionaries—both Anglo- and Spanish-American. Vessie D. Hargrave was founder of the school, and its president from 1947 to 1953. Wayne McAfee was president from 1953 until its discontinuation in 1954. It was discontinued because of the belief that native workers could be better and more economically trained in their homelands. During the history of the school, there were students enrolled from more than twenty countries.

dent of Latin America, and having sent one of his Colombian members to I.P.I. for two terms.

In San Antonio Outhouse felt much impressed to unite with the Church of God. However, he and Hargrave agreed that he should wait until returning to Chile to make his final decision. The matter should be considered carefully on the field. On February 22, 1954, Outhouse and his wife united with the Church of God. The first church was organized in Santiago, from which there was immediate and favorable growth. Within eight months about eight missions were opened in Chile, and two small Bible schools were begun.

§ 7. OVERSPREAD OF LATIN AMERICA

Paraguay was reached by the Church of God in the winter of 1953, when Jose Minay of Chile asked to be sent there. He immediately opened a mission in Asuncion, and began to preach in the villages and towns nearby.

Miguel Flores of El Salvador was appointed to Nicaragua in 1951. The faithful servant of God sacrificed his home and other personal property to work in Nicaragua. Within a year he organized four churches and established the converts in the faith. In 1952, Flores was succeeded by Pedro Abreu of the Dominican Republic, who was a skilled builder. Abreu erected several churches throughout the country, the principal one in the capital city of Managua. In this same manner of self-sacrifice, most of the Latin-American countries have been reached by the Church of God.

The Church of God entered Colombia quietly in 1955 when two Pentecostal preachers in Bogota united with the Church and began to preach under its sponsorship. Protestant missionary work in Catholic Colombia was a difficult and dangerous business, but Ricardo Moreno and Mesias Juarez labored discreetly with some success. About a year later, in April 1956, Paul Childers of North Carolina was sent to Colombia by his business firm. Childers and his wife, Candita, joined with Moreno and worked toward establishing a congregation in Sogamoso, which was organized in November 1956. Within a year other congregations were also established in Apulo and Villavicencio. Despite difficulties of Protestant missions in Colombia, the Colombian people were hungry for the gospel and received the Word gladly.

§ 8. TUNISIA

The Pentecostal message reached Tunisia in North Africa as early as 1911, when Josephine Planter went there as a missionary. For forty-one years this lady labored alone in Tunis in the ministry of the full gospel. In about 1947 Miss Planter established contact with the Church of God, after which time she received support from the Church. Even though the solitary missionary worked faithfully and won converts to the Pentecostal faith, few, if any, of the converts actually received the baptism of the Holy Ghost.[9]

About this time there was in Lee College a young lady on whose heart the Lord had laid a burden for Tunisia. When the Missions Board deferred to send a twenty-year-old woman alone to a field where there were no other Church of God missionaries, she paid her own passage. She went to Tunis in April, 1952. For one year she assisted Miss Planter, after which she moved from Tunis to the small village of Megrine. Margaret Gaines, a singularly pious young lady, opened a small mission in her home, which was officially recognized by the Tunisian government on February 4, 1954. It was a happy beginning.

Converts were won to Jesus Christ slowly, but patiently they were established in the faith of the Scriptures. On June 8, 1954, one of the converts in Tunisia received the baptism of the Holy Ghost—in the same manner as the early Church of God people at Camp Creek in 1896. This convert, Yvette Pelissier, became Miss Gaines's assistant in the tremendous task of sowing the seed of the full gospel in the Arab nation where once was ancient Carthage.

---

9. Correspondence from Miss Margaret Gaines, undated, but received on October 12, 1954.

§ 9. Zeal for Missions

The Missions Department was strengthened in November, 1953, when Johnnie Milton Owens was appointed missions representative. While Owens was in the U. S. Army in Egypt during World War II, he was converted and came under the influence of a Salvation Army brigadier who had the baptism of the Holy Ghost. When he returned home, he attended the Riverside Church of God in Atlanta.

Remembering conditions he had seen over the world, Owens obtained a list of all Church of God mission fields and began to work in their behalf. He raised money for the erection of mission stations and gathered clothing for the missionaries to distribute among the needy natives in their fields. The success of his endeavors was astounding. By the time he was appointed missions representative in 1953 he had raised the money to build 110 mission stations around the world.

As missions representative, Owens traveled widely to conventions, prayer conferences, and other meetings in behalf of the Church of God world missions program. Owens was the first of numerous missions representatives who were to spread the challenge of world outreach.

§ 10. Assembly of 1954

Approximately ten thousand delegates attended the Assembly of 1954 (Forty-fifth) in Memphis, Tennessee. Few changes were made in the administration of the Church, and the accustomed love and fellowship prevailed. Physical incapacity due to an automobile accident, which occurred while he was visiting state conventions in the summer of 1953, forced the retirement of John C. Jernigan. He was succeeded as Assistant General Overseer by James A. Cross, overseer of South Carolina. Cross, a brilliant thinker and solid administrator, possessed multiple abilities long noted and admired by his colleagues. The son of pioneer preacher W. H. Cross, the newly elected Assistant General Overseer was well beyond his forty-three years in experience, ability, and influence.

H. L. Chesser, ineligible to succeed himself as General Secretary-Treasurer, was replaced by H. D. Williams, overseer of Alabama.[10] In many ways Williams resembled the man he succeeded, methodical and meticulous, popular among the ministers of the Church and forthright in his associations. Both Cross and Williams had been impressive as members of the Council of Twelve for two years preceding their election to their executive posts. There were no other immediate changes in the Executive Committee, although it was decided that effective in 1956 the office of editor in chief should be separated from the Committee. This decision was made because of the vast difference in the responsibilities of the editorial and administrative fields, and in order to provide greater attention to the publishing interests of the Church.[11]

§ 11. A PUBLISHING SURGE

By 1954, the Church had become manifestly aware of the tremendous but heretofore neglected opportunities in the editorial field. This had been proved in 1952 when the erection of a new publishing plant was recommended by the Supreme Council and approved by the General Council.[12] Construction was begun in the spring of 1953 and completed in the spring of 1954.

In the fall of 1952 an art department was created with Chloe Stewart, a remarkably gifted young illustrator, as chief artist.* In the spring of 1954, the production of Sunday school literature was reorganized with W. Perdue Stanley as editor of Sunday school literature. Before coming to the Editorial Department Stanley served as Sunday school and youth director of Georgia. *The Pilot,* a quarterly youth worker's publication, was begun in 1952-1953 by the National Sunday School and

---

10. *Minutes of the Forty-fifth General Assembly,* 1954, pp. 17, 27.

11. *Ibid.,* p. 30.

12. *Minutes of the General Council,* 1952, p. 23.

*Earlier artists who served the editorial needs of the Publishing House were James C. Rickles of Alabama (1945) and A. S. Erickson during his interim as missionary to Peru (1949). These men served briefly and did not begin a continuing graphics department such as that in 1952.

Youth Board and Cecil M. Truesdell was named its first editor. Beginning in 1954 this periodical was supervised by O. W. Polen, the new assistant Sunday school and youth director.

In addition to these editorial advancements, the business offices were strengthened by the appointment of E. C. Thomas as circulation, credit, and sales manager. Thomas majored in business administration at Queens College while he was pastor of a local church in Charlotte, North Carolina. The new $750,000 publishing plant was ready for occupancy about Assembly time, 1954. Shortly after the dedication of the new plant, Cecil Bridges submitted his resignation as business manager, whereupon E. C. Thomas was elevated to the vacant office.[13] Bridges on April 1, 1955, accepted the position of assistant superintendent of the Home for Children in Sevierville.

With these editorial and publishing developments, the Church of God demonstrated a growing concern for publishing excellence. There was a new consciousness of training and technique in its use of the printed word. Increasingly the Church would use more sophisticated methods in its proclamation of the gospel.

§ 12. SOUTH CAROLINA HOME FOR CHILDREN

As North Carolina had done in 1944, the Church of God in South Carolina instituted a Home for Children in 1956. The new regional home was brought about through the efforts of H. B. Ramsey, overseer of South Carolina, and his state ministers' council. The home was located six miles northwest of Gaffney on a 125-acre farm donated to the Church for that purpose. J. B. Camp, veteran minister of the Church of God, was named superintendent of the home which began its operation on January 13, 1956 with the arrival of four homeless children.[14] The facility, which could accommodate twenty children, was filled to capacity by the end of the first year's opera-

---

13. *Church of God Evangel,* March 26, 1955, p. 2.
14. J. D. Free, *Church of God Evangel,* August 20, 1956, p. 13.

tion. The home remained in Gaffney until 1969 when it was moved to Mauldin, near Greenville. As in North Carolina, the South Carolina Home for Children was supported by the congregations in that state, who contributed to it in lieu of the national home in Sevierville.

Opening of the new home was consistent with the Church's desire to de-emphasize the centralization and institutional nature of its care for orphans and homeless children. It was a step toward providing a more homelike atmosphere to those tender lives already scarred by tragedy and disappointment.

§ 13. A Time to Reap

The decade of the 1950s was a time of missionary reaping for the Church of God. Several mission fields that had tantalized and eluded the Church for many years were at last entered with permanent missions; some of the victories were gained by unexpected but fortunate means. Following World War II, when defeated Japan lay as a fertile field for Christian missionary work, many zealous soldiers in the Army of Occupation witnessed for Christ to the Japanese people and sowed good seed of evangelism. Such efforts eventuated in the opening of the Church of God in Japan. Among the soldiers who did this work of evangelism were Henry E. Flowers, Leon Simms, James Joplin, Arthur Shannon, and Robert L. Orr. In response to possibilities in the Shinto land, the Church of God sent L. E. Heil, a young minister from West Virginia, and his wife, Letha, to Japan as missionaries. The Heils arrived in Yokohama on August 19, 1952. Heil's work was slow and difficult but fruitful in the Land of the Rising Sun.[15] It was good fruit from the tragic seeds of war.

The improbable Gilbert Islands, sixteen tiny specks in the Pacific Ocean, became a mission field of the Church of God in 1955. These islands lie near the equator, about two-thirds of the way between the United States and Australia. Edward Kustel, a native of the Gilbert Islands living in the United

---

15. Conn, *Where the Saints Have Trod*, pp. 232-236.

States, felt a divine call to return to his homeland with the full gospel. On January 20, 1955, after two years of preparation, prayer and travel, Kustel, with his wife, Alma Lee, landed on Betio, a small coral islet on the south end of Tarawa. In the tiny land, 11,000 miles from the United States, the Kustels began a good and promising work.[16]

Nearer home, in the Caribbean area, some obdurate fields were either opened to the Church or began to yield to the influence of the gospel. Delayed success was realized in July, 1956, on Trinidad, Grenada, and Tobago when Edward D. Hasmatali, a native Trinidadian, brought his native missionary work into the Church of God. With sixteen churches and missions, fifteen ministers, and three hundred fifty members, it was already a substantial organization when Hasmatali extended his efforts into the islands of Grenada and Tobago.

Guyana, on the South American continent, was another late success for the Church in the 1950s. The Church of God had made efforts in what was then British Guiana since 1942, but the work there was vague and mercurial. The impetus of Hasmatali's work in Trinidad spilled over into Guyana, however, and in 1956 Guyana became a stable and promising section of the Church of God.[17]

§ 14. England's Immigrated Church

The extension of missions went farther still. During the decade immediately following World War II, large numbers of West Indians immigrated to England. As subjects of the British Commonwealth they had this right to settle in the English homeland. When these Jamaicans, Bahamians, and Barbadians migrated to England, they carried their religious worship and beliefs with them. Many were members of the Church of God in the Caribbean and formed the foundation of the Church in their new homeland.

In 1951 O. A. Lyseight of Jamaica and his wife moved

---

16. *Ibid.,* pp. 214-217.
17. *Ibid.,* pp. 111-114.

to the Midlands in England. By September 1953 Lyseight and a few Jamaican friends began promising Pentecostal missions in Wolverhampton and Birmingham in the industrial heartland. Although a few Englishmen attended the worship services, the congregations were principally blacks from Jamaica and other Caribbean islands.

In 1955 the two missions were organized as the first congregations of the Church of God in England. This was accomplished when Paul H. Walker, the indefatigable executive secretary of world missions, visited England after attending the Pentecostal World Conference in Stockholm, Sweden. Walker officially organized the congregations on June 18, 1955.[18] Almost immediately new congregations were established in other cities and towns. Within three years there were thirteen churches with more than a thousand members among England's transplanted Jamaicans and other West Indians.

§ 15. Underground in Spain

Of the late-flowering mission fields, Spain was probably the most rewarding. The Church of God entered Spain surreptitiously in much the same way that early Christianity spread from country to country. Although the Church was not officially organized until 1956, the Pentecostal faith had worked quietly like leaven for more than a decade prior to that time. A citizen of Spain named Custodio Apolo was converted to the Pentecostal faith in New York City in 1934 and almost immediately felt an urge to return to Spain with the gospel. Apolo united with a Spanish-speaking Church of God in New York City which supported and sponsored his return as a missionary to his own people. This was not easy. The revolutionary status of the Iberian nation in those oppressive days made Protestant missionary work an exceedingly treacherous business. Apolo suffered considerable persecution when he conducted secret worship services in his house after the Spanish authorities refused him permission to conduct public services.

18. *Ibid.*, pp. 252, 253.

Twice, on July 26, 1951, and September 6, 1955, Apolo was so bold as to conduct baptismal services for the new converts.[19] The Missions Department of the Church of God supplied Apolo with literature which was distributed and read in secret, much as the earliest Christian literature must have been read in the days of the apostles.

There are times when the army of the Lord enters a campaign boldly and gains its victory on a grand scale. There are other times when the army, outmanned and outnumbered, must enter the field covertly, work with stealth and enjoy its victory without fanfare. Such quiet victory is also glorious.

Early in 1956 Ray H. Hughes, who was on a preaching tour of other European countries, visited Apolo in Badajos, Spain, near the Portuguese border. After preaching first in Madrid and Barcelona, Hughes arrived in Badajos on February 29, where he was met by a small band of believers in Apolo's home. In the old saint's home the young American formally organized the Church of God. In the worship service that night two of Apolo's converts received the baptism of the Holy Ghost; these were the first to receive the blessing during the years Apolo had worked in Spain. This experience was like a divine amen to the enterprise of the Church.

Conditions in Spain ultimately improved, and the work of the Lord was at last carried on openly. Even though its beginning was covert and its progress slow, the work of the Church of God in Spain represented one of its finest endeavors. It was reminiscent of olden times, and yet it opened the door for the future. In a wonderful way it was like the threshold to a new era.

---

19. *Ibid.,* p. 250.

Part Six
The Threshold
of Greatness
1956-1976

Chapter 27
THE CHANNEL
BROADENS

§ 1. The Stream of Maturity

A river is a lively and exciting thing as its headwaters start their flow to the sea. High in the mountains crystal freshets cascade down the slopes to be joined by bubbling springs and icy rivulets along the way. The water is clear and fresh and invigorating as it courses across the plains of its youth. The splashing freshet becomes a stream, then a brook, and at last a clear and shallow river. As other streams empty into it, the fledgling river swells and flows all the more. It teems with life and rolls with joyous energy down the mountainsides and across the meadows, still far from the sea. Animals of the forest and field make their way to its grassy edge; men find rest and inspiration on its banks and in its bracing waters.

As the stream flows on, growing larger each mile, broadening its breast and deepening its channel, it changes from a lovely mountain stream into a mighty river. The change is not in substance or quality or basic nature, but in size and capacity. The dash and excitement may be less than before, but the stream's usefulness and power are greater than ever. The turgid river seems more ponderous and sluggish than the mountain stream, but that is only an illusion; the river has force and capabilities the stream never dreamed of. The deep, relentless river, now more murky than crystalline because of silts gathered by its flow through the land, seems impersonal and treacherous in comparison to the mountain stream. But that too is an illusion; the river has qualities of life and service the

301

brook could never know. Now it can irrigate the valleys and plains, generate power to illuminate cities and operate factories, carry provisions and vessels upon its ample breast and in many ways supply life and vitality to its region. What it loses in splashing excitement it gains in usefulness and effectiveness.

Men are also like that as they progress from infancy to maturity. So are nations and institutions. And so is the Church of God. In its formative stage everything in the Church of God was new, innovative, exciting; it was of necessity bold and venturesome. As the Church gained maturity, it gained efficiency in those issues and concepts it hammered out in the early days. Its boldness and daring remained as great as ever—just less conspicuous than in the days of lonely beginning. Innovations of the Church are as numerous as ever, possibly more numerous; these individually exciting tributaries are often muted by the roar of the main stream in its well-defined channel.

By 1956 the Church of God had outgrown its infancy and youth; as a church, it had become youthfully mature. It was seventy years old, and two generations had passed since its birth. With its survival and growth assured, its service and character became the pressing issues; it was time to assert itself in mature and responsible ways. In short, the Church of God had come of age.

§ 2. EXECUTIVE SUCCESSION

When Zeno C. Tharp concluded his tenure as General Overseer at the Assembly of 1956 (Forty-sixth) and went into retirement, Houston R. Morehead, who had served as First Assistant General Overseer, was elected to the office.[1] His election set a pattern that has never been broken: the person serving as First Assistant at the time of a change in the General Overseer has always been elevated to the high office. There has been no exception since the multiple assistantships began in 1964; despite the number of Assistants, the General Overseership has been attained only through the office of First

---

1. *Minutes of the Forty-sixth General Assembly,* 1956, p. 15.

Assistant. In fact, the trend was set even earlier, with the election of H. L. Chesser in 1948 and Zeno C. Tharp in 1952, both of whom were elected General Overseer from the office of Assistant General Overseer when there was only one Assistant.

This pattern has assured the Church of God of experienced leadership despite the frequent changes brought about by the limitation on executive tenures. Unlike the law of limited tenures, however, the pattern of succession is not required. It just happens. Changes and shuffles have frequently been made in the other offices of the Executive Committee, but never in this most vital step of succession.

Houston R. Morehead came to the leadership of the Church from a background of broad experience. A native of Illinois, the fifty-year-old leader had gained distinction in varied capacities, among them as pastor in Tennessee, youth worker in Michigan, and overseer of Missouri, Michigan and South Carolina. A member of the Executive Council since 1946 and the Executive Committee since 1950, Morehead was highly respected by his colleagues and the general membership of the Church. He brought spiritual sensitivity to the office of General Overseer and gave the Church conscientious leadership. Morehead was eligible for only one two-year term; he came to the office with six of his maximum of eight years on the Executive Committee already expired.

Chosen to serve with Morehead were James A. Cross, First Assistant General Overseer; Earl P. Paulk, Sr., Second Assistant; and H. D. Williams, General Secretary-Treasurer. For Paulk, this was a return to the post he had held twelve years earlier, 1941-1944. In keeping with action of the previous Assembly (1954), the office of editor in chief was dropped from the Executive Committee so there would be no unnecessary dilution of departmental responsibilities.

§ 3. THE PATHWAY IMPRINT

At the Publishing House the years 1955 to 1960 brought significant advancement to the publishing interests of the Church. Throughout 1956, in observance of the seventieth anniversary of the Church of God, the *Evangel* adopted an editorial theme for the year and featured each week a particular aspect or ministry of the Church of God. During that year a modern off-set multicolor printing process began to be used extensively for production of the *Evangel, The Lighted Pathway* and Sunday school literature.

An equally ambitious program concerned book publication. In 1956 the Publishing House undertook to become a serious publisher of Pentecostal books. From its outset, the Pentecostal Revival consisted mainly of the preached Word and publications of an immediate, but impermanent, nature. Little attention was given to book publication. The Publishing House took a step toward correcting that deficiency by adopting the trade name, "Pathway Press," so future books could be distributed to a broader market than the Church of God constituency.[2] The first two books published under the new imprint, in the spring of 1956, were *Pillars of Pentecost* by Charles W. Conn and *Religion on Fire* by Ray H. Hughes. These were followed by a spate of other Bible-based works.

Another bold step of that time was the opening of retail bookstores that would feature Pentecostal materials. Broadening on the Pathway name, the retail stores were called "Pathway Bookstores." The first store opened was in Tampa, Florida,[*] with others opened soon afterward in Charlotte, North Carolina; Akron, Ohio; Atlanta, Georgia; and Chattanooga, Tennessee. Under Thomas's direction the Pathway Bookstore system began to provide a much-needed service to numerous areas of the country.[†] In recognition of his business skills and achievements as business manager of the Publishing House, his title was changed to Publisher in 1960.[3] This raised the dignity and

2. *Ibid.,* p. 24.

3. *Minutes of the Fiftieth General Assembly,* 1960, p. 43.

*The Tampa store was actually begun in 1955 under a different name. In 1956 the name was changed to Pathway Bookstore and it became the first of the Pathway Bookstore system.

†In 1971 a franchising system was developed to give even wider opportunities for the retail bookstores. Individual owners and managers are franchised as Pathway retailers in cities where they wish to open a store.

emphasized the importance of what had come to be one of the most responsible offices of the Church of God.

§ 4. SEEDS OF EVANGELISM

From its beginning the impulse of the Church of God was evangelistic outreach; every effort was in some way aimed at winning men to the Lord Jesus Christ. Despite the itenerant, largely personal, evangelistic efforts of the very earliest ministers, the Church of God relied almost altogether on mass evangelism in its efforts to win men to Christ. Local church revivals, city-wide meetings, camp meetings and even youth camps were of the same kind. Some attention was given to personal evangelism, but this remained minimal for many years. At the 1956 Assembly a first step was taken toward coordinating the evangelistic energies of the Church: a National Evangelism Committee was named which would constitute the possible beginning of a permanent department of evangelism.*

> This committee shall have the status of a standing board, and shall form the possible beginning of a Department of Evangelism. This board shall make a study of all forms of Christian evangelistic effort—mass evangelism, personal evangelism, child evangelism, etc. This board shall promote the general evangelistic interests of the Church by whatever means of publicity, records and guidance are beneficial or necessary. They shall make to the Supreme Council whatever recommendations they feel necessary for the vigorous pursuit of a Biblical, balanced, abiding evangelistic emphasis in the Church.[4]

The committee, C. Raymond Spain, Doyle Stanfield and

4. *Minutes of the Forty-sixth General Assembly,* 1956, p. 28.

*A "department" should be defined as an area of church operation that has both an executive head and a managing board. Generally a department is set in motion by the naming of a committee or person to serve a particular need of the Church. If the need warrants it, a permanent board and executive director are named later. It is then that the area of service becomes a full-fledged department. Frequently a committee with the status of a standing board is appointed that may (or may not) grow into a department. Similarly, particular functions are frequently performed by a person or an office, but this is regarded as an office and not a department.

Ray H. Hughes, proved to be as vigorous and creative as was expected, and the evangelistic efforts of the Church soon began to reflect a new cohesion and effectiveness. The energetic work of the group was like good seed in fertile ground, soon to bear fruit of every good kind.

Named at the same time was a National Music Committee,* which did not eventuate into a department. Instead, it would ultimately merge with the evangelism thrust of the Church and become a part of that ministry. Evangelism in the Church of God soon came to full flower; the Church emphasized its strong point and grew thereby.

§ 5. THE YOUNG PIONEERS

Two of the most exciting programs of Christian growth and maturity in the late 1950s concerned and involved the young people of the Church of God. Both programs demonstrated how enthusiastically young people respond when they are challenged and entrusted with responsibility.

The first was incubated on the Lee College campus and represented the brightest star of the scholastic firmament in what was a rather doleful decade for the college. Through the combined efforts of Lee College, the newly-appointed Evangelism Committee and the Sunday School and Youth Department, strong emphasis was placed on personal evangelism and Christian witnessing on the campus. Existing Youth for Christ groups became very active under the leadership of Charles R. Beach, a member of the language faculty at Lee. In 1956 the energetic professor and a few student leaders began evangelistic excursions into cities of nearby states. The name "Pioneers for Christ" was ultimately chosen for the intrepid group, which soon became the most inspiring outreach effort of the Church of God.

Beach was the driving force behind PFC. His energies brought into being a new breed of youth and lay evangelists, who applied serious training and native skills to the primal evangelistic impulses of the Church. "Pioneers for Christ" was

---

*G. W. Lane, W. E. Tull, C. S. Grogan.

a happy choice of name for the campus evangelists, who were in many ways like the earliest pioneers of the Church. They walked from door to door in towns and cities to witness to the people that Christ is the Lord of life. They visited jails, nursing homes and hospitals to proclaim the good news of redemption; they conducted services on street corners and in local churches —or anywhere else there might be a listener.

"Invasions" were organized by Beach and such student leaders as G. A. Swanson, Terry Beaver, Bill Wooten and Robert Blackaby; an invasion being a group of students—scores of them at times—conducting massive personal evangelism efforts in a particular town. Hundreds of homes were visited, and numerous worship services were conducted. And there were also seminars to help the local members understand the best methods of leading a sinner to Christ.

Summers were especially busy, when student teams spent their entire vacations doing this evangelistic work. They went to such places as Salt Lake City, Boston, Albuquerque, and New York City. Eventually, they spent summers outside the United States, in the Bahamas, Trinidad, Jamaica and other target cities and countries. Donald S. Aultman, as the assistant national Sunday school and youth director, gave assistance to the program and personally led some of the missions invasions.

Each year even now the same happy, dedicated work is done. The Pioneers have become a movement in themselves. Not only have they done massive evangelistic work personally, but they have motivated and trained hundreds of laymen to evangelize their towns. PFC has brought a dynamic new element to the Christian responsibility to tell men about Christ.

§ 6. YWEA: Youth and Missions

The second youth evangelistic emphasis centered in world missions support. O. W. Polen, veteran youth leader from Ohio who was elected national Sunday school and youth director in 1956, spearheaded in 1957 a program called Youth World

Evangelism Appeal.[5] This program of missions education and giving, undertaken in conjunction with the Missions Department and the Evangelism Committee, aimed at making the youth of the Church conscious of missionary work. Local Sunday school classes and youth groups raised funds to assist missionaries with needed equipment and supplies. Young people were encouraged to pray daily for the missionaries and give daily from their earnings or allowances.

Proceeds of this youth giving were used to buy such things as bicycles, mules, burros, boats and other items needed by missionaries in their travel and work. Needs of individual missionaries were supplied by individual youth groups. It was a good program, and like many good programs, it became even better.

When Cecil B. Knight, who was Polen's assistant for four years, was elevated to the national directorship in 1960, he introduced a plan that greatly enlarged the YWEA endeavor. Funds would be raised for building substantial church buildings, youth centers and training institutes around the world, with one project for each year.* The first such project, in 1961, was a church in Brasilia, Brazil; then came such major projects as a youth center in Tokyo, a seminary in Djakarta and a Bible college in Durban, South Africa. The young people of the Church of God dug deeply into their pockets and built

---

5. Conn, *Where The Saints Have Trod,* p. 48.

*The YWEA projects are as follows: (1961) $21,109.19 for a church in Brasilia, Brazil; (1962) $18,181.27 for a church and youth center in Tokyo, Japan; (1963) $34,753.47 for a church in Bombay, India; (1964) $43,836.44 for a church in Manila, Philippines; (1965) $45,349.54 for a church home for displaced Zulus in Durban, South Africa; (1966) $55,951.08 for a Bible school in Hermosillo, Mexico; (1967) $46,311.99 for a church in Port-au-Prince, Haiti; (1968) $74,995.84 for a seminary in Djakarta, Indonesia; (1969) $72,054.88 for a Bible school in Nassau, Bahamas; (1970) $124,814.69 for a Bible institute in Gallup, New Mexico; (1971) $116,708.40 for a seminary in Balboa, Panama; (1972) $148,164.87 for a servicemen's center in Pearl Harbor, Hawaii; (1973) $214,333.92 for a Bible school in Durban, South Africa; (1974) $292,000.00 for a European Bible School; (1975) $307,803.58 for churches in Mexico City, Mexico; San Salvador, El Savador; Managua, Nicaragua; (1976) $262,326.64 for mission centers at Lee College, Northwest Bible College and West Coast Bible College.

in all parts of the world impressive facilities that will endure in fact for a lifetime and in consequence forever.

§ 7. Forward in Faith

For years the Church of God entertained dreams of a national radio program, but the recurring dream was slow in being fulfilled. Numerous ministers conducted successful and attractive local broadcasts, some with wide listening audiences over vast interstate areas. The desire for a national broadcast was very real, but it was not always equally practical. As early as the mid-1940s the Church had a brief fling at such a broadcast when General Overseer John C. Jernigan and other prominent leaders of the Church preached over a powerful Mexican border station. The idea did not work well and was soon discarded.

Finally the Church came to grips with its desire for a broadcast—but still with some hesitation. The Assembly of 1956 called simply for the Supreme Council to "initiate a national radio and television program in interest of the Church of God."[6] More than two years passed before the program was actually put on the air waves.

In late 1957 and early 1958 the Supreme Council conducted a series of auditions for the posts of radio speaker and the program director. Earl P. Paulk, Jr., popular pastor in Atlanta, was selected as speaker; Bennie S. Triplett, Sunday school and youth director of Tennessee, was chosen as announcer and program director. In a very real sense each man held a special place in the affections and admiration of the ministry and membership of the Church. Paulk was the prominent son of a prominent father; Triplett was an accomplished son of the Home for Children. Both men were highly personable and immensely gifted. Paulk, long admired as a pastor, scholar and writer, served as radio speaker in addition to his duties as pastor in Atlanta. Triplett, a talented composer and musician, became the first full-time appointee to the radio ministry. He organized a choir and special music groups from the Cleveland area.

---

6. *Minutes of the Forty-sixth General Assembly,* 1956, p. 30.

Following a "Forward in Faith" rally at the Assembly of 1958, a Radio Commission was appointed, with H. D. Williams as chairman, to expedite and direct the radio ministry.[7] The first program was broadcast on December 7, 1958, heard on a network of six stations located in strategic sections of the country.* Named "Forward in Faith," the program was recorded weekly in the chapel at the General Offices. Almost immediately, more stations were added to the special network. Within six months Forward in Faith was carried by more than forty stations.[8] Before the first year ended, it was broadcast on fifty stations, in most parts of the United States and in several other countries.[9] At long last a dream had come true.

§ 8. ACADEMIC NADIR

Despite the progress of the Church on almost every other front, its educational program remained discouraging during the late 1950s. Enrollment at Lee College continued to drop and the regional schools in North Dakota, California and Saskatchewan remained marginal in their operation. The Church of God was apparently not yet aware of the changes that had taken place in the field of education—its new emphasis in modern life, its new demands and its new directions. In that time of uncertainty in the Church regarding education, the status of its educational institutions reached a depressing level. An academic malaise spread through the Church.

In some desperation the Lee College Board of Directors, administration and faculty sought to turn the tide and win the Church's confidence in the academic quality of its college program. In May 1957 the Board elevated Rufus L. Platt, Dean of the Junior College, to the presidency.[10] Retiring President R. Leonard Carroll returned to a local pastorate. At the time of

---

7. *Minutes of the Forty-seventh General Assembly,* 1958, p. 37.
8. *Church of God Evangel,* June 8, 1959, p. 2.
9. *Ibid.,* October 26, 1959, p. 2.
10. *Minutes of the Lee College Board of Directors,* May 21, 1957.
*Birmingham, Alabama; San Francisco, California; Baxley, Georgia; Detroit, Michigan; Chattanooga, Tennessee; and Charleston, West Virginia. (H. D. Williams, *Church of God Evangel,* December 1, 1958, p. 2.)

the change in presidents, the enrollment was 436. For the new term in September 1957 it declined to 397. Eventually, in the spring of 1960 the enrollment dropped to a discouraging 337. Despite Platt's efforts and the assistance of those around him, the time of upturn had not yet come. The Church had not yet caught up with the forward surges and opportunities in the world of education.

§ 9. A New Black Vitality

Following the separation of the black and white sections of the Church of God in 1926, there was separate supervision for the black congregations, which also had their own National Assembly. Except for the General Assembly, in which a dutiful section was always reserved for black delegates and there was generally a special worship service by and for them, there was little contact between the two races. The comparative lack of growth among the blacks was a nagging concern to the leadership of the Church. The Executive Committee and Supreme Council gave intermittent consideration to ways of increasing black vigor and involvement in general Church outreach. In the setting of that period, however, the answers were difficult to find, or, they were typically superficial. In many ways the Church of God was victim of the national frustration and inertia of the times.

In May 1958 the Executive Committee appointed an energetic, experienced white minister to the national overseership of the Negro churches: J. T. Roberts, pastor in Tampa and member of the Supreme Council. This was a bold, unprecedented action; the six previous national overseers were all respected black leaders.

Announcement of Roberts's appointment at the National Assembly in Jacksonville, Florida was greeted with some question and considerable optimism among both the blacks and whites. It was with much hope and faith that General Overseer Morehead announced:

> The Assembly was blessed with high interest and good attendance from the beginning to the end. The excellent

cooperation of the ministers was commendable and indicated good progress for the future. We have high hopes
for the expansion of our colored work. . . . Pray much
that the Lord will bless (Overseer Roberts) in his work
and that the work may grow and prosper under the blessing of the Lord.[11]

Under Roberts's guidance and evangelistic verve, the black
work soon showed a welcome, almost dramatic, new energy and
motivation. New churches were organized and numerous new
buildings were erected. There was a brief new vitality, with a
resultant sense of identity, among the black membership of the
Church. It seemed that the answer, though long in coming,
had come at last.

§ 10. THE VERGE OF DIVISION

When the ordained ministers gathered in Memphis for the
Assembly of 1958, they had little reason to suspect that the
unity of the Church of God would be tested to its limits. An
apparently innocuous measure to permit the wearing of wedding bands precipitated one of the rockiest Assemblies the
Church had ever had. The debates became so emotional and
intense that the concord of the ministers was stretched to its
thinnest point. Some of the men feared that the wearing of
wedding bands would open the floodgate to abuses, that members would begin to wear "unnecessary jewelry," a violation of
the holiness dress code held by the Church from the beginning.
Others felt that the Church's restriction on unnecessary jewelry
was never intended to include wedding bands. Still others felt
that circumstances of the times required a degree of relaxation
in the strict code.

The General Council adopted the measure by a narrow mar-
gin and presented it to the General Assembly, where the debate
was continued by laymen and licensed ministers as well as ordained ministers. This was the first time in the memory of
most persons present that any measure had been debated on
the Assembly floor; measures from the Council were generally

---

11. *Church of God Evangel,* July 21, 1958, p. 2.

adopted by the Assembly without discussion. After the spirited debate ended, the proposal to permit the wearing of wedding bands was adopted.

For awhile it seemed that there might be a deep schism within the body regarding the problem of worldliness and that this debate only served as the occasion that exposed it. But the Church was made of sterner stuff; there were allowances for such differences of opinion within the great expanse of brotherhood and love. The resilience and tenacity of its spiritual love won the victory; the true unity of the body was not broken, only proved.

The Church of God was like a river that splits momentarily around a rock in its bed and then flows together again without interruption. The river may gurgle around many stones as it flows to the sea, but it is always the same river on its way to the same sea.

Chapter 28
MIDPASSAGE

§ 1. THE OLD-NEW LEADERSHIP

The tension-filled Assembly of 1958 marked the end of Houston R. Morehead's abbreviated tenure as General Overseer. Due to the eight-year limitation on Executive Committee service, Morehead was ineligible for a second term in office. James A. Cross, who had been First Assistant General Overseer, was elected to succeed Morehead. Predictably, the remaining members of the Executive Committee moved up in position: Earl P. Paulk, Sr. to First Assistant General Overseer and H. D. Williams to Second Assistant General Overseer. Added to the Committee was A. M. Phillips, overseer of Florida, who was elected General Secretary-Treasurer.

James A. Cross's rich background in the Church of God ideally prepared him for the office of General Overseer. The son of a minister, he was reared in a parsonage and was a distinguished student at Lee College (then Bible Training School). Cross entered the ministry early in life and was a successful pastor of numerous congregations. At age twenty-four he was appointed overseer of Nebraska, the first of an impressive list of responsible assignments. He was noted for his keen, analytical mind and for his stable leadership. Of greatest importance was the fact that Cross commanded the confidence and respect of the Church everywhere.

§ 2. NEW FACES FOR MISSIONS

Significant changes were made in the supervision of the growing world ministries of the Church. Paul H. Walker,

pioneer preacher and missions representative, was replaced
as executive missions secretary by L. H. Aultman, popular
overseer of North Carolina. Walker returned to the Dakotas
as overseer of the rugged region of his birth and childhood.

There was also a change in the office of missions field representative in 1958; Wade H. Horton, who had held the post
for six years, was replaced by C. Raymond Spain, overseer of
Michigan. To complete the personnel sweep, Johnny Owens
left the Missions Department, where he had served as a representative since 1953; his post was not refilled. Aultman and
Spain were well-received by missionaries and the Church in
general. The initial concern of some regarding the changes
was soon dispelled; the world missions enthusiasm and mo-
mentum continued without abatement.

§ 3. THE HALFHEARTED ENTERPRISE

As early as 1954 there were some business-minded leaders
who so lamented the high cost of insurance on Church of
God properties that they dreamed of a Church-contained insurance program that would reduce or eliminate the heavy
expenditure. What began as a simple dream grew to greater
proportions, the institution of an insurance company that
would not only reduce costs but would provide revenue for
the Church as well.

But this was a halfhearted dream. From the beginning the
Church had a double mind on the subject. When the idea
was presented to the Supreme Council, some felt it was a good
idea, and others felt it smacked of commercialism contrary
to the principles of Scripture. They wanted no part of it.
The Church operated a Tennessee Music and Printing Company and managed the investments of its Aged Ministers
Funds, but these were regarded as spiritual in either nature
or purpose. An insurance company seemed to be business
pure and simple.

A few individuals began such a business venture in 1956
and developed it as a private company named Pathway Mu-

tual Insurance Company. With virtually all of its policies written on properties of the Church of God, the owners and investors offered to sell the business to the Church at the Assembly of 1958.

With considerable ambivalance, the Church purchased the company in January 1959 and operated it as one of its departments; Arlis Roberts was appointed president, and E. C. Thomas was named chairman of the board.[1] Even though the company did well, there was a nagging, ever-present attitude among many that the Church should not be involved in such business enterprises. These objections ultimately prevailed, and the Assembly of 1966 called for discontinuation of the company.[2]

In October 1967 the company was sold to outside business interests, and the matter was put in the past.

§ 4. INTERCHURCH STUDY COMMISSION

Encouraged by its sense of brotherhood, the Church of God also followed elusive dreams in other, more significant areas. Because of their several similarities, especially in regard to the doctrine of holiness and the experience of sanctification, the Church of God and the Pentecostal Holiness Church frequently entertained thoughts of union. The first official dialogue on that possibility occurred in 1947-1948 under the overseership of John C Jernigan. Although no progress was made toward merger, the hope remained alive to germinate anew in 1959.

That year each denomination appointed members to an Interchurch Study Commission,* to explore the possibility of

---

1. James A. Cross, *Church of God Evangel,* February 16, 1959, p. 2.
2. *Minutes of the Fifty-first General Assembly,* 1966, p. 56.
*Church of God members were James A. Cross, Earl P. Paulk, Sr., H. D. Williams, A. M. Phillips and Charles W. Conn. (Later members were Wade H. Horton, R. Leonard Carroll, Ralph E. Williams and C. Raymond Spain.) Representng the Pentecostal Holiness Church were J. A. Synan, W. H. Turner, R. O. Corvin, W. Eddie Morris and Byon A. Jones. (Later members were J. Floyd Williams, A. D. Beacham, R. L. Rex.)

318   *Like a Mighty Army*

closer fellowship and cooperation between the two church groups." At the initial meeting in Des Moines, Iowa, on October 25, 1959, a brief resolution was adopted regarding the "many similarities and mutual interests" of the two denominations.[3]

The meetings continued for ten years, alternating between Cleveland and Franklin Springs, Georgia. Strong fraternal ties were increased and enlarged by a liberal interchange of speakers in denominational conferences, camp meetings, and college seminars, and by frequent cooperative editorial and publishing endeavors.[4]

The Church of God and Pentecostal Holiness fellowship was dramatized with a series of four biennial "Holiness Conferences" between 1963 and 1969.[*] The conferences were well attended and did much to foster fellowship and undergird the Pentecostal experience and the holiness tradition. The final meeting of the Interchurch Study Commission was September 24, 1969—exactly ten years after the group was organized.[5] No effort was ever made to merge the two churches; each retained its own identity and operation. The result was something even more precious, something that exemplified the Christian ideal of brotherhood: a fellowship and cooperation that have outlived the Commission itself.

§ 5. The Making of a Memory

In 1960, fifty years after R. M. Evans and Edmond S. Barr first took the Pentecostal message to the Bahamas, the Church of God celebrated the event with a tour to the Islands. L. H. Aultman and C. Raymond Spain organized and directed the tour, which was made by 750 persons. As nearly as possible, the tour route followed the trail of Evans from Durant, Florida, to Miami, to Nassau.

---

3. *Church of God Evangel,* December 7, 1959, p. 2.
4. *Ibid.,* May 30, 1960, p. 2.
5. From the official files of the Church of God.
*In Charlotte, North Carolina (September 1963); Falcon, North Carolina (May 1965); Atlanta, Georgia (May 1967); and Greensboro, North Carolina (May 1969).

The large group of tourists sailed from Miami on New Year's Day, 1960, and arrived in Nassau the following day at noon. The ship was greeted by a throng of Bahamian believers singing on the docks. It was a joyful time with a weekend of services in several of the Nassau churches. American delegates and Bahamians filled the churches and the city. On January 4 the anniversary celebration climaxed at noon with a mass rally in a ball park. Thousands were present. It was the same day and hour of R. M. Evans's arrival in 1910. Carl M. Padgett, a young man who accompanied Evans on that historic day, was also present on this day of commemoration; the now aged missionary gave a testimony to the gathered delegates.

Trouble with the ship on the return trip to Miami gave the tired tourists an unplanned taste of the peril and inconvenience missionaries face every day. Following a flash fire below deck, the immobilized vessel wallowed in the sea for about twenty-four hours. With food supplies exhausted, the delegates filled the desultory day with impromptu worship and inescapable fellowship. Tugboats from Miami arrived at last and towed the ship and its weary cargo safely home.[6]

Memory being what it is, the pleasures of the trip soon stood out in bold relief to those who made the excursion, while the fright and inconvenience served only to heighten its drama and sharpen its memory.

§ 6. THE MISSIONARY IMPULSE

Even while the missions impulse of the Church of God was being celebrated in the Bahamas, it asserted itself in other parts of the world. On January 1, 1960, the Church entered the South American country of Bolivia.[7] Late in 1959 a young Chilean pastor named Daniel Cubillos felt a divine urge to go into Bolivia with the gospel; he and his small family moved to their new land just before the new year began. On the

---

6. Conn, *Journal,* January 5, 1960.
7. Vessie D. Hargrave, *Church of God Evangel,* June 27, 1960, p. 3.

first day of the year, while they were singing in Nassau, he conducted the first worship service in Sucre, a city of forty thousand in the Bolivian Andes. As most of the Latin American countries have been, mountainous Bolivia proved to be a fertile field for the Church of God.

In Europe, the redoubtable Herman Lauster extended the perimeters of the Church beyond his native Germany. He was called upon to conduct services in Switzerland late in 1959. This resulted in the organization of a church in Schaffhausen in February 1960.[8]

Lauster, already legendary in Germany, also directed his attention toward the Alsace Lorraine, a bilingual region on the German-French border. A church was organized in the delightfully medieval city of Colmar in April 1960.[9] Later Lauster would also organize a church in Muenster. A gifted German minister, Karl Otto Boehringer, whose wife was English, was assigned to pastor the Colmar congregation. He was succeeded by another young German minister, Eberhard Kolb, a product of the new German Bible School. Although the organization of these churches in aged and advantaged Europe did not represent traditional missionary work, they did reflect the same spiritual urges and hungers that had motivated the Church of God from the beginning. In a similar way more congregations would be organized in other towns and countries.

The German Bible School, instituted in Krehwinkel in October 1958, with E. Lamar McDaniel as president, became a missionary fountainhead for several countries of Europe, Africa and the Middle East. In addition to supplying workers for Germany, the school would see its graduates go into such lands as Israel, Nigeria, Ghana, and the Alsace Lorraine. The day had come when the evangelized lands would in turn evangelize still others. That is the true missionary impulse. That is the true Christian way.

---

8. Herman Lauster, *Church of God Evangel,* December 19, 1960, p. 14.
9. Lauster, *Ibid.,* December 12, 1960, p. 7.

§ 7. SAARLAND AND FRANCE

The Church of God in France had a German beginning and spoke at first with a German accent. Even before Herman Lauster organized the church in Colmar, his son Walter moved to Heiligenwald, a city of the industrial Saar region, and began evangelistic work. With his wife, Bobbie, the young Lauster preached in several towns and cities of the Saar. The Saar, like Alsace Lorraine, was a border region, half-German, half-French, with a blend of both cultures and fluent in both languages. A congregation was established in the town of St. Ingbert early in 1958, and in May of that year a second was organized in Saarbrucken, capital of the district.[10]

In 1959, through the intervention of J. H. Saayman of South Africa, a young French pastor named Andre Weber joined with Lauster and opened a church in Troyes, deeper into the French interior. Weber, who was ministering in Belgium when he met Lauster, was a relative of the renowned Pierre Nicole, Pentecostal pioneer in France. A native of the Troyes area, Weber had long felt a burden to start a church in the city of his youth. The young pastor conducted revival meetings, then organized the church in 1959; he later pitched a tent in the slum sections of the city and evangelized the prostitutes, hoodlums, Gypsies, and other down-and-out segments of society. Weber was an earnest minister of the gospel accustomed to difficulty and eager to win men to Christ. Under his leadership the church in Troyes became an effective center of the Pentecostal message.

Back in and near the fluid borders of the Saarland, Lauster started churches in Pirmasens, Germany in 1961 and Saarlouis in 1962. Encouraged by those successes, the Missions Board, in 1964, sent Lauster to Chatellerault in the Loire Valley of central France. The purpose was to spread the Pentecostal faith more fully to other parts of the spiritually destitute French nation. But France was not to become the fertile ground for the gospel Germany was.

---

10. Interview with Walter Lauster, January 14, 1977.

§ 8. 1960: Assembly of Regrouping

The Church of God was shaken deeply at the Assembly of 1958, and two years later the tremors were still ominous. It was a time of regrouping for the days ahead. Delegates arrived in Memphis with an emotional admixture of anxiety because of disappointments and optimism because of faith.

At the Assembly of 1960 James A. Cross was reelected General Overseer as expected. Then Wade H. Horton, overseer of Mississippi and former field representative of missions, was elected First Assistant General Overseer. Horton had long been a favorite of the Church of God; his sudden emergence to the high office confirmed the Church's confidence in, and affection for, him. Earl P. Paulk, Sr., whom Horton replaced, was not reelected to the Executive Committee, but H. D. Williams was reelected Second Assistant General Overseer and A. M. Phillips was reelected General Secretary-Treasurer.

There were other changes at the Assembly, the most conspicuous being Ray H. Hughes's simultaneous assignments as president of Lee College and national radio minister. Few men of the Church could have survived such arduous responsibility. Horton and Hughes were marked for long and distinguished leadership of the Church.

A third man thrust into a leadership role in 1960 was Cecil B. Knight, elected national Sunday school and youth director. Knight would bring the youth work to new levels of achievement and innovation. The outlook of the Church was promising as the Church of God entered what has been called its "Decade of Destiny."

§ 9. A Divine Interruption

After the tensions of the Assembly of 1958, there was some concern that those tensions might carry over into the meeting of 1960. They might have, but God intervened in a remarkable way. It started at a session of the Supreme Council preceding the Assembly, at a session when the Council discussed the Church's need to reaffirm its belief in, and practice of, holiness. The Council adopted a resolution to that effect and then had a period of prayer and personal affirmation. The Holiness Resolution stated:

> The foundation of the Church of God is laid upon the principles of biblical holiness. Even before the Church experienced the outpouring of the Holy Ghost, its roots were set in the holiness revival of the past century. It was, and is, a holiness church—holiness in fact and holiness in name.
>
> The passing of three-quarters of a century has not diminished our holiness position or convictions. The years have, instead, strengthened our knowledge that without holiness it is impossible to please God.
>
> We hereby remind ourselves that the Scriptures enjoin us at all times to examine our own hearts. The continuing and consistent life of holiness requires this. Conditions of our day desperately require it. The subtle encroachment of worldliness is a very real and unrelenting threat to the Church. We must therefore beware lest *we* become conformed to the world, or lest a love for the world take root in *our* hearts to manifest itself as lust of the flesh, lust of the eye, or the pride of life.
>
> For these reasons, we present the following:
>
> *Whereas,* the Church of God is historically a holiness church, and
>
> *Whereas,* we are enjoined by the Scriptures to be so and
>
> *Whereas,* a tide of worldliness threatens the spirituality of the Church,
>
> *Be it resolved,* that we, the Church of God, reaffirm our standard of holiness, in stated doctrine, in principles of conduct, and as a living reality in our hearts.
>
> *Be it further resolved,* that we, as ministers, maintain this standard in our own lives, in our homes, and in our pulpits.
>
> *Be it further resolved,* that we, as ministers and members, rededicate ourselves to this purpose, and guard our lives against conformity to the world in appearance, in selfish ambition, in carnal attitudes, and in evil associations.

> *Be it further resolved,* that we, as ministers and mem-
> bers, seek to conform to the positive virtues of love, mercy,
> and forgiveness as taught by Jesus Christ.[11]

As the resolution was read to the ordained ministers, both
the speaker, who had also drafted the resolution, and the
audience were overcome with weeping. Ministers began to
kneel at their seats in prayer. Then came such a time of confessions and testimonials that all business had to be suspended. The praying, weeping and testimonies continued for two
full days in what was a great time of personal and denominational renewal. It was noted that "the resolution relative
to principles of holiness of the Church of God was unanimously
adopted in the General Council on Thursday, August 18,
1960, with unity and genuine purpose."[12] The spirit of the
spontaneous outbreak was so salutary and overwhelming that
it left a permanent imprint on the Church of God.

§ 10. Concern With Image

The Church of God had long been large enough that the
news media were eager, sometimes determined, to report its
affairs. In 1958, the customary publicity committee was
changed to a public relations committee,* whose primary
function at each Assembly was to assist newsmen and protect
the public view of the Church of God. A press box and
press room were provided for newsmen, even in the formerly
exclusive ordained ministers' sessions. The committee inter-
preted Church of God beliefs, customs and Assembly actions
for the inquiring press, helped set up special features and
issued press releases to national wire services. The Church
made friends with what had not always been a friendly press.

In 1960 the editor in chief was appointed public relations
director in connection with his editorial responsibilities. He
was to publicize church activities and handle matters of

---

11. *Minutes of the Forty-eighth General Assembly,* 1960, pp. 51, 52.
12. *Loc. cit.*
*Charles W. Conn, O. W. Polen and Earl P. Paulk, Jr.

Church image; he was to assist various news and information media—newspapers, radio and television stations and networks, magazines, encyclopedias, researchers and historians —in gaining accurate information and correct understanding of Church of God affairs. A public relations office was set up in 1960, but it did not become full-time until six years later.

§ 11. MINISTRY TO THE MILITARY

From the time of World War II the Church of God saw increasing numbers of its young men drafted into military service. Uprooted from family and church, these servicemen were often lonely and discouraged, and some ran into severe spiritual difficulties. In 1961 the Church expressed its concern for these young men by initiating a servicemen's department. Overseer Cross assigned H. D. Williams, Second Assistant General Overseer, to gather a mailing list of Church of God members and friends in military service and begin a program of regular correspondence with them. Williams began such correspondence with a mailing list of about one thousand servicemen; he also made the Church of God constituency aware of this area of responsibility with a servicemen's page in the *Evangel*.[13]

This was the beginning of one of the most exciting and rewarding ministries of the Church. Through it the Church would extend its care and support to sons around the world; and in return those uprooted sons would become missionaries and evangelists to press the gospel into new parts of the world. The Church of God would soon witness a dramatic new dimension in worldwide evangelism.

---

13. H. D. Williams, *Church of God Evangel*, February 20, 1961, p. 6.

Chapter 29
REJUVENESCENCE

§ 1. THE SECOND WIND

In many ways the Church of God got its second wind in 1962. A new burst of energy touched almost every area of Church ministries, and there was a general surge forward. Ever since the outstanding Assembly of 1960, the Church had been filled with a deep sense of blessing and responsibility; every department had engaged in plans for advancement and increased effectiveness.

Preparations for the Assembly of 1962 were positive and progressive, including an unprecedented schedule for ministers and laymen to do personal evangelism in the city of Memphis. For the first time ever, business of the Assembly was suspended, and the delegates went in groups to many sections of the city to witness for Christ. This massive demonstration of evangelistic outreach was spearheaded by the Evangelism Committee and the Pioneers for Christ organization. Experienced Pioneers from Lee College and summer witness teams accompanied and directed the ministers and members as they witnessed for Christ. More than the immediate results could have shown, the massive effort set a new tone of evangelism for the future.

General Overseer Cross spoke in the finest keynote tradition on the subject, "Let the Church Speak," which was a call for aggressive Christian living and labor. The remaining services were positive, optimistic and dynamic; inspiration ran like an electric current through the entire Assembly. Much time was devoted to planning for the future in every department of the denomination. The Church showed itself to be vibrantly alive and happily unified. It was like an army moving forward at double time. Like a church that knew its mission.

§ 2. THE NEW LEADERSHIP

The men chosen to lead the Church in this period of rejuvenescence made an interesting configuration. Predictably, Wade H. Horton was elected General Overseer; and A. M. Phillips was elevated to the office of First Assistant General Overseer. Then, instead of selecting the next Executive Committee members from among the state overseers as was recently customary, the ministers chose two department leaders to fill the remaining executive posts. Charles W. Conn, who had been editor in chief for ten years, was elected Second Assistant General Overseer; and C. Raymond Spain, missions field representative for the past four years, was elected General Secretary-Treasurer. This deviation from recent patterns did not indicate any new direction for the Church; in reality it was a return to an earlier time when departmental leaders were frequently chosen for the Executive Committee.

Even the new General Overseer, Wade H. Horton, was more experienced in missions than in the supervision of a state. He had been overseer of Mississippi for two years, 1958-1960, but as missions field representative for six years, 1952-1958, he had enjoyed a highly effective ministry in many parts of the world. Still earlier, this native of South Carolina had served as pastor in several states and Washington, D.C. He was best known, however, for the personal magnetism of his leadership and the quality of his pulpit ministry.

Before the end of 1962 the four-man Executive Committee was reduced to three. A. M. Phillips became terminally ill shortly after the Assembly during the course of his travels for the Church. The normally ebullient minister carried on his duties as long as he was able, but in November he was confined to his bed, the victim of incurable cancer. Phillips gradually became weaker. On a snowy day in December, he gave a final victorious testimony to his family and Executive Committee associates, who were at his side, and quietly died. It was December 24, Christmas Eve.

Since there was no provision for the selection of a successor, Phillips's responsibilities were redistributed to Conn and Spain. The Executive Committee continued with only three members for the next two years.

§ 3. THE DEPARTMENTAL PHALANX

To say that the Church of God was like an army moving forward at double time is to say that its several departments were moving forward together. Its various ministries were specialized agencies of a unified whole. Each department advanced its particular function and, thereby, contributed to the progress of the entire body. The Church had become an organized, closely-knit phalanx of individual units in one coordinated effort to penetrate the world for Jesus Christ. Whatever the functions might be, the purpose was one. Like the body Paul described to the Corinthians, the Church of God was one body composed of many members. The victory of one was victory for all; the invigoration of one gave vigor to all.

It was a time of rejuvenescence. New departments were born and the old were improved; new projects were begun, and the old were enlarged. New hopes were born and old hopes were fortified and confirmed.

§ 4. A SUPERINTENDENT FOR EUROPE

.At the Assembly of 1962 a superintendent of Europe was named to supervise the rapidly-growing Church of God interests on that continent. The European churches, because of their gradual origins under missions sponsorship, were reckoned as sections of the World Missions Department. But the European churches were not "missions" as such; they were only overseas from the United States. Vessie D. Hargrave, well-known for his long-time work in Latin America, was named to fill the position. He established his headquarters in Basel, Switzerland and assumed supervision of the European churches from that neutral point. It was believed that the Swiss center of operations would best serve the strong demands of the growing works in other countries without giving advantage to any. With strong churches in Germany and England, and smaller but promising works in France and Spain, and single congregations in numerous other countries, the Church of God made a full commitment to the interests of the "Old World."

§ 5. EVANGELISM AND HOME MISSIONS

The many evangelism endeavors of the Church grew to the point that a program of coordination and direction was needed. In its March 1963 meeting, the Supreme Council authorized the institution of an Evangelism and Home Missions Department.[1] The Executive Committee appointed Walter R. Pettitt, overseer of Pennsylvania, to direct the new department. Pettitt, who had three years' experience on the Evangelism Committee, entered his new work with energy and enthusiasm.

In connection with his work in evangelism, Pettitt would also supervise the architectural services of the Church.[2] Since 1962 an Architectural Committee, composed of ministers and licensed architects, had provided plans for the construction of church edifices and facilities.[3]

§ 6. NEW LIFE AT LEE

One of the most dramatic reversals in the history of the Church of God happened at Lee College during the 1960s. Immediately following the appointment of Ray H. Hughes to the presidency in 1960, the already-low enrollment dropped lower still, to 312; then the decline was arrested, and all trends of the school turned upward. Hughes, ever the evangelist, led a renewal of spirit reminiscent of that in Ezekiel's valley. After a steady increase in enrollment, an unbelievable 629 students registered for the fall 1963 semester. Lee's resuscitation re-

1. *Minutes of the Supreme Council*, March 6, 1963.
2. Wade H. Horton, *Church of God Evangel*, July 8, 1963, p. 4.
3. Charles W. Conn, *Church of God Evangel*, June 4, 1962, p. 3.

quired simultaneous advancement on three fronts—student recruitment, faculty recruitment, and development and improvement of the physical facilities.

Academic recognition resulted from, and then added to, the new life at Lee. The Bible College had been accredited by the Accrediting Association of Bible Colleges in 1959, and the Junior College was accredited by the Southern Association of Colleges and Schools in 1960. Hughes also led in a stimulating enlargement of facilities: a new administration building was built in 1963 and a new science building in 1965.

One innovation of the period was an annual "College Day," in which high school juniors and seniors were invited to the campus *en masse* as guests of the College. Sponsored jointly by Lee and the National Sunday School and Youth Department, the first such day was April 25, 1964. The visitors, more than a thousand of them, were introduced to the academic, spiritual and social phases of college life. This proved to be an exceptionally good student recruitment opportunity and soon became a high point of the school calendar.[4] It brought beneficial, if momentary, excitement and fullness to the customarily uncrowded campus.

This temporary turgidity accelerated growth, and school morale rose along with the enrollment and campus expansion. At long last higher education would take its rightful place in the ministries of the Church of God.

§ 7. FORWARD IN FAITH MOVES FORWARD

At the same time that Lee College was being revitalized under the presidency of Ray H. Hughes, the radio broadcast Forward in Faith became a respected Pentecostal voice under his ministry. Its special network grew from forty-two to 120 stations in thirty-seven states, five foreign countries, and several United States Armed Forces overseas stations.[5] A recording studio was built for the program in the old quarters of

4. Ray H. Hughes, *Church of God Evangel*, April 6, 1964, p. 11.
5. Bennie S. Triplett, *Church of God Evangel*, December 2, 1963, p. 11.

Tennessee Music and Printing Company. Delton L. Alford, a
talented young musician newly come to Lee College, joined the
staff as music director and built a commendable music organization. Because of the increased demands of both Lee College
and Forward in Faith, it became necessary for Hughes to give
up one responsibility so he could devote full time to the other.
He remained at Lee and resigned from the radio ministry in
September 1963. After a summer of one-month trial series by
four prominent preachers with radio experience, G. W. Lane
of Cincinnati, who had a broadcast of considerable merit in
that city, was chosen radio minister.[6] Bennie S. Triplett remained as program director.

§ 8. A New Look for Publications

The format and physical appearance of Church publications,
under the supervision of Lewis J. Willis, newly appointed
editor in chief, made such striking improvements that the
Evangel moved into the forefront of denominational journals.
Improvements approved for the *Evangel* at the Assembly of
1962 were put into effect in January 1963; these included art
layout and design, off-set printing process, the weekly use of
color and an increase of pages. The *Evangel's* excellence was
acknowledged by the Evangelical Press Association in 1964
and 1965, when the paper won several awards, among them
the coveted Denominational Publication of the Year Award.
With color, art design and increased size added to its editorial
content, the *Evangel* reached impressive heights in Pentecostal
journalism.

Willis demonstrated personal editorial skills and built around
himself a strong editorial staff. The result was one of the finest
Christian journals of the time.*

Similar improvements were made in the *Lighted Pathway*

---

6. Charles W. Conn, *Church of God Evangel,* September 9, 1963, p. 4.
*Willis secured the service of two outstanding editorial assistants during his
editorship. Duran M. Palmertree, a member of the Lee College faculty, served
from 1963 to 1967. He was succeeded by Heinrich Scherz, who returned to
his native Germany as president of the European Bible Seminary in 1973.

under the direction of Clyne W. Buxton, who became editor in 1962. Buxton, an experienced youth minister, had most recently been Sunday school and youth director of Alabama. In 1964 the youth publication was also cited by the Evangelical Press Association for its appearance and content.[7]

§ 9. TRAINING FOR SERVICE

With its Church Training Courses, the Sunday School and Youth Department made a lasting contribution to the general education needs of the Church of God. Begun as a series of workers training courses in 1955, the program had grown to great proportions involving studies in teaching methods, Bible survey, doctrine and other themes of benefit to the Church. Because of its growing emphasis on excellence in all areas of Christian education, the department would eventually become, in name as well as service, the Youth and Christian Education Department.

On August 19-23, 1963, this vigorous arm of the Church sponsored a Leadership Training Conference "to give advanced training in Christian education to all persons who are connected with the educational ministry of the Church."[8] The conference, conducted on the Lee College campus, was especially designed for pastors, youth leaders, Sunday school teachers and Christian education directors. It was a serious effort with a faculty of seventeen instructors with appropriate academic degrees. Under the direction of Cecil B. Knight, the ambitious seminar attracted more than four hundred Christian educators for the four days of intensive training. Results of the conference were good—and it marked another step in the Church's growing emphasis on training for all areas of church service. Response was sufficient for future conferences to be scheduled. The motion toward educational requirements and provisions for Church of God leadership was begun and, once begun, could only continue its forward course.

---

7. Duran M. Palmertree, *Church of God Evangel,* June 29, 1965, p. 5.
8. Palmertree, *Ibid.,* September 16, 1963, p. 6.

§ 10. The Nourishing Link

The progressive mood of the Church of God manifested itself all over the world as demands for evangelism and Christian training came from every quarter. The Evangelism Board of the Full Gospel Church of God in South Africa urgently requested evangelistic help from America. In late August 1963 the Executive Committee responded by commissioning three outstanding ministers to South Africa. Paul F. Henson of Mississippi, J. Frank Spivey of Georgia, and Albert H. Batts of Tennessee spent three months preaching in forty-five churches of South Africa and Rhodesia. More than six hundred were converted under their ministry before they returned home in early December.[9]

> The evangelistic group the Executive Committee sent to South Africa in August returned today. The Executive Committee was at the airport to meet them. The men had glowing reports of their separate trips through South Africa, and they were still aglow today. I pray that this fervor and enthusiasm they have will spread all across the Church in renewed evangelism here in the States. Already the Africans are asking for a similar campaign next year. England is also requesting one. The evangelists all feel that such efforts should be repeated year after year.[10]

In a similar vein, Cecil B. Knight and Donald S. Aultman of the Sunday School and Youth Department went to the South African republic in the spring of 1964 for Christian education conferences. In seventeen days the two men lectured to more than six hundred pastors and teachers and 2,500 members. The South Africans set as their aim for the decade—"a Christian education building for every church of the Full Gospel Church of God."[11]

§ 11. The Forgotten Americans

Great as the Church's emphasis on evangelism always was, it was increased during the years 1962-1965 with attention

---

9. Palmertree, *Ibid.,* December 30, 1963, p. 4.
10. Conn, *Journal,* December 5, 1963.
11. W. J. DeKock, *Church of God Evangel,* May 4, 1964, p. 5.

given to new methods and new directions. One new direction was toward the forgotten Americans—the American Indians. Although the first such efforts were begun much earlier than 1962-1965, Indian evangelism was given new purpose and emphasis in those years. The Church had sponsored a ministry to the Indians of North Carolina as early as 1948 when Pastor R. P. Fields began evangelistic efforts among the Lumbee, Smiling and Seminole Indians of Eastern North Carolina. Members of numerous tribes were converted and formed the nucleus of Church of God Indian missions. A church organized in the Saddle Tree territory grew to seventy members and in 1950 was influential in starting a congregation in Pembroke. Churches were soon organized in numerous other Indian communities in North Carolina.[12]

In 1959 a campground was developed in Pembroke for an Indian camp meeting. Attendance at the meetings quickly grew to three thousand and above. One of the Lumbee natives, Millard Maynard, an experienced minister of the Church, assisted in the development of the Indian outreach. Other Indian tribes of the Southeast were also reached—the Cherokees in North Carolina and the Creels in South Carolina. This presaged a vigorous and determined Indian ministry in the soon-to-be formalized evangelism department of the Church.

Evangelistic efforts were also begun in the Dakotas among the Sioux, Cheyenne and Mandan tribes. The Dakota Indian work was initiated by Hilbert and Victor Nelson in the late 1950s and early 1960s. These dedicated brothers gave up their North Dakota farmlands in order to work with the Indians. Their main mission station was established in Eagle Butte, South Dakota, near Wounded Knee, where the Sioux made their last valiant stand against the white man. Other missions were established in LaPlant and Dupree. The evangelistic efforts were particularly successful among the Sioux, a once warlike tribe now hungry for the Prince of Peace. In 1963 State Overseer Paul H. Walker wrote, "A group of Sioux Indians

12. Interviews with R. P. Fields and Millard Maynard.

once darkened by sin now have a Savior and rejoice in their newfound joy."[13]

The Church in 1963 extended its arm to the Navajo and Zuni Indians of the Southwest. Early in the year W. M. Horton, overseer of New Mexico, began meetings on the Navajo Reservation near Gallup. The spiritually-hungry Indians were receptive to the gospel, and a considerable number were converted. In May 1963 Charles W. Conn, Assistant General Overseer, visited the Navajo and Zuni reservations with Horton and conferred with the Indian leaders about membership in the Church of God. Horton and Conn toured much of the expansive territory on the Arizona-New Mexico border and went into numerous hogans to visit and pray with the gentle, trusting folk. On the evening of May 27, the two churchmen met with the Indian representatives in Gallup, New Mexico. During the long conference, conducted in the Navajo language through a young Navajo interpreter, Harry Begay, fourteen of the leaders joined the Church of God.[14]

Immediately the hungry-hearted Indians became a ripe mission field for the Church. An Indian camp meeting was soon begun at Two Wells, New Mexico, and large numbers attended from all parts of the sprawling, picturesque Navajo land. Earnest attention would at last be given to the earliest, most poignant of all Americans.

---

13. Paul H. Walker, *Church of God Evangel,* June 24, 1963, p. 8.
14. Conn, *Journal,* May 28, 1963.

Chapter 30
A NEW DIMENSION

§ 1. An Unplanned Partnership

Missionaries of the Church of God in several parts of the world gained support and fellowship—and sometimes an additional responsibility—from an unexpected source at the end of World War II. With the armed conflict ended, Church of God members in the American military forces frequently took their weekend leaves on mission compounds and in missionary homes. There, in hospitable company, the weary, lonely young men found the fathers and mothers and sisters and brothers they had read about in Scripture. They attended worship services off base, which they could not always understand, instead of, or in addition to, chapel services on base, with which they could not identify.

The servicemen began to sing and work in the services; they helped the missionaries and gave needed financial assistance. In return, the missionaries gave encouragement and fellowship to the uprooted young men. Then, with their own spiritual zeal either renewed or preserved, the servicemen became increasingly aware of the spiritual needs around them. They saw the needs of the nationals where they were stationed, and they saw the needs of their own military companions. They saw, and they cared.

The missionaries and the servicemen supported one another in the finest form of teamwork. In some places it became hard to tell one from the other. Many a young man came home from the occupied lands spiritually safe because the missionaries were there; and many a congregation in those war-scarred lands came into existence because the servicemen were there. It was spiritual sharing at its best.

§ 2. MISSIONARIES IN UNIFORM

Unfortunate circumstances sometimes produce fortunate results. Such was the case of Pentecostal young men who were drafted into military service during and after World War II. Uprooted from their families and friends, these young men were sent to strange and distant parts of the world. In many instances the results were beneficial because the men banded themselves together in what they called Pentecostal Fellowships. Through these ephemeral fellowships many men were saved from wallowing in their loneliness and from drifting into carnal vices. They formed islands of fellowship in a sea of sin. Church of God servicemen found that the cords of home and church were strong enough both to hold and to nourish them while they were away.

In their surroundings, the Christian soldiers saw both evangelistic and missionary needs. They saw the needs of the servicemen and became evangelists; they saw the needs of the people and became missionaries. And so, what had been spontaneous and temporary in the late 1940s and 1950s began to take on the aspects of continuity and cohesion in the 1960s.

One of the most prodigious works was in Europe, where numerous servicemen's fellowships were organized by a former soldier who became burdened for such a work while he was in military service. He was J. Don Amison, a native of Florida. As impressed with the evangelistic possibilities among the military population as he was depressed by the sin he saw in several sections of the world, Amison requested the Missions Board to send him to Europe as a missionary to the servicemen. When his application was denied because of lack of funds, the young soldier struck out on his own. With a touch-and-go experience equal to that of any regular missionary, Amison returned alone to Germany in January 1961. His wife, Wilma, and small family would join him later. Servicemen from all parts of Europe attended an introductory service in the little town of Krehwinkel, Germany, on February 22, 1961. Then, with encouragement from such persons as Walter Lauster in the Saarland; Lamar McDaniel at the German Bible School, with whom he lived at the beginning; and Chaplain Robert D. Crick, Amison traveled to military bases, organized meetings and enjoyed much initial success.

Amison began a servicemen's magazine, *On Guard,* to publicize the new evangelistic effort. He generated such enthusiasm that about ten servicemen's fellowships were organized by the end of the year.[1] These fellowship groups, with the approval of the post chaplains, had their meetings in homes or rented buildings near the bases. Other men, such as B. R. Butler in Evreux, France, and O. M. Shepard, in Mannheim, Germany, were instrumental in developing the burgeoning fellowships. Then as the responsibilities increased, a servicemen's council was organized to assist Amison and direct the growing evangelistic outreach.[*]

§ 3. SPIRITUAL RETREATS

A step of great importance was the initiation of a spiritual retreat program for the military personnel. In September 1962 Charles W. Conn, newly-appointed director of the servicemen's work, made a tour of Germany with Amison and negotiated with the Army Chaplaincy for a Church of God Servicemen's Retreat. The petition was approved, and a retreat was scheduled for the fall of 1963.

Amison, after having launched the highly effective work, returned to the United States before the Servicemen's Retreat began. G. A. Swanson, who went to Europe in January 1963 as Amison's assistant, succeeded him as servicemen's representative. Swanson, a native of Arizona who had done

---

1. J. Don Amison, *Church of God Evangel,* January 8, 1962, p. 11.

*This council included at various times such men as Chaplain Robert D. Crick, Chaplain James N. Layne, Colonel Lawrence B. Owens, Leon Groover, Paul Bright, Lee Butcher, Robert Seyda, Jr., Marvin C. Freeman, B. R. Butler, Vessie D. Hargrave and William D. Alton.

much to organize the Pioneers for Christ at Lee College, gave the servicemen's work steady leadership, and its growth continued unabated. Under Swanson's direction the fellowship in Kaiserslautern became the center of the servicemen's operation. Both a church and a servicemen's center were established there. Swanson, with his wife, Treasure, made Kaiserslautern the headquarters of the widespread ministry to the military.

The first Church of God Servicemen's Retreat was conducted in Berchtesgaden September 9-13, 1963, with the director as retreat master and Chaplain Robert D. Crick, retreat coordinator. The 181 retreatants came from Germany, France, Switzerland, England and Libya. The meeting was such a success that it was scheduled as a regular event of the European servicemen's year.

The retreat was conducted in the spectacular mountains of Obersalzburg, where Hitler had retreated to his "Eagle's Nest" for rest during World War II. All services were in the General Walker Hotel, once a luxury hotel for high-ranking Nazi officers. Now the facility was used for the rest and recreation of American servicemen, with a religious retreat every week of the winter.[2] That was a point of righteous irony.

§ 4. THE ASIAN FRONT

While the military fellowships were prospering in Europe, similar programs were also in progress on the other side of the world. In Japan a servicemen's fellowship was begun as early as 1952 when Robert Orr organized such a group at Misawa Air Force Base on Honshu Island. After getting the work started in Japan, Orr was transferred to Germany, where he also worked with the fellowships. Through military rotation the servicemen were often transferred from one part of the world to another, a condition which weakened some fellowships while it strengthened others.

In 1961 the Misawa group, under the strong leadership of

---

2. Lewis J. Willis, *Church of God Evangel,* October 21, 1963, p. 6.

George F. Matheny, became very active. Through the rotation system, Leon Groover, who had been instrumental in the European work, came to Misawa and assisted Matheny. Worship services at first were conducted in the Matheny home,³ and then the group leased a building for eighteen months. This was undesirable, so the men set out to have a building of their own. Matheny twice requested a six-months' extension of his duty in Japan so he could secure permanent facilities for the fellowship. Property was purchased, and a small building was erected in the military community.⁴ The servicemen deeded their property to the Japan Church of God so it could be used as a missions church if the servicemen's work should ever cease to operate. Missionary L. E. Heil, an experienced builder, was of great assistance to the group.

In 1958 a fellowship was organized in Fukuoka on the southern Island of Kyushu, but this group never expanded to the proportions of the Misawa church.

§ 5. OKINAWA

South of Japan, on the island of Okinawa, largest of the Ryukyuan Islands a vigorous fellowship was begun in 1963. The group was organized in Naha, on April 17, 1963, by Jack Landers, Douglas Lane, Don Prewitt and Lucas Matthews.⁵ These Christian servicemen worked diligently among their military colleagues and witnessed as much as possible to the Japanese-speaking Ryukyuan natives.

On July 2, less than three months after the Okinawa fellowship was organized, the servicemen's director went to Okinawa to intervene for a young airman who had been subjected to severe discrimination because of his religious beliefs.* During the course of his negotiations with the Air Force

---

3. H. D. Williams, *Church of God Evangel,* March 5, 1962, p. 5.
4. L. E. Heil, *Church of God Evangel,* April 8, 1963, p. 11.
5. Doug Lane, *Church of God Evangel,* October 14, 1963, p. 6.
*Ultimately the airman was cleared of accusations against him, and he was restored to his former rank. Soon thereafter he left the Air Force and attended Lee College.

authorities, the director met with most members of the young fellowship and was deeply impressed by their earnestness and dedication.[6]

The next spring, April 12-15, 1964, Conn returned to Okinawa for the first Church of God Servicemen's Retreat in the Far East. The opening meeting was of such spiritual nature that he recorded at the time:

> Okinawa. This is the first anniversary of our servicemen's church. About one hundred were present when I preached this morning. We then had a basket lunch at the church; it was almost like a homecoming back in the States. In the afternoon we had a song and testimony service. We had a large crowd present tonight. After I spoke four adults came to the altar for salvation. Brother Landers and the group here are very spiritual, deeply consecrated.[7]

The servicemen in Okinawa also extended their efforts to the Ryukyuan people, whose principal religion was Shinto. Such efforts at native evangelism were customary wherever Pentecostal servicemen were stationed.

§ 6. KOREAN BEGINNING

The Church of God in Korea is the result of work by servicemen stationed there. Many of the American troops in Korea following the Korean War, 1950-1953, became burdened by the misery of the prostrate land and tried to help the sad, friendly people. Because of the great number of beggar orphans, largely the offspring of American soldiers and Korean women, a number of homes were begun for the homeless waifs. Just as World War II had left the country divided, the Korean War had left it poor and devastated. Soldiers stationed in South Korea were on a "hardship tour," without wives and families, always on alert. North of the 38th Parallel was Communist North Korea, threatening, belligerent —the dreaded enemy.

---

6. Conn, *Journal*, July 2, 3, 1963.
7. *Ibid.*, April 12, 1964.

One company, through the influence of Church of God men, established an "Angel Orphanage" and supported seventy orphans. Significantly, a soldier wrote back to the Church, "Pray that we who are here may give the impression to the Korean people that there are still many good Christians that come from America."[8]

One young airman from Georgia, Joseph L. Comer, who went to Korea in 1962, applied himself to such intensive study of the Korean language that within six months he was able to testify and preach to the Korean people.[9] With Frank T. Stansell and Richard A. Jackson, both of California, and other members, Comer began missionary work for the Church of God.[10] Chaplain Richard Y. Bershon was also assigned to Korea at that time and assisted the work.

In April 1964, Director Conn, following the retreat in Okinawa, went to Korea for a meeting with the servicemen. The meeting was scheduled as a full retreat, but it was monsoon season, and the land was wet, cold and gloomy. The weather was so wretched that it took nearly three hours to go by bus from Osan, where the plane landed, to Seoul, thirty miles away. The Korean countryside was drenched.

> It was raining, cold and miserable when our bus got to Seoul. Then the driver left the bus standing in the city center with a farewell word that that was as far as he was to take us. A few servicemen and I were left stranded— all in Korea for the first time. Then I saw Chaplain Bershon running across the square through the rain to the parked bus. How we accidentally got together I don't know, for everything had gone wrong.[11]

A small group of Christian servicemen met at the Eighth Army Retreat Center in Seoul, but because of the almost impassable weather and military restrictions, only five servicemen were present. With the Americans was Kim Doo Hwan, a young

---

8. George W. Jones, *Church of God Evangel,* June 5, 1961, p. 5.

9. Joseph L. Comer, *Church of God Evangel,* March 30, 1964, p. 15.

10. Charles W. Conn, *Church of God Evangel,* March 9, 1964, p. 5.

11. Conn, *Journal,* April 17, 1964.

Korean minister, whom they had introduced to the Church of God and secured to pastor the church they planned to build. The men had purchased property in the Moon Lae Dong section of Seoul, near the Kimpo Airport. In spite of this modest beginning, the foundation of the Church of God was laid in Korea for an inspiring missions outreach.

§ 7. Korea Again

A year later, on October 1, 1965, Conn, accompanied by Lewis J. Willis, returned to Seoul for official organization of the Church of God in Korea. The tent church was filled with worshipers—eight of whom united with the Church. Kim Doo Hwan, whose name was Americanized to David Kim, was assigned to pastor the congregation and supervise the missions endeavor.[12] Before another year passed, a lovely church was erected on the spot, and new workers were added to the Korean Church of God. The work grew rapidly in the fertile field and became one of the fruitful areas in the Far East.

When Kim left Korea to attend Lee College in 1966, he left the work under the supervision of Yung-Chul Han, another dedicated young minister. The Missions Board made the appointment of Han permanent in 1970. The Church of God has had a highly effective ministry in the Republic of Korea. Under Yung-Chul Han's energetic leadership a Bible school was founded in Seoul and new churches were begun in all parts of South Korea. By 1976 there were thirty-five organized churches, eleven missions, and almost six thousand members. Wonderful fruit grew from the tragic seeds of war, planted by lonely hands that wanted only to be good Christians.

§ 8. The Home Front

The Assembly of 1964 gave impetus to the forward directions and creative attitudes of the Church. The Executive Committee was increased to six members, and a procedure of succession was adopted in the event death should again occur

---

12. *Ibid.*, October 1, 1965.

on the executive body, as it had when A. M. Phillips died in 1962. Horton, Conn and Spain were reelected to the Committee; and R. Leonard Carroll, pastor in Lenoir City, Tennessee, was elected Third Assistant General Overseer. Ralph E. Williams, pastor in Charlotte, North Carolina, was elected General Secretary-Treasurer. The office of director of world missions was added to the Committee, and Vessie D. Hargrave, superintendent of Europe, was elected to fill it. William D. Alton, also of Latin American experience, replaced Hargrave in Europe. General Overseer Horton assigned each member of the Executive Committee specific responsibilities for the next two years, a plan that would give continuous executive representation to the numerous ministries of the Church. Inasmuch as the General Overseer was *ex officio* chairman of all committees, the other men served as his liaison representatives to the various boards and departments.

In the area of youth and Christian education, Donald S. Aultman was elected national Sunday school and youth director, and Paul F. Henson was named his assistant. Both men were experienced youth directors and preachers of great popularity. They made an exciting, progressive team.

§ 9. THE EXECUTIVE COUNCIL

At this Assembly the name Supreme Council was changed to Executive Council, a change long sought by some. It was felt that the early name was a misnomer; the highest continuing council of the Church was executive, but hardly supreme. Only the name was changed; the body would still be composed of the Executive Committee and the Council of Twelve sitting in joint session as one body.

> *Be it resolved,* By the Church of God, duly and regularly met in its Fiftieth General Assembly, That the Council of the Church heretofore known as the "Supreme Council" and consisting of the Council of Twelve and the Executive Committee of this Church shall henceforth be known and designated as the "Executive Council."
>
> *Further resolved* that this action shall not impair the validity of any valid action heretofore taken by that Coun-

cil under the designation of "Supreme Council," nor shall it prohibit the use of the term "Supreme Council" to designate that said Council where, because of pending matters or prior commitments, it is necessary or desirable that said Council be so designated.[13]

§ 10. A Women's Auxiliary

The Ladies Willing Worker Band was made a national department of the Church of God in 1964. The LWWB had been a service arm of the denomination for thirty or more years, but without a director and governing board. Appointed to the post of executive secretary was Ellen B. French, who had served with her husband, C. E. French, as missionary in India, Puerto Rico, Haiti, Dominican Republic and Peru.

The wife of the General Overseer was to remain titular president and chairman of the board with other Executive Committee wives serving as board members.

§ 11. Decision for Cleveland

When office space in the General Offices became impossibly inadequate for efficient operation of the Church, attention was given to either building larger quarters in Cleveland or relocating in another city. In 1963 a serious study was begun on the matter, a study that continued for more than a year. Sites were considered in such places as Atlanta, Memphis, Chattanooga and Cincinnati; less thought was given to remaining in Cleveland.

Officials of those cities were present at the Assembly of 1964 to press their cases, but the overwhelming decision of the General Council was to remain in Cleveland. Plans were begun immediately for a new general offices building, which would be nearly four years in planning and construction.

§ 12. German Victory

Even at the Assembly, plans were laid for military retreats on distant mission fields. The "Ministry to the Military" was

---

13. *Minutes of the Fifty-fifth General Assembly,* 1974, p. 56.

coming into full bloom as one of the Church's greatest evangelistic opportunities. The new outreach was pressed with such vigor and enthusiasm that Director Conn made two round-the-world trips in 1964, conducting retreats and conferences in several lands where American troops were stationed— Okinawa, Turkey, Vietnam, Korea, Philippine Islands, Germany and Japan. Coincidentally, the two main areas were Germany and Japan, one-time enemies of America. Fittingly, in each of these fall meetings there would be evidences of divine providence.

In Germany, September 7-10, 1964, attendance was up to 235, more than fifty more than the previous year. It was a memorable meeting in many ways and especially because of Herman Lauster's presence. The aging missionary, who had defied Hitler in the evil days of the Nazis, was now to preach to American servicemen under the shadow of Hitler's "Eagle's Nest." Speaking on "The Whole Armor of God" to the rapt servicemen, Lauster recalled much of his time of trial during the Nazi nightmare.

Then the hero of the faith faltered and stopped. He said, "My heart is growing weaker; I cannot go on. God bless you. Amen." The heart that had beat so strongly for so long in the work of the Lord stopped its sturdy beat at last. Lauster died in the pulpit, surrounded by his loved ones and friends, a death as victorious as his life had been valorous. That evening a lonely friend who had spent the final week with Lauster, recorded:

> Brother Lauster once fought aganst the Nazi tyranny and was imprisoned for his efforts. Yet he died today preaching the gospel in the very place where Hitler once reveled and attempted to stamp out religion. In a very real way this has been a day of victory. Yet I feel a deep sense of loneliness tonight, for I have lost a dear and treasured friend. He and I had plans for a tour today, but he is now in heaven and I am left alone.[14]

---

14. Conn, *Journal,* September 9, 1964.

§ 13. Japanese Victory

The retreat in Japan on November 23-26, 1964, was a further testament to the providence of God. The meeting, which was conducted in the picturesque little town of Hakone, was attended by fifty-eight excited retreatants from five Asian countries: Japan, Korea, Okinawa, Taiwan and the Philippine Islands.[15] Hakone was a lovely town high in the mountains of the Hakone-Fuji National Park, much like Berchtesgaden in Germany. With hot springs and pleasant climate, the town had long been a health spa for weary Japanese. Now American servicemen found rest and repair of heart and mind in the healing environs. Services were in the Gohra Hotel, a resort facility used for retreat and recreational purposes. Testimonies of the young servicemen were so touching and relevant that they could well have been a part of the book of Acts. Some attended after much difficulty and against great travel handicap. Weary and lonely, they found strength in fellowship; gradually the knots of stress loosened into bands of spiritual blessings.

Under the direction of Chaplain Richard Y. Bershon, L. E. Heil, Lovell Cary, Lewis J. Willis and the executive director, the retreat was a spiritual blend of military duty and missionary opportunity. Even before the retreat adjourned, plans were underway for another meeting the next year. The retreat closed on Thanksgiving Day with a traditional American Thanksgiving dinner prepared by the Japanese hosts.

And, indeed, there was much—very much—for which to be thankful.

---

15. *Ibid.,* November 23, 1964.

Chapter 31
PEOPLE, PLACES AND PLANS

§ 1. Evangelism By Union

In 1965 the Church of God was organized in Greece, Portugal, Holland, Ghana, Syria and Antigua. This expansion was accomplished by taking into the fold of the Church indigenous congregations already functioning in those countries. Frequently the congregations were small and poor, in need of membership with a worldwide organization. By union with the Church of God the congregations were able to expand their efforts; by union with the congregations the Church of God gained immediate entrance to lands that might otherwise be closed to it for years.

The Pentecostal Movement overspread the world in much this fashion. Small congregations experienced the baptism of the Holy Spirit in their lands without association with, or even knowledge of, the worldwide revival. As metal is drawn to a magnet, these independent congregations were later drawn to the fellowship and strength of the Church of God. These small beginnings were then nourished and strengthened until they became the foundation for evangelism in their lands. In this way the local groups became vital parts of a greater whole, and the Church was able to accelerate its effort to preach the gospel in all the world.

§ 2. Metropolitan Evangelism

In keeping with its increased evangelistic emphases elsewhere, the Church of God in 1965 turned its attention to

349

neglected areas of the American homeland. Strangely, the big cities of the United States constituted one such area. From its beginning the Church of God had made its principal efforts in rural areas and smaller cities, a fact that probably reflected the origins of the Church.* Many of the metropolitan areas of the United States had no Church of God witness at all, or at best far too little to reach the masses.

In an effort to correct this situation and go where the people were, a metropolitan evangelism program was begun in 1965. Experienced evangelists were sent to such cities as Chicago, Philadelphia, Milwaukee, Boston, Denver and New York. Some of these cities already had thriving congregations, but it was recognized that they should have many more: the population masses were not being reached with the gospel.

The metropolitan evangelists were fully supported by the evangelism funds of the Church. They were to work without worrying about financial support, living quarters or worship facilities; they were to locate suitable sections of the cities, generally by survey, and do the work of evangelism. Then, when a congregation was built up, it would be left to a pastor, and the evangelist would move on to another section of the city and begin anew.

Under this program the Church had notable success in starting new churches in the large cities. But each success was only a beginning, which at its best still made no real dent in the masses in the cities. In reality, the world still waited to hear the gospel of the Lord Jesus Christ.†

§ 3. COUNCIL OF ADVISORS

In December 1965 the Executive Committee convoked a meeting of all surviving former members of the Committee. These earlier leaders of the Church were called upon to serve as an "Advisory Council" to the Executive Committee to share

---

*See p. 423 for a survey of where Church of God churches are located.
†The efforts of Ray H. Sanders in Chicago and Denver, Gerald Johnson in Milwaukee, and J. D. Golden in New York were especially fruitful.

with the present leaders their insights and experiences in handling the affairs of the Church. It was not to be an executive body, but advisory and honorary.

At the first meeting of the Advisory Council on December 14, 1965, a wide range of subjects was discussed.[1] The body was not empowered to make policy but only to counsel with those who did have such responsibility. Of thirteen eligible delegates, eleven were present.[*] The group was duly constituted and established an annual meeting for the future.

§ 4. Experienced Leadership

The Assembly of 1966 brought few surprises and much confidence for the future of the Church of God. As the delegates gathered in Memphis for the August 10-15 conference, there was a general feeling that all was well and would be even better. Charles W. Conn was elected General Overseer, after having been Assistant General Overseer for four years. Chosen to assist Conn in the affairs of the Church were R. Leonard Carroll, First Assistant General Overseer; C. Raymond Spain, Second Assistant General Overseer; and Ray H. Hughes, Third Assistant General Overseer. Ralph E. Williams was re-elected General Secretary-Treasurer and Vessie D. Hargrave, director of world missions. There were no surprises, no new faces; all of these choices had been anticipated for a year.

Hughes's election to the Executive Committee ended his distinguished presidency at Lee College, where he was succeeded by James A. Cross, overseer of Florida. There seemed to be little mood among the delegates for the untried or the inexperienced. This desire for experienced leadership was also reflected in the election of the Council of Twelve; only one man without prior service was elected to that body.

---

1. Lewis J. Willis, *Church of God Evangel*, February 7, 1966, p. 3.

*Delegates present were: J. H. Walker, Sr., John C. Jernigan, Zeno C. Tharp, Houston R. Morehead, James A. Cross, Earl P. Paulk, Sr., A. V. Beaube, J. D. Bright, Paul H. Walker, R. R. Walker and H. D. Williams. Serving Executive Committee members present were: Wade H. Horton, Charles W. Conn, C. Raymond Spain, R. Leonard Carroll, Ralph E. Williams and Vessie D. Hargrave.

In his acceptance speech, General Overseer Conn declared:

> I believe that we stand on the threshold of greatness . . .
> the Church of God has now gathered the strength, mo-
> mentum and direction for which our forefathers prayed
> and yearned and wept. We are left with the responsibility
> to achieve in our day that which they longed for [in their
> day].[2]

§ 5. THE UNTAPPED RESERVOIR

It was in many ways an Assembly that focused upon people
more than issues. Laymen were drawn back into the affairs of
the Church. They sat in the galleries of the General Council
sessions and used their right to speak in the forum of the
General Assembly. What had been shaping up in recent years
came into being in 1966. Lay importance was made explicit
with the creation of a National Laymen's Board. In the empowering resolution it was frankly stated that "evangelization
of our day will require the united efforts of the total membership of the Church."[3] Laymen were seen as a vast reservoir
of services that the ministry of the Church had overlooked,
neglected or relegated to mere supportive roles. Now the
reservoir was to be tapped and its pent-up powers released.*

§ 6. THE BROKEN WALL

Of equal moment was the matter of human rights, which
was also dealt with boldly. For forty years, or since 1926, the
Church of God had been divided, however benignly, into two
groups, one black and one white. Each had its separate function, albeit with unity and fraternity, and each maintained re-
spectful detachment from the other. The black constituency
had a National Overseer, a National Assembly and separate
state overseers. Those who attended the General Assemblies
sat in a special section reserved for them.

---

2. *Minutes of the Fifty-first General Assembly,* 1966, p. 29.

3. *Ibid.,* p. 61.

*The first members of the Laymen's Board were: Lynwood Maddox, Charles
R. Beach, Arthur Hodge, H. A. Madden and J. D. Silver (*Ibid.,* p. 68).

The Assembly of 1966 moved toward eliminating all such racial discrimination. The stage had been set in 1964 with the adoption of a strong "Resolution on Human Rights" that recognized the dignity and worth of every individual. The resolution asserted "that no American should, because of his race or religion, be deprived of his right to worship, vote, rest, eat, sleep, be educated, live and work on the same basis as other citizens."[4] Along with its rhetoric, the resolution flexed spiritual muscle by declaring that "no Christian can manifest a passive attitude when the rights of others are jeopardized."

The leadership of the Church of God, both black and white, worked to forge the rhetoric into reality. At the 1966 Assembly another resolution was adopted that would eliminate the separation of ethnic or racial groups in the Church of God.[5] All references to race or color were to be stricken from Church of God records, and all racial barriers broken down. Thereafter all members of the Church of God could attend, or become members of, any local congregation they wished, attend any conference or convention, or enroll in any college, without regard to race or color.

While other denominations still debated these basic human rights, the Church of God acted on them positively and determinedly. The wall that appeared, however innocently, in 1926 was broken down in 1966. There would still be problems, but the Church would work toward resolving them. To assist in the mending process, Overseer Conn named veteran minister H. G. Poitier as a special envoy to the black constituency of the Church. This was a temporary assignment until the merging process could be completed.

§ 7. Ministers Retreats

Concern for the welfare and competency of its ministry led the Church to initiate several programs of ministerial enrichment during this period. One such program begun in 1967

---

4. *Minutes of the Fiftieth General Assembly*, 1964, pp. 67, 68.
5. *Minutes of the Fifty-first General Assembly*, 1966, p. 62.

was a schedule of ministers' retreats in most of the States. Impressed with the deleterious effects modern-day pressures were having on pastors and other ministers, the Executive Committee proposed to the state overseers that they arrange for a time of rest and inspiration in their territories. This proposal was made at an Overseers Promotional Meeting on January 10; before the end of the year there were twenty-two retreats. Thereafter the retreats became a regular and welcome part of each year's schedule.[6]

The ministers saw the benefits of Jesus' invitation to His tired apostles, "Come ye yourselves apart into a desert place, and rest a while" (Mark 6:31). The retreats were conducted in places that invited relaxation—in sylvan settings where possible, or places that provided broad recreational possibilities. No business was allowed; the preachers were given respite from nerve-jangling intrusions. Slowly their bruised emotions were touched with the healing hand of rest, and they were fortified by the common fellowship.

Mornings generally featured relaxed discussions of mutual interests, and the evenings usually offered worship and fellowship. All the rest of the day was filled with rest and recreation. The results were so salutary that the ministers retreats soon spawned ministers' wives retreats. Later, still other retreats followed—for laymen, married couples and related groups.

§ 8. THE INDONESIAN VISION

The Church of God dream of an Indonesian mission was long and slow in coming to reality, but when it came, it was far greater than anyone ever dreamed of. In 1955 Dalraith N. Walker went as a missionary to the new island republic. He worked with Ho L. Senduk and the Bethel Full Gospel Church that had been organized three years earlier, in 1952. Wade H. Horton also visited Indonesia and preached with Ho and Walker on several of the islands. Nothing immediate came of these efforts, and the vision waned.

6. Hollis L. Green, *Church of God Evangel,* January 29, 1968, pp. 6, 7.

Indonesia consisted of the former Dutch East Indies, a vast archipelago of three thousand islands spread for three thousand miles along and below the equator. These were the fabled Spice Islands. The Dutch colony won independence from the Netherlands in 1949 and established itself as a republic, Indonesia, in 1950.[7] There was a great amount of distrust toward Europeans and Americans among the East Indian people who had only recently been freed from Western domination. Moreover, the republic flirted briefly with Communism. Hopes of the Church of God were delayed.

Ho L. Senduk and his wife visited the United States in 1958 and joined the Church of God. Then Ho worked toward the day that the Bethel Full Gospel Church would be united with the Church of God. That dream was to come true in 1967, after Indonesia broke off its growing ties with international Communism.

On a tour of Indonesia, James L. Slay learned of the Bethel desire for amalgamation with the Church of God. Responding to the news, General Overseer Charles W. Conn went to Indonesia in February 1967, where he was joined by C. Raymond Spain and W. E. Johnson. Spain was in Asia in connection with the Ministry to the Military, to which he had only recently been assigned; W. E. Johnson was chairman of the World Missions Board.

The three Americans were met in Djakarta, the capital city, on February 2, 1967, by Ho and his executive committee. The negotiations were productive and successful despite the cultural differences, the language difficulties and the vast geographic span that separated the two groups. America and Indonesia are on exact opposite sides of the world; they are East and West; the one is spiritually Moslem and the other is nominally Christian.

Articles of amalgamation were drafted after the Americans conferred with officers and ministers of the Bethel Church

---

7. *Tanah Air Kita,* B.P.U. Perusahaan Pertjetakan Dan Penerbitan Negara, Djakarta, c. 1965, pp. 12, 13 ff.

and visited numerous local congregations. The General Overseer reported to the Church:

> Carefully we drafted articles of amalgamation. It was a memorable night (on February 5) when we gathered in the home of Brother Ho to refine and sign the document. Due to an electric power failure we had to work by candlelight. Following the signing, we American and Indonesian brethren joined hands in a circle around the table on which the document lay; we prayed for God's blessing upon our union.[8]

Signatories for the Church of God were Charles W. Conn, General Overseer; C. Raymond Spain, Second Assistant General Overseer; and W. E. Johnson, Chairman, World Missions Board. Signatories for the Bethel Full Gospel Church were Ho L. Senduk, National Overseer; The Sean King, Assistant Overseer; Ong Ling Kok, First Secretary; Khoe Soe Liem, Second Secretary and A. I. Pelealu, Treasurer. The Indonesian body took the English name Bethel Full Gospel Church of God and the Indonesian name Gereja Bethel Indonesia.

§ 9. HANDS AROUND THE WORLD

The Indonesian church reported 71,127 members in 431 local congregations on seven islands—Java, Sumatra, Borneo, Celebes, Maluccus, Timor and New Guinea. Under conditions of the amalgamation, the Indonesian church would be indigenous, with its ministers members of the Church of God General Council when they were in the States, and the National Overseer a member of the Executive Council. Similarly, Church of God ministers would be members of the Indonesian ministers' council and the General Overseer would be a member of the Executive Council.

The Church appointed W. H. Pratt and Larry Bonds to Indonesia as missionary teachers in the seminary built in Djakarta by the YWEA program. Frequent trips to Indonesia by Church of God leaders and to America by Bethel leaders

---

8. Conn, *Church of God Evangel*, July 24, 1967, p. 3 ff.

knitted the two groups even closer together. Several Indonesian students enrolled at Lee College.

With all these contacts the Church of God reached its hand of fellowship and brotherhood to the other side of the world. At the same time, the Church was awakened to an exotic part of the world, to warm and friendly hearts that beat as its own.

§ 10. "Perpetuate Pentecost"

On Pentecost Sunday, 1967, the Church of God conducted a nationwide "Perpetuate Pentecost" campaign. A special issue of the *Evangel* was distributed to the local congregations for use in door-to-door witnessing. On the afternoon of May 8, Pentecost Sunday, hundreds of workers visited homes with personal testimonies and the special literature. Approximately one million homes were visited in one day. Testimonies of those who received the Pentecostal baptism indicated the success of the project. The massive effort was a blessing to the Church in many ways, not the least of which was its public relations benefit.

The campaign was also used in other countries, especially South Africa, with similar success. Concern for the perpetuation of Pentecostal doctrine and experience was real. It was felt that the Pentecostal Revival was in its finest period of opportunity and acceptance. The Church of God must not fail to spread the gospel in as many places as possible.

The Church demonstrated concern for its Pentecostal identity and integrity in still another way. A survey was made in 1967 to determine how many members had actually received the baptism of the Holy Spirit. Results of the survey showed that sixty-one percent of the members had the blessing, and thirty-nine percent did not.[9] The Church was concerned that it be Pentecostal in continued fact as well as in doctrine. The program to perpetuate Pentecost became much more than a catchy phrase. It would be a way of life.

---

9. General Overseer's Newsletter, March 4, 1968.

Chapter 32
PATTERNS OF PROGRESS

§ 1. ENLARGED HOME BASE

Several times in its history the Church of God outgrew its headquarters facilities and was forced to expand. There was never a time of more acute need than the period of 1963 to 1968, when the burgeoning Church experienced mounting desperation regarding adequate space. Expansion became a critical necessity. Construction of a new General Offices Building was approved by the General Assembly of 1964,[1] and actual construction began immediately prior to the Assembly of 1966. The preparation spanned two years of Horton's tenure as General Overseer, and actual construction spanned two years of Conn's tenure. Clifford V. Bridges was named construction liaison officer.

On May 22, 1968, the imposing new building was dedicated. It was a structure of such architectural beauty and artistic design that it immediately, and has ever after, attracted the admiration of the knowledgeable public. The quiet serenity of the four-story building with its sculpted fountain and spacious grounds was carried over into the two-story lobby, which featured a Byzantine mosaic mural depicting the Day of Pentecost. An adjoining rotunda continued the vast mural of vignettes from the history of the Church of God.

The offices themselves were adequate and attractive, with the most functional and modern equipment for the work of the Church's many ministries. Three thousand citizens of

---

1. *Minutes of the Fiftieth General Assembly,* 1964, pp. 56, 57.

Cleveland passed through the building during open house; fifteen hundred attended the dedication. In the dedicatory address, the General Overseer said:

> This building upon this hillside is like a watershed of the past and the future . . . It is more than steel or stone, glass or timber: it is more than man has the ability to create. It is a memory of a godly heritage and a vision of a great future.[2]

The gleaming structure, which was built on twenty-two acres at the corner of Twenty-fifth and Keith Streets, dominated the north side of Cleveland. The total project cost $2,317,000 for the site, building and furnishings.[3]

When the General Offices moved into the new facility, the Publishing House took over the entire building on Montgomery Avenue. An expansion program was then undertaken for the publishing needs of the Church. The older facility was virtually doubled so it could house the greatly enlarged plant.

§ 2. To the Far Regions

The magnificent new Headquarters Building was not an ornament of pride, but a vessel of service. It was the fountainhead from which the worldwide ministries of the Church would flow. Before the end of 1958, world missions endeavors were begun in the landlocked African country of Chad, in Yugoslavia, Taiwan, Tortola and Guadeloupe. The arms of the Church embraced these lands of Asia, Europe and the Caribbean in a desire to reach the world for Christ. Independent missionaries who had dug out struggling works brought their labors into the nurturent fellowship of the Church. So the Church of God increased its outreach and opportunities in the far regions of the world.

Of these beginnings, the works in Chad and Yugoslavia were particularly inspiring and promising. The Chad mission was opened in 1961 by Andre Girod of France, who went into the

---

2. Conn, *Church of God Evangel*, July 22, 1968, p. 10.
3. General Overseer's Newsletter, c. June 1, 1968.

central African country soon after his conversion. He and his sister jointly started the mission, which was the only Pentecostal work in the black and Arab land. In the spring of 1968 James L. Slay, missions field representative, passed through Chad as he crossed Africa and accepted the Girods into the fellowship of the Church of God. The union was immediately fruitful; new workers joined the missionaries in Chad and had much success in winning souls to Christ.

The Church entered Yugoslavia by means of an amalgamation with a small organization known as the Evangelical Church of Christ. With headquarters near the capital city of Belgrade, the group consisted of ten congregations and 220 members. For more than twenty years the Yugoslav church had promoted the Pentecostal doctrine in the Communist nation. Union with the Church of God, brought about by contacts with William D. Alton, superintendent of Europe, was effected on March 16, 1968. The Yugoslav leader, Pavlov Milivoj, spearheaded the amalgamation and successfully melded the congregations with the worldwide ministries of the Church.[4]

§ 3. Assembly of 1968

In a period of such progress, few changes were expected at the General Assembly in Dallas, but there were some rather significant changes after all. Charles W. Conn was reelected General Overseer, and R. Leonard Carroll, First Assistant. Then Ray H. Hughes was elevated to the Second Assistant post, and C. Raymond Spain, who had been Second Assistant, was elected General Secretary-Treasurer, where he had served four years earlier. Wade H. Horton was returned to the Committee as Third Assistant after an absence of only two years. Then the Assembly removed the office of director of world missions from the Committee and restored its former title and role as executive secretary of world missions. It simply was not a workable idea for departments of the Church to

---

4. Heinrich C. Scherz, *Church of God Evangel,* July 29, 1968, p. 23.

be given this double role in church administration. For years the Church of God toyed with the idea that the Executive Committee could be strengthened by the addition of one of the department executives. Idealistic as that temptation always seemed, it never did work. It was no more practical with the missions director than it had been earlier with the editor in chief or the president of Lee College. So, in 1968 the Executive Committee once again consisted of only those members elected specifically to it.

James L. Slay succeeded Vessie D. Hargrave in the missions post when the latter was appointed overseer of South Carolina. This terminated Hargrave's long and distinguished service of twenty-four years in the missions work of the Church. Another significant change made at the Assembly of 1968 was in the Youth and Christian Education Department. Retiring Director Donald S. Aultman went to Lee College as vice-president and dean, succeeded in the youth post by Paul F. Henson, who was rapidly gaining attention as a skilled leader and preacher. Aultman would do much at Lee College as he had done in youth work, to improve the effectiveness of his charge. He was especially instrumental in bringing the College to the academic level necessary for accreditation. The Church took great pride in the plethora of its capable young leaders who gave much promise for the future.

At the Assembly of 1968 Cecil B. Knight, overseer of Indiana, was elected director of evangelism and home missions. Knight was an innovative and dynamic leader who brought continued vigor to the evangelistic ministries of the Church. Knight pressed the work among the Indians of the Southwest, Northwest and Southeast forward with special attention.

The women's work of the Church also had a change in administrative leadership at this Assembly. Willie Lee Darter of Texas, a member of the LWWB Board of Directors, was named executive secretary of the energetic auxiliary. With all of these changes at what promised to be a routine Assembly, the Church actually girded itself for a fresh surge forward.

§ 4. GENERAL BOARD OF EDUCATION

A standing board was created at the 1968 meeting to "concern itself with the elementary, secondary and higher educational programs in the Church of God."[5] To be known as the General Board of Education, the highly specialized body would be responsible for the Church's wide-ranging and growing interests in education. Principally, it was "to review objectives of educational institutions in relation to the doctrine, belief and polity of the Church, and promote loyalty of Church of God constituents to its educational institutions." The board was created to complement and not supplant existing boards of individual schools: "to function in an advisory and consultative capacity to the educational institutions without impinging upon the authority of the boards of control of these institutions."[6]

The new board was a reflection of the Church's concern for quality education at all levels; it was a creation of the Church's accelerated emphasis on education's role in the Kingdom of God. R. Leonard Carroll was named executive director of the general education program in connection with his duties as First Assistant General Overseer.*

§ 5. CONTINUED MILITARY MINISTRY

At the 1968 Assembly much attention was given to the growing Ministry to the Military. This effort to "take the Church to those who have been taken from the Church" excited the imagination and appreciation of the people as few things have ever done. Servicemen's Director C. Raymond Spain, who projected himself into the ministry with great effectiveness, was successful in opening new ways of reaching the men in uniform. Working with the Military Command in the States, he was able to go into many restricted areas

---

5. *Minutes of the Fifty-second General Assembly,* 1968, p. 34.
6. *Ibid.,* p. 35.
*Members of the first General Board of Education were H. D. Williams, James M. Beaty, Robert E. Fisher, Albert M. Stephens and Robert White.

where American servicemen were stationed. This included the battlefields of Vietnam, where the United States was involved in its most tragic and divisive conflict.

Spain organized an annual retreat in Baguio, Philippine Islands and secured a Far East servicemen's director, James E. Garlen, of New Mexico. American servicemen were stationed in ninety-nine countries, Spain reported, and Pentecostal fellowships were organized in many of them.[7]

G. A. Swanson returned to the States in 1968 and was succeeded as European servicemen's representative by Roy F. Stricklin of Missouri who had gone to Europe as Swanson's assistant two years earlier. He and his wife, Margy, as pastor of the center in Kaiserslautern for four years, had become a kind-of parental image to the men in uniform.[8] Stricklin headed the European work for six years, during which time it was multiplied several times over. At first there was only the one servicemen's center in Europe, in Kaiserslautern, Germany. In order for the men to have a church home away from home, new centers were opened in several parts of Germany and other cities from Holy Loch, Scotland, to Madrid, Spain, to Adana, Turkey. These centers provided sleeping quarters for weekend visits, game rooms for recreation, libraries for reading, kitchens for meals, chapels for worship, and friends for caring and sharing. Within six years there were ten centers and fifty-three fellowships in Europe. With annual retreats, camp meetings, youth camps and leadership training conferences, the servicemen's work had become a church within a church.

§ 6. New Norms in Education

One of the most encouraging ministries of the Church during this period was in the field of higher education, where that which had been budding for several years came into full flower. Lee College, under the guidance of President James A.

---

7. C. Raymond Spain, *Church of God Evangel,* January 1, 1968, p. 22.
8. Spain, *Ibid.,* October 21, 1968, p. 4.

Cross, merged its formerly separate colleges into one unified institution with three divisions—Arts and Sciences, Education, and Religion. The College's high academic quality was recognized by full accreditation by the Southern Assocation of Colleges and Schools on December 3, 1969. This accreditation as a four-year institution gave the Church justified pride in its oldest school. President Cross reported:

> There were two events that were very significant in making accreditation possible: the transition from a junior college to a four-year college, and the combining of the four-year Bible college and the liberal arts college under one academic structure. This last action made it possible for both our biblical education and Christian education majors to receive degrees with the same academic values as those of the liberal arts students.[9]

A step toward upgrading Northwest Bible College and West Coast Bible College was taken in 1964 when those formerly regional schools were placed under the general sponsorship of the Church. This meant that they would thereafter conform to the same policies and provisions as Lee College, except that they would be two-year rather than four-year institutions. Until 1964 the overseer of the Dakotas had been *de jure* president of Northwest Bible College and the overseer of California, *de jure* president of West Coast Bible College. Under the new policy separate presidents could be named by the appropriate board of directors.

Laud O. Vaught, who had been at Northwest for eleven years, was immediately named the first full-time president of that institution. There has been no further change. West Coast Bible College, on the other hand, did not name a full-time president until 1969, when R. Terrell McBrayer, former dean of students at Lee College, was named president.[10]

Northwest Bible College grew steadily under Vaught's leadership. From sixty students in 1964, it doubled in enrollment in a three-year period. A disastrous flood destroyed

---

9. James A. Cross, *Church of God Evangel*, April 27, 1970, p. 20 ff.
10. Lewis J. Willis, *Church of God Evangel*, June 16, 1969, p. 15.

much of the campus in 1969, but this only made it possible for the campus to be greatly improved in subsequent years.[11] The College was accepted as a member of the American Association of Bible Colleges in 1966. The academic program of Northwest Bible College was sufficient to warrant approval by the University of North Dakota for credit transfer in 1967. In addition to the academic enrichment of the College, Vaught led in physical expansion of the campus. A new administration building was erected in 1966 and a president's home in 1968.

West Coast Bible College took new life during the brief tenure of McBrayer. The enrollment increased from sixty-four to 109. Three new facilities were constructed: a library, chapel and the administration building. The College was accepted as a correspondent to the Western Association of Schools and Colleges in 1970, an achievement that would lead to academic accreditation.

§ 7. "Project '70"

As the Church of God approached the decade of the '70s much thought was given to problems and opportunities that would be faced during the period. Plans were laid for projects that would span the decade without interruption by the changing tenures of different leaders. On April 16, 1969, the General Overseer wrote to the ministry of the Church regarding what the Executive Committee called "Project '70" and named three large study commissions.[12] These commissions were to give a year of study to such areas as education, publications and stewardship; evangelism, world missions and spiritual life; communications, Sunday schools and youth activities. Recommendations for implementation would be presented during the early 1970s.

The Church correctly perceived the significance of its next decade. And perceiving the time and its opportunities, it moved into the '70s with confidence and hope.

---

11. Laud O. Vaught, *Church of God Evangel,* June 16, 1969, p. 4; February 9, 1970, pp. 11, 12.

12. General Overseer's Newsletter, April 16, 1969.

Chapter 33
SURGE OF THE SEVENTIES

§ 1. The Changing Scene

In the face of steady growth and extensive planning, the Assembly of 1970 began with a mood of well-being and good will. Most of the sessions in St. Louis, August 25-31, were filled with worship and positive discussion about the future of the Church. Much thought was given, as it had been for the past two Assemblies, to the possibility of modifying the tithe-of-tithes system of the Church. The desire to modify the plan in order to retain a greater portion of local tithes in the local church was in itself an expression of confidence in the health of general and state funds.

Despite the beneficent mood of the meeting, the 1970 Assembly occasioned a large number of administrative changes. R. Leonard Carroll, an Assistant General Overseer for the past six years, was elevated to the office of General Overseer. A native of South Carolina, Carroll had earlier served as pastor in Tennessee. Also elected to the Executive Committee were Ray H. Hughes, First Assistant General Overseer; Wade H. Horton, Second Assistant General Overseer; Cecil B. Knight, Third Assistant General Overseer; and G. W. Lane, General Secretary-Treasurer. The limitation of eight consecutive years on the Executive Committee began to have a telling effect on the office of General Overseer at this Assembly. Carroll was eligible for the high office only two years because he

367

attained it after having been on the Committee for six years. In fact, four successive General Overseers would come to the office for abbreviated two-year tenures. The decade of the '70s would not see a full four-year tenure in the office.

Charles W. Conn, retiring General Overseer, went to Lee College as its fourteenth president. C. Raymond Spain, retiring General Secretary-Treasurer, was elected director of evangelism and home missions. Changes were made in two long-term tenures at the Publishing House, where Lewis J. Willis had been editor in chief eight years and E. C. Thomas, publisher for fifteen years. O. W. Polen was named to the editorial and F. W. Goff to the publications posts. Both men were experienced Executive Council members and state overseers. A further departmental change of moment was in the area of world missions. James L. Slay left missions for a teaching post in the Chair of World Missions at Lee College; he was succeeded as executive secretary by W. E. Johnson, former chairman of the board.

§ 2. BETTER CARE FOR CHILDREN

There was also a change at the Home for Children in Sevierville: P. H. McCarn, who had served as superintendent for six years, was succeeded by E. K. Waldrop. The tenure of McCarn had seen much progress in developing cottage housing for the children of the Home. From its origin as an orphanage, and from the peak year 1952 when it had a population of 297 children, the Home had become a shelter for children made homeless by desertion, neglect, mental illness, child abuse and other social ills. The institutional approach had given way to smaller houses, with house parents and a sense of family.[1] Each of the modern homes housed twelve children and the house parents. The units became a community of neat houses on a neighborhood street, and the children could more nearly simulate normal, happy childhood. The concern of the Church impelled a search for better ways.

---

1. E. K. Waldrop, *Church of God Evangel*, December 14, 1970, p. 14.

§ 3. Voice Around the World

Under the guidance of Floyd J. Timmerman, radio minister since 1966, Forward in Faith was aired on 250 stations in virtually every state of the nation. In addition, the weekly broadcast was heard around the world on powerful short-wave stations in Europe and the Far East. Correspondence reached the radio offices from many parts of the listening world. Encouraged by listener response and impressed with their requests for prayer, in January 1971, Timmerman initiated a telephone ministry of prayer. A special telephone line was installed so those who needed prayer could call direct to the radio offices at any hour of the day or night.[2]

§ 4. European Command

W. D. Alton ended his tenure as superintendent of Europe in 1970. His successor was J. Herbert Walker, Jr., who took over the post from a rich background of service. Walker, with his wife, Lucille, was associated with Lee College where he was academic dean from 1957 to 1968. Prior to that, he had been assistant superintendent of Latin America, 1955-1957. In 1947-1952, the couple served as missionaries to Haiti.

Walker did a good work in Europe, and gave the churches of the Old World confident leadership. After only a year in Europe, Walker moved the continental headquarters from Switzerland, where the work of the Church was negligible, to Urbach, Germany, a strong center of church activity and outreach. The European Bible Seminary was moved to Rudersburg, Germany, only seven miles from historic Krehwinkel, where the Church of God began in Europe, and earliest home of the school.

§ 5. The Tragic Tenure

R. Leonard Carroll's tenure as General Overseer, already abbreviated by limitation, was shortened further by death. The

---

2. Floyd J. Timmerman, *Church of God Evangel,* May 24, 1971, p. 22.

fifty-one-year-old church leader traveled for the Church of God widely following the Assembly of 1970 and represented it beyond its own walls. Holder of a doctorate in education from the University of Tennessee, Carroll was the author of several books, the latest being a comprehensive study of Christian stewardship, titled *Stewardship: Total Life Commitment.* Christian stewardship had been the emphasis of his recent ministry.

On January 26, 1972, Carroll and his wife Evelyn, attended a prayer conference in his native South Carolina. In the morning session he addressed the ministers on the theme of "Counting the Cost." Almost prophetically the General Overseer said:

> After you count the cost and press on, don't look back. I want to set my face like a flint. I want to go on, even if there is a fight, or if it is a burden all the time, or if there is suffering every step of the way, or if there is a valley that is unpleasant and disagreeable; I want to walk on. If someone asks, "Where are you going?" I will say, "I have my eyes fixed on the banks of that distant shore. I am making my journey with an onward step and with confidence, knowing that anything can happen which could rule out the stepping stones that we have planned. But we have the consolation that as we go God will open up the way before us step by step."[3]

Strangely weak after the address, Carroll returned immediately to his home in Cleveland. In the early evening he succumbed to a massive heart attack and quietly died. Friends and associates rushed to the hospital where he was taken, but it was too late.

The Church of God was shocked and grieved as was the Christian world. For the second time in its history the Church had lost its General Overseer by death—F. J. Lee in 1928 and R. Leonard Carroll in 1972. A. M. Phillips, Assistant General Overseer, had died in 1962. The Church created an R. Leonard Carroll Ministerial Student Loan Fund in mem-

---

3. R. Leonard Carroll, *Church of God Evangel,* February 28, 1972, p. 8.

ory of the leader; Lee College named a large new housing complex for married students "Carroll Court" in his honor.

§ 6. The Orderly Succession

In accordance with the procedure of succession adopted by the Church in 1964, Ray H. Hughes was elevated to the office of General Overseer, Wade H. Horton to First Assistant General Overseer, and Cecil B. Knight to Second Assistant General Overseer. The Executive Council came together on January 31 for the installation ceremony. The solemn body of men, with prayer and laying on of hands, installed the new General Overseer in office, and adjusted the rank of his Assistants.[4] The General Secretary-Treasurer was not changed.

Then a Churchwide election was conducted to name the Third Assistant General Overseer. Balloting by mail, the ministers elected W. C. Byrd, overseer of Georgia, to the vacant post.[5] The Executive Committee was able to carry on its work without unusual delay or interruption. The Church of God was saddened by the death of its General Overseer but encouraged by the smooth and competent transition.

Floyd J. Timmerman, radio minister, was appointed to the Georgia overseership to succeed Byrd, and Carl Richardson, a Florida pastor, was named to the vacated radio post. The total transition was completed June 15, 1972.[6]

§ 7. Assembly of Confidence

When the fifteen thousand delegates arrived in Dallas for the Fifty-fourth General Assembly, August 12-21, 1972, the air was filled with confidence and optimism. Every member of the Executive Committee was reelected without change in position, a phenomenon that had not happened since the Assembly of 1943, or twenty-nine years. The numerous changes prior to the Assembly accounted in part for this unusual mat-

---

4. O. W. Polen, *Church of God Evangel,* March 13, 1972, p. 3.
5. Polen, *Ibid.,* May 8, 1972. p. 20.
6. Polen, *Ibid.,* July 10, 1972, p. 18.

ter, but the unity of the Assembly was the greatest factor. This confidence and unity prevailed throughout the meeting even as sensitive issues were discussed.

§ 8. Modified Financial Plan

Since 1966 there had been an active effort on the part of numerous ministers to modify the financial system of the Church. The historic system, adopted in 1917, provided for ten percent of all local tithes to be paid to General Headquarters and ten percent to state headquarters, with eighty percent remaining in the local church. This double tithe on local treasuries enabled the Church to carry on general programs of evangelism, education, superannuation and administration at levels otherwise impossible. The Church grew well under the plan. As annual revenues increased and the national and state funds were enlarged, the local churches sought relief from the double tithe. From 1970 to 1972, a fifteen-man committee studied ways of making a reduction without crippling the general ministries of the Church.

The Assembly of 1972 adopted a plan that would halve the amount sent to General Headquarters and state headquarters, five percent to each, with ninety percent remaining in the local church. This reduction was to be made carefully over a twenty-year period, two percent at four-year intervals.* This long process would enable the general and state treasuries to hold their receipts at constant levels through Church growth while the local congregations kept more of their tithes for local use. This theory proved accurate at the time of the first adjustment in 1974; hopefully it would work with those to follow.†

---

*The following plan of adjustment in the 20 percent tithing program:

Date	Total Percentage	General	State
1. January 1974	18%	9%	9%
2. January 1978	16%	8%	8%
3. January 1982	14%	7%	7%
4. January 1986	12%	6%	6%
5. January 1990	10%	5%	5%

†See Table 34, "General Church Receipts," p. 427.

§ 9. "Total Evangelism"

General Overseer Hughes was always an evangelist; regardless of his position or forum, his work was evangelism. Under his urging, the Assembly of 1972 adopted a program of "Total Evangelism." The measure designated 1973 as a "Year of Total Evangelism" and set an ambitious program of a "new church a day" for the two-year period, 1972-1974.[7] In his closing remarks to the laymen of the Assembly, Hughes made a bold, almost audacious, challenge:

> Every member must be a witness. The pulpit alone cannot do the job. The pulpit can only touch a very small group. So we must have your help. There must be public witnessing to complement the pulpit preaching. I am calling upon you, as Aaron and Hur held up the hands of Moses, to hold up the hands of ministers and help reach out to the lost of the world . . . We are believing that by June 1974 the Church will have mobilized its forces so that one new church a day will be organized throughout the Church of God.[8]

It was an ambitious program. But then, it was an Assembly of confidence. And Church of God people are traditionally a people of confidence.

---

7. *Minutes of the Fifty-fourth General Assembly,* 1972, p. 43.
8. *Ibid.,* p. 61.

Chapter 34
THE HERITAGE
AND THE HOPE

§ 1. INTERNATIONALISM

During the 1970s the Church of God became truly international in its outreach. In many parts of the world the missionaries and church leaders were from countries other than
the United States. The Church of God had developed and
trained capable leaders in many lands that carried the light to
other lands.* In still other countries the work had become
indigenous and largely self-contained, without any missionary

---

*For example, Luke R. Summers of Canada went to the Virgin Islands as
a missionary, then to Barbados, to Jamaica, and finally to the West Indies as
superintendent; O. A. Lyseight of Jamaica went to England as founder and
overseer; S. E. Arnold of England went to Ghana as missionary; Gerhard Becker
of Canada went to Nigeria; Walter Greiner of Germany went to Palestine; Willie
Ruoff of Germany went to Nigeria; Arthur W. Pettyjohn of Canada went to
the Philippine Islands as missionary-overseer; Andre Girod of France served as
overseer of Chad; Andre Marcelin of Haiti went to Chad as educational director; Curtis Grey of Jamaica went to England and then to Liberia; Jeremiah
McIntyre of Jamaica went to England and then to Canada; Ridley Usherwood
of Jamaica went to England and then to the European Bible Seminary; Samuel
Robeff of Argentina went to Indonesia; Tommy Sands of the Bahamas went to
the seminary in Indonesia; Juan Alzamora of Peru went to Northwest Guatemala
as overseer; Enrique Guerra of Guatemala went to Costa Rica and then to
El Salvador as overseer; Francisco Son of Guatemala went to El Salvador as
educational director; Joaquin Guadaloupe of Puerto Rico went to Panama as
educational director of the Bible Institute; Jose Minay of Chile went to
Paraguay, Uruguay and to Guatemala; Abel Sanchez of Mexico went as educational director of Panama and then to El Salvador; Silvestre Pineda of Mexico
went to Chile as educational director and then to Peru as overseer; Roberto
Rodriguez of Puerto Rico went to Colombia as overseer. Such interchange is
too profuse in Latin America to make a full list.

375

presence. Canada, Mexico, Puerto Rico, England, France, Korea, Argentina and Egypt were a few such lands.

Especially influential in the internationalization of the Church were the strong bonds of amalgamation formed in South Africa and Indonesia. These channels of mutual exchange brought a continuing interflow between the united sections of the Church of God.

The young people of the Church developed and maintained strong involvement in worldwide outreach through their YWEA projects. Their funds were translated into soaring steel and stone and timbers around the world as beautiful structures were erected in Brazil, Japan, India, the Philippines, South Africa, Mexico, Haiti, the Bahamas, Indonesia, Germany, Panama, El Salvador and Nicaragua.*

A further encouragement to the internationalizing process was the increase of travel between countries where the Church was located. As the travelers visited other countries, the Americans encountered many of their non-American brothers and sisters, and were in return seen in other sections of the world. In 1967 the Lee Singers, led by Director Delton L. Alford, made the first of numerous tours in Europe. This premier choral group of Lee College traveled widely in Western Europe and behind the Iron Curtain on subsequent tours. A sister group, the Ladies of Lee, led by Director Roosevelt Miller, also made several overseas tours. Similarly, the United States was visited by choral groups from England, Germany and Korea. Smaller musical groups also traveled abroad and shared in the fellowship.

The blending of cultures was very much a part of the Ministry to the Military, where brothers and sisters in Christ were found in all parts of the world. One convert of the servicemen's work, Jake Popejoy, was appointed overseer of the

---

*Another prominent project of the YWEA program was an Indian Bible Institute for the Navajo and Zuni tribes in Gallup, New Mexico. This institute opened its first semester in the spring of 1971. Under the leadership of A. M. Stephens, superintendent for Indian affairs in the Southwest, the institute quickly developed into a productive part of the Evangelism and Home Missions Department of the Church.

Church of God in Italy in 1976. If the constant blending together of its people did not fully homogenize the many sections of the Church, it did make the diverse national elements appreciative of one another.

The Assembly of 1972 reflected and accentuated the international aspects of the Church by its multilingual proceedings. The program materials were printed in several languages and sections of the vast auditorium in Dallas were reserved for Spanish, German, French and other translations for the benefit of the non-English-speaking delegates.

§ 2. INTERNATIONAL EVANGELISM CONGRESS

On August 9-12, 1973 the Church of God conducted an International Evangelism Congress in Mexico City, the first event of such magnitude conducted outside the United States. Besides its practical aspects on evangelism, the meeting dramatized the international character of the Church. Between nine thousand and ten thousand delegates from twenty-five countries attended the conference, two thousand of which came from the United States. The delegates were educated regarding Mexico. Instead of an uninteresting, blank splotch on a map, they found a varied land, green and colorful. Crossing the towering Sierra Madre Oriente Mountains, they saw a spectacular part of their own hemisphere. Instead of the adobe dwellers they imagined in stereotype, they found a warm and friendly people. Instead of strangers, they found brothers and sisters.[1]

The theme of the meeting was "Until All Have Heard." Its five objectives, as enunciated by Overseer Hughes, were "(1) to make the Church world-conscious in its vision, (2) to emphasize the urgency and emergency of last-day evangelism, (3) to stress total evangelism for the total Church, (4) to teach techniques for outreach, and (5) to renew our commitment to the Great Commission."[2]

---

1. Conn, *Journal,* August 8, 16, 1973.
2. Interview with Ray H. Hughes, March 9, 1977.

Speakers from the Far East, Jamaica, Chile, South Africa and the United States addressed the mass meetings in the Olympic Sports Palace. There were fifty-eight workshop sessions on all phases of evangelism. The total experience was inspiring and educational to the assemblage of international delegates. The evangelistic results were good, with two new Mexican churches organized as fruit of the Congress. The Congress was so stimulating to the evangelistic and missionary ministries of the Church that a second such meeting was scheduled for San Juan, Puerto Rico in August 1977.

§ 3. HIGHLAND BOYS RANCH

While the genius of the Church manifested itself in worldwide ministries, it also multiplied and reached out on the American scene. A group of concerned laymen in Louisiana were successful in starting a youthcare facility there similar to the Homes for Children in Tennessee, North Carolina and South Carolina. In January 1971 a Boys Ranch was opened on a forty-acre tract of land donated for that purpose in Loranger, Louisiana. Because most of the men who organized the home for needy boys were members of the Highland Park Church of God in Baton Rouge, and it was sponsored principally by that congregation, the new facility was named Highland Boys Ranch.

Located eight miles northeast of Hammond, the Ranch consisted of the forty-acre tract, a residence, barn, house trailer and farm equipment. Under the leadership of Jack Dyer, president of the corporation, and John Gray, ranch manager, the project was developed as a home for boys between the ages of ten and sixteen in need of physical and spiritual nurture. It was quickly filled to its resident capacity of sixteen boys.

In May 1972 the ministers of Louisiana, led by Overseer Clifford V. Bridges, petitioned the Executive Council for permission to use funds raised in that state to "direct, further develop, and support" the Boys Ranch in lieu of supporting the general Home for Children in Sevierville. The Council approved the request on January 16, 1974,[3] and later made a loan of $60,000 to the Ranch for enlargement and improvement of the facility. The Highland Boys Ranch and its sixteen young residents became a part of the Church's general care for the homeless and the needy. This was a further step in providing regional or state homes for children orphaned by death, desertion, neglect or abuse.

§ 4. The "Big Brother" Program

In keeping with the total evangelism emphasis introduced at the General Assembly, the Evangelism Department announced a plan in 1973 for states with large membership and more ample resources to assist states with smaller works. This sharing of strength was designed to elevate mission states (those that required financial subsidy from the general funds) to self-supporting status. For example, the churches in South Carolina contributed $15,000 to a new church in Vermont, and the churches in West Virginia sponsored a full-time new-field evangelist in Idaho. These illustrate how the plan worked between eighteen "big brother" states and their twenty "little brother" states.[4]

§ 5. The Blunted Edge

Having reached a period of peak efficiency, the Church of God grew in every area—evangelism, education, communications and stewardship. Delegates approached the Assembly of 1974 with high hopes. Every department of the Church had shown progress and innovation: the body was in an upward mode. Yet the gathering in Dallas on August 6-12 became enmeshed in divisive debate that threatened to blunt the Church's growing edge. The debate regarded proposals to specify certain practices believed to be inimical to the holiness standards and heritage of the Church of God. Whether or not the desire for specificity was justified, the issue became emo-

---

3. *Minutes of the Executive Council,* January 16, 1974.
4. Ray H. Hughes, *Church of God Evangel,* July 23, 1973, pp. 4, 5.

tional and intense. The pervasive love and confidence of the ministers and people asserted themselves in the end. Those who did not have the perspective of other turbulent Assemblies, such as those of 1946 and 1958, worried about the future. The following items were added to the official body of "Church Teachings":

> That our members dress according to the teachings of the New Testament. 1 John 2:15, 16; 1 Timothy 2:9; 1 Peter 3:1-6.
>
> Against members attending movies, dances, and other ungodly amusements; further, that extreme caution be exercised in viewing and in the selectivity of television programs. 1 John 2:15, 16; Romans 13:14; 1 Thessalonians 5:22; Philippians 4:8; 2 Corinthians 6:14-7:1.
>
> Against members going in swimming with opposite sex other than the immediate family. 1 John 2:15, 16; 1 Timothy 2:9; 1 Corinthians 6:19, 20; Romans 6:13; 2 Peter 1:4; Galatians 5:19.
>
> That our members adhere to the scriptural admonition that our women have long hair and our men have short hair as stated in 1 Corinthians 11:14, 15.[5]

§ 6. THE RETURNED OVERSEER

Wade H. Horton, who had been General Overseer from 1962 to 1966, was elected to the office for a second tenure in 1974. Never before had anyone been reelected General Overseer for a second tenure. Several men had been reelected to the Executive Committee, but none to the highest administrative office. Horton was a popular leader. It is unlikely that any person of the Church since A. J. Tomlinson or F. J. Lee had enjoyed such great popularity as he. Because of the law of limitation on Executive Committee positions, Overseer Horton would be eligible for only two years. In the usual pattern of administrative succession, Cecil B. Knight was elevated to First Assistant General Overseer.

Following Knight's election, three new members were

---

5. *Minutes of the Fifty-fifth General Assembly,* 1974, p. 51.

elected to the Committee—T. L. Lowery, pastor of the North Cleveland church, was elected Second Assistant General Overseer; J. Frank Culpepper, overseer of South Carolina, was elected Third Assistant General Overseer; Floyd J. Timmerman, overseer of Georgia, was elected General Secretary-Treasurer.

There were other administrative changes. T. L. Forester, who had served as interim executive missions secretary since W. E. Johnson's retirement in May 1973, was appointed to continue in that post. John D. Nichols was elected evangelism and home missions director; B. A. Brown was appointed superintendent of the Home for Children. Cecil Guiles continued as youth and Christian education director, where he had served since 1972.

§ 7. EMERGENCE IN SPAIN

Following a 1967 change in Spanish policy that recognized evangelical churches and permitted them to operate openly, the Church of God emerged from its covert and shaky beginning. The work began in a piecemeal fashion, principally by congregations accepted into the fellowship of the Church by William D. Alton, superintendent of Europe at the time of the change in Government policy. Ironically the valiant work of Custodio Apolo in Badajos played no significant role in the emerging churches. Apparently the Badajos mission did not survive the old saint's death in 1966. The small cell-like congregations were in Barcelona, Madrid, Tarragona, Miranda de Ebro, and Ceuta, across the Strait of Gibraltar in North Africa. Actually, the Ceuta congregation was the oldest of those identified with the Church of God; this group, not on the Spanish mainland, united with the Church in 1960 during a visit by Vessie D. Hargrave from Latin America. With pastors such as Jose A. Caballos, Luisa O. Parga, Alfredo Rodriguez, and Miguel B. Trallero these congregations formed a nucleus for a greater effort in the future.

In September 1975, the Missions Board appointed James E. Lewis and his wife, Tarose, as its first American missionaries to the overwhelmingly Catholic country. Lewis, like Apolo before him, soon found the hearts of the people warmly responsive to the gospel of Jesus Christ. The young missionary couple likewise responded with enthusiasm to the warmth of the Spanish hearts.

§ 8. MILITARY VANGUARD

Even before the Church of God appointed its first missionary to Spain, the Church was represented there by its Ministry to the Military outreach. As had happened in the Philippines, Japan, Korea, and Okinawa, Christian servicemen were in the vanguard of missionary penetration. A servicemen's center was organized at the Torrejon Air Force Base in Madrid in February 1975. Larry G. Hess, who had extensive Pioneers for Christ experience at Lee College, was assigned director of the new center.

In the same manner, servicemen's leaders in other countries have doubled as missionaries where there are no Church of God missionaries. Among these are Charles A. Page in Adana, Turkey, and Ron L. Byrne on the Pacific Island of Guam. This effort is an expeditious and successful blending of missionary and evangelistic enterprises.

§ 9. A GRADUATE SCHOOL

The Assembly of 1974 set in motion two educational programs that had been planned in the "Project '70" proposals. The first of these was a Spanish Institute of Ministries, located in Houston, Texas. James M. Beaty, professor of religion at Lee College, was named president. The school opened on September 3, 1975, with seventeen students.

The second was the Church of God Graduate School of Christian Ministries, which began operation in 1975. The Graduate School did not come about easily or quickly. In 1965 General Overseer Horton appointed a committee to study the prospects for such a school. The first official call for a seminary was made by General Overseer Conn in an address at the Golden Anniversary Commemoration of Lee College on

January 8, 1968.[6] Plans for the school were included in "Project '70," and the 1970 General Assembly passed the following measure:

> That the General Assembly authorize the Executive Council to proceed with a study leading to the establishment of a Seminary and Bible Institute, and if found feasible, that the Executive Council initiate the first phase of the program.[7]

After five years of planning and preparation, the school opened its first term on September 1, 1975, with seven full-time and eleven part-time students. R. Hollis Gause, former academic dean of Lee College, and F. J. May, pastor in Louisville, Kentucky, were named director-dean and associate professor of the fledgling school. The General Overseer of the Church of God was designated president, which made Wade H. Horton the first Graduate School president, *de jure*.

The school was located on Centenary Avenue, in a remodeled Lee College apartment house known as College Arms. The two institutions shared libraries and adjunct faculty but were otherwise unrelated.

On July 27, 1976, the Graduate School graduated five students: Ralph Douglas, Darrell Kilpatrick, Lukie L. Magee, M. Dwain Pyeatt and Marvin Woods. These were awarded Master of Arts or Master of Science degrees. Speaker for the first commencement service was H. D. Williams, chairman of the General Board of Education, who had been instrumental in bringing the ambitious school into being. It was a small beginning of what promised to be one of the most important steps ever taken in the academic ministry of the Church of God. It was also one of the first graduate schools in the Pentecostal Movement.

§ 10. AN EDUCATION EXPLOSION

Opening of the Graduate School was part of a general upsurge in the educational energies of the Church of God. The

---

6. Conn, *Church of God Evangel,* February 12, 1968, pp. 13, 22.
7. *Minutes of the Fifty-third General Assembly,* 1970, pp. 57, 58.

period 1968 to 1976 saw a burst of creative genius in the academic ministries of the Church, with an introduction of exciting new programs and the enhancement of the old. What happened amounted to an explosion of ideas, interests and institutions. The creation of a General Board of Education in 1968 was followed by the appointment of a general director in 1974. He was Robert White, overseer of such states as Montana, Arizona and West Virginia, and a member of the General Board of Education from its beginning.

A Continuing Education Program was initiated by the General Board of Education and Lee College as a way to extend quality training to those who could not attend college full time. The program officially began on January 1, 1976, and enrolled four hundred students during the first year of its operation.* The program was designed for a combination of independent and classroom study which would lead to a baccalaureate degree from Lee College.

Also a part of the education explosion was a continuing series of Bible Institutes for Ministerial and Lay Enrichment. Initiated in September 1971, the Institutes were conducted annually in more than a hundred cities with four thousand students enrolled. With the Continuing Education and Bible Institute programs, the Church of God brought advanced training to its grassroots level.

§ 11. School for the East Coast

In addition to the Graduate School and the Spanish Institute, the period also saw the creation of an East Coast Bible College in Charlotte, North Carolina. Under the leadership of C. Raymond Spain, overseer of North Carolina, the new Bible

---

*The Continuing Education Program was developed by a special committee, with Martin Baldree, Stanley Butler and Charles Paul Conn from Lee College; and Robert Fisher, David Lanier and A. M. Stephens from the General Board of Education. Delton L. Alford, dean of the College, and Robert White, general director of education, served as *ex-officio* members, and H. D. Williams as advisor. The courses were prepared by a Continuing Education faculty of thirty-five teachers. E. C. Christenbury served as acting director during the development and first year of operation.

college was built on the state campground. George D. Voorhis, a minister of North Carolina, was named president. The school opened with 122 students on September 12, 1976.

While new schools were organized, the older colleges took on new life and vigor. West Coast Bible College, under the presidency of Horace S. Ward, former dean of students at Lee College, enjoyed record-breaking enrollment virtually every semester from 1971 to 1976, when more than two hundred students registered for the fall semester. In 1976 the college was accredited by the Western Association of Schools and Colleges and the American Association of Bible Colleges.

Northwest Bible College, under President Laud O. Vaught, and International Bible College, under President Philip Siggelkow, also made consistent gains. With the promising new educational institutions and the robust health of the old, it was manifest that the day of higher education in the Church of God had come to full flower at last.

§ 12. A SENSE OF HERITAGE

If the Church's hope for the future lay in its institutions, so was its heritage preserved by them. In its formative days the Church had only a future; in the 1970s it also had a past. Now the denomination could look in two directions, with the present always the focal point of the past and the future. The advantage that maturity has over youth is its capacity for reflecting on the past as well as contemplating the future. Youth can look in only one direction while maturity can look in two. With the perspective gained from the past, the Church of God could keep its bearing on the future.

Early in the 1970s Lee College undertook programs to preserve the Pentecostal heritage for succeeding generations. A Pentecostal Research Center was established by the College and its Alumni Association in the spring of 1971. The Center was designed for graduate and special research. Its goal was to house in one place, as nearly as possible, everything ever written by or about the Pentecostal Movement.

A primary focus of the Pentecostal Research Center is the history of the Church of God. "To preserve for future generations those things of the past that have made us what we are" is the stated purpose of the Center . . . Scholarly investigation of all dimensions of Pentecostalism comes within the scope of the Center, and materials collected at the Center are available for reserach. The Pentecostal Research Center is housed in the Lee College Library and is accessible for serious graduate research.[8]

Soon the growing collection of rare and vital materials filled the space designated for the Center, and in 1976 an entire floor of the Lee College Library was provided for it.

In 1972 the College began a Heritage Week program, when pioneers of the Church were invited to the campus to share their experiences with the college community. For one week each year the students were exposed to the rich ministry of such veteran ministers as Houston R. Morehead (1972), Paul H. Walker (1973), J. H. Ingram (1974), Frank W. Lemons (1975), Zeno C. Tharp (1976), and Earl P. Paulk, Sr. (1977). The present generation learned much about its roots as these venerable ministers related how God had blessed and directed the Pentecostal people when faith and hope were about the only commodities they had in abundance.

This program "enabled the students to gain new perspectives of their magnificent heritage. An appreciation of the past gives confidence for the future. And that future is as bright as our heritage is glorious."[9] The more the current generation increased in knowledge of the past the more it increased in confidence for the future. From its heritage it gained perspective, and from perspective it gained hope.

---

8. Evaline Echols, *Church of God Evangel*, November 11, 1974, p. 19.
9. Echols, *Ibid.*, May 10, 1976, p. 24.

Chapter 35
THE UNFINISHED JOURNEY

§ 1. YEAR OF CELEBRATION

In 1976 the United States indulged itself in a year-long celebration of its past. It was the Nation's Bicentennial Year, a year of reflection and projection, a year to honor the past and chart the future. This time of National celebration had special meaning for the Church of God, which was ninety years old in 1976. The cultural roots of the Church were American even though its branches extended to much of the world and its spiritual roots were set in the eternal Word of God.

The Church was honored as part of the Nation's heritage when Lee College was declared a Bicentennial Campus by the National Bicentennial Committee. The Heritage Week series and the Pentecostal Research Center were singled out as two of the reasons for this designation and honor. In addition, the now-famous Lee Singers were featured as the Tennessee artists in a series of concerts honoring the states at Kennedy Center in Washington, D.C.

In many parts of the country local congregations had lecture series, seminars and festive events to honor the Church's ninetieth year and the Nation's 200th birthday. But the Church did not indulge in a euphoric celebration of past victories. It was too occupied with its vision of the future.

§ 2. NATIONAL TELEVISION DEBUT

The Church made a giant communications breakthrough in 1974 and 1976, when the Radio and Television Department, under the aggressive leadership of Carl Richardson, produced two national television programs. The first was telecast in November 1974 on a network of 187 television stations across the country. Called "New World Coming," the program was aired during prime-time evening hours and was seen by a possible seventeen million viewers.[1]

This was only preliminary to the second television special which was broadcast nationally in July 1976. Titled "Freedom Celebration," the hour-long program was filmed in Washington, with the principal segment being a prayer service on the Capitol steps. Approximately five thousand persons were present for the service. Other segments were filmed at such historic sites as the Lincoln Memorial and Mount Vernon. This prime-time broadcast, seen by approximately twenty million viewers across the nation, featured several prominent musical groups, interviews with national leaders and a sermon by Carl Richardson. Open telephone lines were provided so viewers could call for prayer at the end of the telecast. The response was so enthusiastic and requests for prayer so numerous that hopes were awakened for more telecasts in the future.

§ 3. EMPHASIS ON LITERATURE

The Publishing House was continually enlarged to meet the growing demands for Pentecostal literature. Publisher F. W. Goff increased the plant capacity and installed sophisticated printing equipment. O. W. Polen, editor in chief, made the *Evangel* circulation a principal cause in his labors. The success was outstanding. In the past the oldest Pentecostal publication generally had a circulation ranging from twenty thousand to twenty-five thousand. This low circulation belied the editorial quality of the journal. Polen doubled and then trebled the circulation, until it reached a high of 76,389 in April 1976.[2] The attainment of "76,000 in '76" brought the venerable publication to a respectable level of distribution.

---

1. Interview with Carl Richardson.
2. Interview with O. W. Polen.

§ 4. THE PENDULUM PATTERN

As time for the Assembly of 1976 approached, there was a mood of apprehension with some anxiety across the Church. The tensions of 1974 were a livid memory to many who dreaded further debate and appearance of division. But the fears were unnecessary, for the meeting in Dallas on August 6-12 was one of harmony and healing.

There is historically a pendulum pattern in Church of God General Assemblies. No two successive meetings have been filled with tension or idealogical division. When there has been an Assembly with an unusual degree of division, the next has been one of unity and tranquility. In 1946 the Church seemed hopelessly divided, but in 1948 the impasse was resolved in love and brotherhood. In 1958 the Assembly verged on open rupture, but in 1960 the Assembly was so bathed in divine love and brotherhood that for two days all business was suspended for testimonies, confessions, prayers and rejoicing. The pattern had been consistent through the years, and it was true in 1976.

§ 5. ASSEMBLY OF HEALING

General Overseer Horton opened the 1976 Assembly with a call to prayer in the General Council. Following a full hour of kneeling prayer by the ministers, the meeting proceeded with such harmony that it was likened to the 1960 meeting. There were testimonies and expressions of love reminiscent of that earlier time of deep emotion. God revealed to the Church of God that He is still on His throne and directs the affairs of His Church.

> Coinciding with America's Bicentennial celebration, the Fifty-sixth General Assembly . . . was characterized by a spirit of unity which was divine in its origin. Without doubt, it will always be remembered as one of the truly great spiritual convocations in the ninety-year history of the Church.
>
> Against a backdrop of unprecedented growth among the world's fastest growing churches, God dramatically brooded

over the business deliberations and gave the Church of
God a divine mandate for accelerated growth over the next
ten years.[3]

Cecil B. Knight was elected General Overseer. He came to
the office after a lifetime of service in the Church of God,
with six years experience on the Executive Committee. Before
coming to the Committee in 1970, Knight had been national
youth and Christian education director, overseer of Indiana
and director of evangelism and home missions. His work as
director of the Ministry to the Military had been especially
fruitful. During his work with the servicemen he developed a
stateside retreat program comparable to that in Europe and
Asia. Now, at age fifty-one Knight brought experience and
enthusiasm to the highest office of the Church of God.

Ray H. Hughes, who had left the office of General Overseer
only two years earlier, was returned to the Committee as First
Assistant General Overseer; J. Frank Culpepper was elevated
to Second Assistant General Overseer; T. L. Lowery was
elected Third Assistant General Overseer; and Floyd J. Timmerman was reelected General Secretary-Treasurer. General
Overseer Knight was surrounded by an experienced Council
of Twelve. The first three men elected to that body were
former General Overseers: Wade H. Horton, Charles W.
Conn and James A. Cross. It was as if the Church had reached
out in its time of opportunity and need for leaders of wide
experience. And yet the Church opened the door to new leadership, and three new members were also elected to the
Council.[4] This was an Assembly of unity, of harmony and
balance. Most of all, it was an Assembly of healing.

§ 6. EDUCATION AND MISSIONS

There were other administrative changes as the Church
geared for the future. Robert E. Fisher, overseer of Maryland
and member of the General Board of Education, was appointed general education director. Fisher, a long-time ad-

---

3. *Minutes of the Fifty-sixth General Assembly,* 1976, Preface.
4. *Ibid.,* p. 74

vocate of quality education in the Church, had earlier served as superintendent of West Coast Bible College. Robert White, who had filled the education post for two years, was appointed executive missions secretary. This placed Fisher and White in vital leadership roles where their youthful vision and vigor were important qualities.

J. Herbert Walker, Jr., after six outstanding years in Europe, came to the Missions Department as coordinator of mission schools, of which there were forty-six in thirty-five countries. Lambert DeLong succeeded Walker as superintendent of Europe. DeLong was a veteran of almost twenty-five years in Germany, having first gone there with his wife, Mary Lauster, in the summer of 1951. Floyd D. Carey, who was elected general director of youth and Christian education, was a long-time youth leader at every level of church operation. To him youth work was a way of life.

§ 7. Quest for Excellence

Specialization in the Church became a distinguishable force during the early and mid-1970s. This came about as men of similar disciplines sought ways of utilizing their training and skills for the glory of God and the good of the Church. It amounted to a selective quest for excellence. In December 1969 an Academy of Christians in the Professions was organized by men from a broad spectrum of disciplines, careers and ministries. This was followed in August 1970, and formally in August of 1972, by a National Association of Church Musicans. A primary function of this association was "to encourage personal proficiency and growth in the areas of spiritual development, academic improvement, and performance of church music."

In November 1970 Church of God educators figured prominently in the formation of an interdenominational Society for Pentecostal Studies. With all members holding graduate degrees from reputable colleges, this organization demonstrated the place higher education has now assumed in Pentecostal ranks.

Further special interests in the Church of God occasioned Christian Writers' Seminars by the Editorial Department in 1973 and 1975. Also in 1975, the National Music Committee sponsored a National Church Music Conference at Lee College. Later, among other popular specializations, a highly ambitious and successful science symposium was conducted on the Lee College campus during the 1976-77 school term. This was sponsored by the "Liaisons," a body of Church scientists and science majors. The rise of these specialized groups and events indicated a growing inclination within the Church to seek excellence in every field.

§ 8. BACK TO THE MOUNTAINS

For their 1976 post-Assembly promotional conference, the department executives and state officers came together on November 9-11 for what was called a "Leadership Retreat." When the men and their wives met in Gatlinburg, a resort town in the mountains of East Tennessee, there were more than three hundred leaders from all fifty states and Europe. The retreat was a relaxed time of instruction, inspiration, rest and renewal. There was something symbolic, however unintentional, about the return to mountains near where the Church of God had been founded ninety years earlier.

The historic meeting began with a special seminar for the college presidents of the Church. Under General Director Fisher, the presidents and other education personnel sought ways of melding the separate units into a potent force for the future growth of Pentecostal knowledge and faith. Following the seminar, General Overseer Knight addressed the total group of Church leaders with spiritual candor:

> At this point in history it appears that we have developed all of the departments and agencies needed to fulfill the mission of the Church.
>
> From here on it is a matter of improving and working together under the four emphases of the Great Commission: evangelism, education, missions and stewardship. The mark of maturity for a denomination is for its departments and leaders to labor together as a team.

It was a call to peak performance by all parts of the mature body. The day of youthful beginnings might be near its end, but the day of maximum efficiency was in its dawn.

§ 9. A REASONABLE HOPE

It was a good time for the Church of God. The Church was now large enough to do many of the dreamed-of things a church should do, and yet not so big that it could not feel the excitement of every worthy enterprise. It was strong enough to be confident of its abilities, but not so strong that it did not feel the struggle of each new challenge. It was old enough to be poised and mature in its affairs without being so old that it was indifferent and unfeeling in its function. It could now see the masses without losing sight of the individual. It could delight in its victories without diminishing its vision.

Like the early Christians, the Church of God stood ready to give every man a reason for the hope that was in it (1 Peter 3:15). Like its own forebears, it possessed, and was possessed by, a militant faith and steadfast hope. It had reason to believe. And it did believe.

The Church was called upon to "double in a decade"—to be twice as large and strong and able ten years hence as it was in 1976—and the Church believed that it could do it. It believed, because it had doubled in every decade of its history. It believed because its trust remained in the leadership of Christ and the empowering of the Holy Spirit. The Church of God believed that He who had charted its course in the past would also chart it for the future.

APPENDICES

DOCUMENTS

TABLES

BIBLIOGRAPHY

INDEX

DOCUMENT A

MINUTES

of the

ANNUAL ASSEMBLY

of the

CHURCHES OF EAST TENNESSEE, NORTH GEORGIA AND

WESTERN NORTH CAROLINA, HELD JANUARY 26 AND 27, 1906
at Camp Creek, N. C.

Note—We hope and trust that no person or body of people will ever use these minutes, or any part of them, as articles of faith upon which to establish a sect or denomination. The subjects were discussed merely to obtain light and understanding. Our articles of faith are inspired and given us by the Holy Apostles and written in the New Testament which is our only rule of faith and practice.

The meeting called to order and devotions conducted by the pastor, A. J. Tomlinson.

After due consideration the Assembly accepted the following motto or ruling: We do not consider ourselves a legislative or executive body, but judicial only.

The question as to whether records should be made and preserved, of this and other like assemblies was duely discussed by deacon J. C. Murphy and others, passed upon and recommended as scriptural.

The assembly discussed the advisability of each local church making and preserving its own records. Consider it in harmony with New Testament teaching, and advise each local church to make and preserve records of all church proceedings. The Acts of the Apostles as example.

Communion and feet-washing were duely discussed by elder R. G. Spurling and others, and it is the sense of this assembly that the communion and feet-washing are taught by the New Testament Scriptures, and may be engaged in at the same service or at different times at the option of the local churches. In order to preserve the unity of the body, and to obey the sacred Word, we recommend that every member engage in these sacred services. We further recommend that these holy ordinances be observed one or more times each year.

Prayer-meetings discussed by brother Alexander Hamby and others. It is, therefore, the sense of this assembly that we recommend, advise and urge that each

397

local church hold a prayer-meeting at least once a week. We recommend further that some one in every church, who may feel led by the Holy Spirit or selected by the church, take the oversight thereof and see that such prayer-meeting is held regularly and in proper order.

Evangelism, discussed by the pastor and others; reports of work done the past year; consecration on the part of a number. After the consideration of the ripened fields and open doors for evangelism this year, strong men wept and said they were not only willing but really anxious to go. It is, therefore, the sense of this meeting that we do our best to press into every open door this year and work with greater zeal and energy for the spread of the glorious gospel of the Son of God than ever before.

A discourse of The Use of Tobacco was delivered by evangelist M. S. Lemons and discussed by others. After due consideration this assembly agrees to stand, with one accord, in opposition to the use of tobacco in any form. It is offensive to those who do not use it; weakens and impairs the nervous system; is a near relative to drunkenness; bad influence and example to the young; useless expense, the money for which ought to be used to clothe the poor, spread the gospel or make the homes of our country more comfortable; and last we believe its use to be contrary to the teaching of Scripture, and as Christ is our example we cannot believe that He would use it in any form or under any circumstances.

We further recommend and advise that the ministers and deacons of each church make special effort to use their influence against its use, deal tenderly and lovingly with those in the church who use it, but insist with an affectionate spirit that its use be discontinued as much as possible. We also, advise the deacons to secure a report at the close of each year, of the number that have been induced to discontinue the habit and delivered from a desire for it, also the number that still continue its use, and carry such report to the general assembly.

Family worship was discussed by Andrew Freeman and others. It is, therefore, the sense of this assembly that we recommend and urge that the families of all the churches engage in this very sacred and important service at least once a day and at a time most convenient to the household and that the parents should see that every child is taught, as early as possible, to reverence God and their parents by listening quietly and attentively to the reading of God's Word and getting down on their knees during the prayer. We recommend further that the ministers and deacons of each church use their influence and make special effort to encourage every family in the church to engage in this devotional exercise every day. And that the deacons ascertain the proper information and make a report of the number of families that have been induced to take up this service during the year, the number that make it a regular practice and those that do not and carry such report to the yearly or general assembly.

The Sunday School was briefly discussed by elder W. F. Bryant, Malissie Murphy and others. We highly favor this important service as a means to teach the children to reverence God's Word and the house appointed for worship, and also, to elevate the morals of a community. It is, therefore, the sense of this assembly to recommend, advise and urge every local church to have a Sunday School every Sunday during the whole year if possible. We advise the workers to do all they can to propagate the Sunday School interests, and search for places where there are none and organize where it is possible to do so. We believe a Sunday

School may sometimes be organized and run successfully where a church could not be established at once, thereby opening and paving the way for more permanent work in the future. It is further recommended that Sunday School be held in the forenoon when it is possible to hold them at that time.

When a member in good standing removes from the vicinity of one church to another, we recommend that a letter of recommendation be given them on request, in harmony with Romans 16:1, 2, "I commend unto you Phebe our sister, which is a servant of the church which is at Cenchrea: That ye receive her in the Lord, as becometh saints."

We recommend a closer union and fellowship of all the churches. We, therefore, conclude an assembly composed of elders and chosen men, and the women, from each church, once each year to be of vast importance for the promotion of the gospel of Christ and His Church. We, therefore, with one accord select and set apart Thursday, Friday and Saturday before the second Sunday in January of each year, for each special yearly assembly. Provided, however, that there are no preventing providences. The place to be selected later as the providences of God and His Spirit may direct.

It seemeth good to the Holy Ghost and us, being assembled together with one accord, with the Spirit of Christ in the midst, and after much prayer, discussion, searching the Scriptures and counsel, to recommend these necessary things and that they be ratified and observed by all the local churches. It is the duty of the Church to execute the laws given us by Christ through His Holy Apostles.

The Assembly concluded: Saturday, January 27, 1906, at 7:30 P.M.

DOCUMENT B

DECLARATION OF FAITH

WE BELIEVE

1. In the verbal inspiration of the Bible.

2. In one God eternally existing in three persons; namely, the Father, Son, and Holy Ghost.

3. That Jesus Christ is the only begotten Son of the Father, conceived of the Holy Ghost, and born of the Virgin Mary. That Jesus was crucified, buried, and raised from the dead; that He ascended to heaven and is today at the right hand of the Father as the Intercessor.

4. That all have sinned and come short of the glory of God, and that repentance is commanded of God for all and necessary for forgiveness of sins.

5. That justification, regeneration, and the new birth are wrought by faith in the blood of Jesus Christ.

6. In sanctification subsequent to the new birth, through faith in the blood of Christ; through the Word, and by the Holy Ghost.

7. Holiness to be God's standard of living for His people.

8. In the baptism of the Holy Ghost subsequent to a clean heart.

9. In speaking with other tongues as the Spirit gives utterance, and that it is the initial evidence of the baptism of the Holy Ghost.

10. In water baptism by immersion, and all who repent should be baptized in the name of the Father, and of the Son, and of the Holy Ghost.

11. Divine healing is provided for all in the atonement.

12. In the Lord's Supper; and washing of the saints' feet.

13. In the premillennial second coming of Jesus. First, to resurrect the righteous dead and to catch away the living saints to Him in the air. Second, to reign on the earth a thousand years.

14. In the bodily resurrection; eternal life for the righteous and eternal punishment for the wicked.

DOCUMENT C

CHURCH OF GOD TEACHINGS

THE CHURCH OF GOD stands for the whole Bible rightly divided. The New Testament is the only rule for government and discipline.

DOCTRINAL COMMITMENTS

1. Repentance. Mark 1:15; Luke 13:3; Acts 3:19.
2. Justification. Romans 5:1; Titus 3:7.
3. Regeneration. Titus 3:5.
4. New birth. John 3:3; 1 Peter 1:23; 1 John 3:9.
5. Sanctification subsequent to justification. Romans 5:2; 1 Corinthians 1:30; 1 Thessalonians 4:3; Hebrews 13:12.
6. Holiness. Luke 1:75; 1 Thessalonians 4:7; Hebrews 12:14.
7. Water baptism. Matthew 28:19; Mark 1:9, 10; John 3:22, 23; Acts 8:36, 38.
8. Baptism with the Holy Ghost subsequent to cleansing; the enduement of power for service. Matthew 3:11; Luke 24:49, 53; Acts 1:4-8.
9. The speaking in tongues as the Spirit gives utterance as the initial evidence of the baptism of the Holy Ghost. John 15:26; Acts 2:4; 10:44-46; 19:1-7.
10. Spiritual gifts. 1 Corinthians 12:1, 7, 10, 28, 31; 1 Corinthians 14:1.
11. Signs following believers. Mark 16:17-20; Romans 15:18, 19; Hebrews 2:4.
12. Fruit of the Spirit. Romans 6:22; Galatians 5:22, 23; Ephesians 5:9; Philippians 1:11.
13. Divine healing provided for all in the atonement. Psalm 103:3; Isaiah 53:4, 5; Matthew 8:17; James 5:14-16; 1 Peter 2:24.
14. The Lord's Supper. Luke 22:17-20; 1 Corinthians 11:23-26.
15. Washing the saints' feet. John 13:4-17; 1 Timothy 5:9, 10.
16. Tithing and giving. Genesis 14:18-20; 28:20-22; Malachi 3:10; Luke 11:42; 1 Corinthians 9:6-9; 16:2; Hebrews 7:1-21.
17. Restitution where possible. Matthew 3:8; Luke 19:8, 9.
18. Premillennial second coming of Jesus.
    First, to resurrect the dead saints and to catch away the living saints to Him in the air. 1 Corinthians 15:52; 1 Thessalonians 4:15-17; 2 Thessalonians 2:1.
    Second, to reign on the earth a thousand years. Zechariah 14:4; 1 Thessalonians 4:14; 2 Thessalonians 1:7-10; Jude 14, 15; Revelation 5:10; 19:11-21; 20:4-6.

19. Resurrection. John 5:28, 29; Acts 24:15; Revelation 20:5, 6.
20. Eternal life for the righteous. Matthew 25:46; Luke 18:30; John 10:28; Romans 6:22; 1 John 5:11-13.
21. Eternal punishment for the wicked. No liberation nor annihilation. Matthew 25:41-46; Mark 3:29; 2 Thessalonians 1:8, 9; Revelation 20:10-15; Revelation 21:8.

PRACTICAL COMMITMENTS

22. Total abstinence from all liquor or strong drinks. Proverbs 20:1; 23:29-32; Isaiah 28:7; 1 Corinthians 5:11; 6:10; Galatians 5:21.
23. Against the use of tobacco in any form, opium, morphine, etc. Isaiah 55:2; 1 Corinthians 10:31, 32; 2 Corinthians 7:1; Ephesians 5:3-8; James 1:21.
24. A New Testament interpretation of the use of meats and drinks in accordance with the following scriptures: Romans 14:2, 3, 17; 1 Corinthians 8:8; 1 Timothy 4:1-5.
25. Christian day of worship. Romans 14:5, 6; Colossians 2:16, 17; Matthew 28:1; Acts 20:7; 1 Corinthians 16:2.
26. That our members dress according to the teachings of the New Testament. 1 John 2:15, 16; 1 Timothy 2:9; 1 Peter 3:1-6.
27. That our members conform to the Scripture relative to outward adornment and to the use of cosmetics, etc., that create an unnatural appearance. 1 Peter 3:3-5; 1 Timothy 2:9, 10; Romans 12:1, 2.
28. That our members adhere to the scriptural admonition that our women have long hair and our men have short hair as stated in 1 Corinthians 11:14, 15.
29. Against members wearing jewelry for ornament or decoration, such as finger rings (this does not apply to wedding bands), bracelets, earrings, lockets, etc. 1 Timothy 2:9; 1 Peter 3:3.
30. Against members attending movies, dances and other ungodly amusements; further, that extreme caution be exercised in viewing and in the selectivity of television programs. 1 John 2:15, 16; Romans 13:14; 1 Thessalonians 5:22; Philippians 4:8; 2 Corinthians 6:14-7:1.
31. Against members going in swimming with opposite sex other than the immediate family. 1 John 2:15, 16; 1 Timothy 2:9; 1 Corinthians 6:19, 20; Romans 6:13; 2 Peter 1:4; Galatians 5:19.
32. Against members belonging to lodges. John 18:20; 2 Corinthians 6:14-17.
33. Against members swearing. Matthew 5:34; James 5:12.
34. Divorce and remarriage. Matthew 19:7-9; Mark 10:11, 12; Luke 16:18; 1 Corinthians 7:2, 10, 11.
35. The Church of God believes that nations can and should settle their differences without going to war; however, in the event of war, if a member engages in combatant service, it will not affect his status with the Church. In case a member is called into military service who has conscientious objections to combatant service, the Church will support him in his constitutional rights.

TABLES

Table 1

GENERAL OVERSEERS

A. J. TOMLINSON (1865-1943)	1909-1923	(14)
F. J. LEE[1] (1875-1928)	1923-1928	(5)
S. W. LATIMER (1872-1950)	1928-1935	(7)
J. H. WALKER, SR. (1900-1976)	1935-1944	(9)
JOHN C. JERNIGAN (1900-)	1944-1948	(4)
H. L. CHESSER (1898-)	1948-1952	(4)
ZENO C. THARP (1896-)	1952-1956	(4)
HOUSTON R. MOREHEAD (1905-)	1956-1958	(2)
JAMES A. CROSS (1911-)	1958-1962	(4)
WADE H. HORTON (1908-)	1962-1966; 1974-1976	(6)
CHARLES W. CONN (1920-)	1966-1970	(4)
R. LEONARD CARROLL[2] (1920-1972)	1970-1972	(1½)
RAY H. HUGHES (1924-)	1972-1974	(2½)
CECIL B. KNIGHT (1925-)	1976-	( )

[1]Died in office October 28, 1928.
[2]Died in office January 26, 1972.
1909-1914, elected by the General Assembly.
1915-1921, there were no elections.
1922-1927, nominated by Council of Twelve, elected by General Assembly.
1928-1929, recommended by Councils of Twelve and Seventy, elected by General Assembly.
Since 1930, nominated by General Council, elected by General Assembly. (Nomination is tantamount to election, since it is made by majority vote, then presented without opposition to the General Assembly. The Assembly can only ratify or reject. No nomination has ever been rejected.)

Table 2

ASSISTANT GENERAL OVERSEERS

M. S. Lemons	1913-1914	(1)
S. W. Latimer[1]	1928	
R. P. Johnson	1929-1933; 1934-1944	(14)
E. C. Clark	1933-1934	(1)
Earl P. Paulk	1941-1944	(3)
H. L. Chesser[2]	1944-1948	(4)
Paul H. Walker[2]	1944-1945	(1)
A. V. Beaube[2]	1944-1945	(1)
E. L. Simmons[2]	1944-1945	(1)
E. W. Williams[2]	1944-1945	(1)
J. D. Bright[2]	1944-1945	(1)
Zeno C. Tharp	1948-1952	(4)
Houston R. Morehead	1952-1956	(4)
John C. Jernigan	1952-1954	(2)
James A. Cross	1954-1958	(4)
Earl P. Paulk	1941-1944; 1956-1960	(7)
H. D. Williams	1958-1962	(4)
Wade H. Horton	1960-1962; 1968-1974	(8)
A. M. Phillips[3]	1962	
Charles W. Conn	1962-1966	(4)
C. Raymond Spain	1964-1968	(4)
R. Leonard Carroll	1964-1970	(6)
Ray H. Hughes[4]	1966-1972; 1976-	( )
Cecil B. Knight	1970-1976	(6)
W. C. Byrd	1972-1974	(2)
T. L. Lowery	1974-	( )
J. Frank Culpepper	1974-	( )

[1]Two days after Latimer's selection as Assistant General Overseer, the death of the General Overseer, F. J. Lee, October 28, automatically elevated him to the office of General Overseer.

[2]Six Assistant General Overseers served concurrently 1944-1945.

[3]Served less than one year; died December 24, 1962.

[4]Succeeded to the office of General Overseer upon the death of R. Leonard Carroll, January 26, 1972.

1913, named by General Overseer, approved by General Assembly.

1928-1929, recommended by Councils of Twelve and Seventy, elected by General Assembly.

Since 1930, nominated by General Council, elected by General Assembly.

Table 3

GENERAL SECRETARY-TREASURERS

E. J. Boehmer	1921-1946	(25)
R. R. Walker	1946-1950	(4)
Houston R. Morehead	1950-1952	(2)
H. L. Chesser	1952-1954	(2)
H. D. Williams	1954-1958	(4)
A. M. Phillips	1958-1962	(4)
C. Raymond Spain	1962-1964; 1968-1970	(4)
Ralph E. Williams	1964-1968	(4)
G. W. Lane	1970-1974	(4)
Floyd J. Timmerman	1974-	( )

This was not an office of official appointment until 1924.

1924-1927, nominated by Council of Twelve, elected by General Assembly.

1928-1929, recommended by the Councils of Twelve and Seventy, elected by General Assembly.

Since 1930, nominated by General Council, elected by General Assembly.

————————————

Table 4

GENERAL EXECUTIVE COMMITTEE[1]

A. J. Tomlinson[2]	1922-1923	(1)
F. J. Lee[3]	1922-1928	(6)
J. S. Llewellyn	1922-1927	(5)
J. B. Ellis	1923-1924; 1926-1932	(7)
T. S. Payne	1924-1932	(8)
S. W. Latimer	1926-1939	(13)
E. J. Boehmer	1926-1944; 1945-1946	(19)
J. W. Culpepper	1926-1927; 1929-1932	(4)
G. A. Fore	1926-1929	(3)
Alonzo Gann	1926-1927; 1929-1932	(4)
Efford Haynes	1926-1932	(6)
M. S. Lemons	1926-1929	(3)
T. L. McLain	1926-1929	(3)
J. A. Self	1926-1932	(6)
R. P. Johnson	1927-1932; 1937-1944	(12)
M. W. Letsinger	1927-1929; 1930-1931	(3)
S. J. Heath	1927-1929	(2)
E. C. Clark	1929-1935; 1942-1944	(8)
J. L. Goins	1929-1930	(1)
E. W. Williams	1929-1932; 1944-1945	(4)
S. J. Wood	1929-1932	(3)
H. N. Scoggins	1930-1932	(2)
J. H. Walker, Sr.	1935-1944	(9)

Zeno C. Tharp	1937-1944; 1948-1956	(15)
E. L. Simmons	1939-1942; 1944-1945	(4)
Earl P. Paulk, Sr.	1941-1944; 1956-1960	(7)
John C. Jernigan	1944-1948; 1952-1954	(6)
H. L. Chesser	1944-1954	(10)
Paul H. Walker	1944-1945	(1)
A. V. Beaube	1944-1945	(1)
J. D. Bright	1944-1945	(1)
R. R. Walker	1946-1950	(4)
Houston R. Morehead	1950-1958	(8)
Charles W. Conn	1952-1956; 1962-1970	(12)
James A. Cross	1954-1962	(8)
H. D. Williams	1954-1962	(8)
A. M. Phillips[4]	1958-1962	(4)
Wade H. Horton	1960-1966; 1968-1976	(14)
C. Raymond Spain	1962-1970	(8)
R. Leonard Carroll[5]	1964-1972	(8)
Ralph E. Williams	1964-1968	(4)
Vessie D. Hargrave	1964-1968	(4)
Ray H. Hughes	1966-1974; 1976-	( )
Cecil B. Knight	1970-	( )
G. W. Lane	1970-1974	(4)
W. C. Byrd[6]	1972-1974	(2)
T. L. Lowery	1974-	( )
J. Frank Culpepper	1974-	( )
Floyd J. Timmerman	1974-	( )

[1]Called Executive Council, 1922-1926; State Overseer Appointing Board, 1926-1952.

[2]Until 1922 the General Overseer made all decisions and appointments alone. The General Overseer is always chairman of the Executive Committee, which has consisted of the following:

1922-1926, General Overseer, Superintendent of Education, Editor and Publisher—total 3.

1926-1932, General Overseer, the Council of Twelve—total 13.

1932-1937, General Overseer, General Secretary-Treasurer, Editor and Publisher—total 3.

1937-1941, General Overseer, Assistant General Overseer, General Secretary-Treasurer, Editor and Publisher, and Superintendent of Education—total 5.

1941-1944, General Overseer, two Assistant General Overseers, General Secretary-Treasurer, Editor and Publisher and Superintendent of Education—total 6.

1944-1945, General Overseer, six Assistant General Overseers—total 7.

1945-1952, General Overseer, Assistant General Overseer and General Secretary-Treasurer—total 3.

1952-1956, General Overseer, two Assistant General Overseers, General Secretary-Treasurer and Editor in Chief—total 5.

1956-1964, General Overseer, two Assistant General Overseers, General Secretary-Treasurer—total 4.

1964-1968, General Overseer, three Assistant General Overseers, General Secretary-Treasurer, General Foreign Missions Director—total 6.

Since 1968, General Overseer, three Assistant General Overseers, General Secretary-Treasurer—total 5.

[3]Died in office October 28, 1928.

[4]Died in office December 24, 1962.

[5]Died in office January 26, 1972

[6]Elected to committee in February 1972, due to changes necessitated by death of R. Leonard Carroll.

Method of Selection:

Look under the offices of those who compose the Executive Committee at any desired period.

—————————————

Table 5

THE EXECUTIVE COUNCIL[1]

The Executive Council is composed of the General Executive Committee with a Council of Twelve who sit in joint session regularly between General Assemblies. A comparison of this table with that of the General Executive Committee will reveal the years any individual served on the Executive Council as a member of the Executive Committee or as one of the twelve councillors.

A. J. Tomlinson[2]	1917-1923	(6)
F. J. Lee	1917-1928	(11)
T. L. McLain	1917-1929	(12)
T. S. Payne	1917-1941	(24)
M. S. Lemons	1917-1929	(12)
J. B. Ellis	1917-1932	(15)
Sam C. Perry	1917-1924	(7)
M. S. Haynes	1917-1924	(7)
George T. Brouayer[2]	1917-1923	(6)
S. W. Latimer	1917-1941	(24)
E. J. Boehmer	1917-1946	(29)
S. O. Gillaspie[2]	1917-1923	(6)
J. S. Llewellyn	1917-1927	(10)
Alonzo Gann	1924-1927; 1929-1932	(6)
John Attey	1924-1926	(2)
G. A. Fore	1924-1929	(5)
Efford Haynes	1924-1935	(11)
J. A. Self	1924-1933	(9)
J. W. Culpepper	1926-1927; 1929-1934	(6)
R. P. Johnson	1927-1948; 1950-1954	(25)
M. W. Letsinger	1927-1929; 1930-1931	(3)
S. J. Heath	1927-1929	(2)
E. C. Clark	1929-1948	(19)
J. L. Goins	1929-1930	(1)
E. W. Williams	1929-1942; 1943-1948	(18)
S. J. Wood	1929-1933; 1934-1939	(9)

H. N. Scoggins	1930-1935	(5)
Zeno C. Tharp	1932-1934; 1935-1960	(27)
J. H. Curry	1932-1938	(6)
E. M. Ellis[3]	1933-1935; 1938-1943; 1944-1945;	
	1948-1952; 1954-1958	(16)
Paul H. Walker	1933-1937; 1942-1948; 1950-1954;	
	1960-1964	(18)
J. H. Walker, Sr.	1934-1948; 1950-1954; 1958-1962	(22)
John C. Jernigan	1935-1954	(19)
John L. Stephens	1935-1939	(4)
R. R. Walker	1937-1944; 1945-1954	(16)
Earl P. Paulk, Sr.	1939-1945; 1946-1950; 1952-1964	(22)
E. L. Simmons	1939-1948; 1950-1952	(11)
H. L. Chesser	1941-1958	(17)
M. P. Cross	1941-1943	(2)
A. V. Beaube	1942-1948; 1950-1952	(8)
J. D. Bright	1942-1943; 1944-1945; 1946-1950;	
	1952-1956; 1958-1962	(16)
B. L. Hicks	1942-1945	(3)
F. W. Lemons	1942-1946; 1948-1950	(6)
U. D. Tidwell	1942-1946	(4)
Clyde C. Cox	1943-1945	(2)
J. T. Roberts	1943-1946; 1948-1952; 1954-1958;	
	1964-1966	(13)
J. Stewart Brinsfield	1946-1950	(4)
Houston R. Morehead	1946-1962; 1966-1970	(20)
Albert H. Batts	1948-1950	(2)
W. E. Johnson	1948-1952; 1954-1958; 1960-1964	(12)
James L. Slay	1948-1952; 1954-1958; 1960-1964;	
	1966-1970	(16)
A. M. Phillips[4]	1948-1952; 1956-1962	(10)
Charles W. Conn	1952-1960; 1962-1974; 1976-	( )
James A. Cross	1952-1966; 1968-1972; 1974-	( )
H. D. Williams	1952-1966	(14)
John L. Byrd	1952-1956; 1962-1964	(6)
T. W. Godwin[5]	1952-1953	(1)
J. H. Hughes	1952-1956	(4)
Wade H. Horton	1952-1956; 1958-	( )
L. H. Aultman	1954-1958; 1960-1962; 1964-1968	(10)
J. Frank Spivey	1954-1958	(4)
Ray H. Hughes	1956-1960; 1962-	( )
Ralph E. Williams	1956-1960; 1962-1972; 1974-	( )
H. B. Ramsey	1958-1962; 1964-1968	(8)
W. C. Byrd	1958-1962; 1968-	( )
C. Raymond Spain	1958-1974; 1976-	( )
D. C. Boatwright	1958-1962	(4)
F. W. Goff	1962-1966; 1968-1972; 1976-	( )
David L. Lemons	1962-1966; 1968-1972	(8)
G. W. Lane	1962-1966; 1970-1974	(8)
R. Leonard Carroll[6]	1964-1972	(8)
Vessie D. Hargrave	1964-1972; 1974-1976	(10)

T. L. Lowery	1964-1968; 1970-	( )
Floyd J. Timmerman	1964-1968; 1970-	( )
William J. Brown	1964-1968	(4)
Cecil B. Knight	1966-	( )
John D. Smith	1966-1970; 1972-1976	(8)
D. A. Biggs	1966-1970; 1974-	( )
O. W. Polen	1966-1970; 1972-1976	(8)
J. Frank Culpepper	1970-	( )
George W. Alford	1970-1974; 1976-	( )
Paul F. Henson	1972-1976	(4)
P. H. McCarn	1972-1976	(4)
John D. Nichols	1972-1976	(4)
E. C. Thomas	1972-1976	(4)
Bennie S. Triplett	1976-	( )
Gene D. Rice	1976-	( )
Raymond E. Crowley	1976-	( )

[1]Called Council of Elders until 1929; Supreme Council, 1929-1964.

[2]Council seats, vacated by impeachment in 1923, were filled at the Assembly of 1924.

[3]Died December 31, 1957. [5]Died May 22, 1953.

[4]Died December 24, 1962. [6]Died January 26, 1972.

1917-1925, the General Overseer selected two, then the General Overseer with these two selected the remaining ten.

1926, elected by the General Council in groups of three, who served four-year terms, expiring alternately, so that each year only three councillors needed to be selected.

1927-1928, the three men to be elected were chosen by the Councils of Twelve and Seventy from six names nominated by the General Overseer.

1929, the General Overseer selected 1, the General Assembly selected 1, total 2; these 2 councillors then selected 1, total 3; the 3 councillors selected 2, total 5; the five councillors selected 2, total 7; the seven councillors selected 2, total 9; the nine councillors selected 3, for the total of 12.

Since 1930, elected by the General Council.

————————————

Table 6

EXECUTIVE DIRECTORS OF SERVICEMEN'S DEPARTMENT

H. D. Williams	1960-1962	(2)
Charles W. Conn	1962-1966	(4)
C. Raymond Spain	1966-1970	(4)
Cecil B. Knight	1970-1976	(6)
J. Frank Culpepper	1976-	( )

Not a full-time office. A member of the Executive Committee is designated by the General Overseer to serve as Executive Director.

Like a Mighty Army

Table 9

OVERSEERS OF NEGRO CHURCHES

Thomas J. Richardson[1]	1922-1923	(1)
David LaFleur	1923-1928	(5)
J. H. Curry	1928-1939	(11)
N. S. Marcelle	1939-1945	(6)
W. L. Ford	1945-1950; 1954-1958	(9)
George A. Wallace	1950-1954	(4)
J. T. Roberts	1958-1965	(7)
David L. Lemons	1965-1966	(1)
H. G. Poitier	1966-1968[2]	(2)

[1]Served less than one year.
[2]National Office was discontinued as black and white churches were integrated.

Appointed by Executive Committee.

————————————

Table 10

REPRESENTATIVES OF BLACK AFFAIRS

H. G. Poitier	1968-1970	(2)
W. C. Byrd	1972-1974	(2)
J. Frank Culpepper	1974-1976	(2)
T. L. Lowery	1976-	( )

1968-1970, appointed by Executive Committee.
Since 1972, filled by a member of the Executive Committee.

———————————— *EDUCATION* ————————————

Table 11

BOARD OF DIRECTORS, LEE COLLEGE[1]

J. B. Ellis	1926-1928	(2)
Frank W. Lemons	1926-1929; 1942-1946	(7)
Alonzo Gann	1926-1936	(10)
J. A. Muncy	1926-1936	(10)
P. F. Fritz	1926-1936	(10)
E. M. Ellis	1928-1936	(8)
H. L. Whittington	1929-1936	(7)
U. D. Tidwell	1936-1943; 1946-1948	(9)

Sam C. Perry	1936-1938	(2)
Robert Bell	1936-1938	(2)
E. C. Clark	1938-1942; 1945-1946	(5)
R. P. Johnson	1938-1941	(3)
M. P. Cross	1940-1942	(2)
E. M. Tapley	1940-1945	(5)
J. D. Bright	1941-1944	(3)
J. T. Roberts	1942-1944	(2)
B. L. Hicks	1943-1944	(1)
R. R. Walker	1944-1946	(2)
J. H. Hughes	1944-1946	(2)
C. J. Hindmon	1944-1952	(8)
J. H. Walker, Sr.	1946-1948	(2)
A. V. Beaube	1946-1950	(4)
Houston R. Morehead	1946-1950	(4)
H. D. Williams	1948-1952	(4)
L. H. Aultman	1948-1957	(9)
James A. Cross	1950-1954	(4)
John L. Byrd	1950-1958	(8)
John L. Meares	1952-1956	(4)
D. C. Boatwright	1952-1966	(14)
H. L. Chesser	1954-1960	(6)
James A. Stephens	1956-1968	(12)
Lewis J. Willis	1958-1962; 1970-1972	(6)
James L. Slay	1958-1962	(4)
Lee Watson	1958-1968	(10)
J. P. Johnson	1958-1962	(4)
A. V. Howell	1960-1964	(4)
W. Paul Stallings	1962-1974	(12)
David L. Lemons	1962-1964	(2)
Virgil W. Smith	1962-1964	(2)
Cecil B. Knight	1964-1968	(4)
Grady P. O'Neal	1964-1968	(4)
H. D. Williams	1964-1966	(2)
Donald B. Gibson	1966-1970	(4)
Philemon G. Roberts	1966-1974	(8)
Ralph E. Williams	1968-	( )
Louis H. Cross	1968-1976	(8)
Thurman J. Curtsinger	1968-1972	(4)
Fred P. Hamilton	1968-	( )
William A. Lawson	1968-1976	(8)
Lynwood Maddox	1968-1974	(6)
F. J. May	1968-1976	(8)
H. B. Ramsey	1968-1976	(8)
Russell C. Miller	1970-1972	(2)
Bill Higginbotham	1972-	( )
William G. Squires	1972-1976	(4)
Garold D. Boatwright	1972-1976	(4)
Paul L. Walker	1974-	( )
H. W. Babb	1974-	( )
Clifford V. Bridges	1974-	( )

E. C. Thomas	1976-	( )
Elton Chalk	1976-	( )
Richard L. Tyler, Jr.	1976-	( )
Robert E. Daugherty	1976-	( )
Paul F. Barker	1976-	( )
Cleo Watts	1976-	( )

[1]Called Board of Education, 1926-1936.

1926, the General Overseer selected the first man, the Council of Twelve the second, the Council of Seventy the third, then the three board members selected the remaining two men.

1927-1942, appointed by General Overseer.

Since 1943, appointed by Executive Committee.

_____

Table 12

PRESIDENTS OF LEE COLLEGE[1]

A. J. Tomlinson	1918-1922	(4)
F. J. Lee	1922-1923	(1)
J. B. Ellis	1923-1924	(1)
T. S. Payne	1924-1930	(6)
J. H. Walker, Sr.	1930-1935; 1944-1945	(6)
Zeno C. Tharp	1935-1944	(9)
E. L. Simmons	1945-1948	(3)
J. Stewart Brinsfield[2]	1948-1951	(2)
John C. Jernigan	1951-1952	(1)
R. Leonard Carroll	1952-1957	(5)
R. L. Platt	1957-1960	(3)
Ray H. Hughes	1960-1966	(6)
James A. Cross	1966-1970	(4)
Charles W. Conn	1970-	( )

[1]Called Superintendent of Education, 1918-1947.

Lee College was known as Bible Training School, 1918-1941; and Bible Training School and College, 1941-1947.

[2]Served 2½ years; the interim was filled by Earl M. Tapley, Dean.

1918-1921, General Overseer served as Superintendent of Education.

1922-1925, nominated by Council of Twelve, elected by General Assembly.

1926-1935, selected by Board of Education.

1936-1941, nominated by General Council, elected by General Assembly.

Since 1942, selected by Lee College Board of Directors.

Table 13

PRESIDENTS OF NORTHWEST BIBLE COLLEGE[1]

F. W. Lemons	1935-1937	(2)
D. C. Boatwright	1937-1939	(2)
Glyndon Logsdon	1939-1943; 1944-1945	(5)
E. E. Coleman	1943-1944	(1)
C. C. McAfee	1946-1948	(2)
T. M. McClendon	1948-1949	(1)
Glynn C. Pettyjohn	1949-1951	(2)
M. G. McLuhan	1951-1953	(2)
L. E. Painter	1953-1956	(3)
W. Paul Stallings	1956-1958	(2)
Paul H. Walker	1958-1964	(6)
Laud O. Vaught	1964-	( )

[1]Known as Northwest Bible and Music Academy until 1958.

1935-1964, The Overseer of the Dakotas was *ex officio* president.
Since 1964, selected by Northwest Bible College Board of Directors.

————————————

Table 14

PRESIDENTS OF WEST COAST BIBLE COLLEGE

J. H. Hughes[1]	1949-1950	(1)
H. B. Ramsey	1950-1954	(4)
Ralph E. Williams	1954-1958	(4)
L. W. McIntyre	1958-1962; 1968-1969	(5)
Floyd J. Timmerman	1962-1966	(4)
Wayne S. Proctor	1966-1968	(2)
R. Terrell McBrayer	1969-1971	(2)
Horace S. Ward, Jr.	1971-	( )

[1]J. H. Hughes served as President from the opening of the school, February 16, 1949, until the Assembly of 1950—or one and a half years.

1949-1969, State Overseer of California was *ex officio* president.
Since 1969, selected by the West Coast Bible College Board of Directors.

————————————

Table 15

GENERAL EDUCATION DIRECTORS

R. Leonard Carroll[1]	1968-1970	(2)
Ray H. Hughes[1]	1970-1972	(2)
Cecil B. Knight[1]	1972-1974	(2)
Robert White	1974-1976	(2)
Robert E. Fisher	1976-	( )

[1]A member of the Executive Committee served as Director, 1968-1974.
Since 1974, appointed by Executive Committee.

Table 16

GENERAL BOARD OF EDUCATION

H. D. Williams	1968-1976	(8)
James M. Beaty	1968-1974	(6)
Robert E. Fisher	1968-1976	(8)
Albert M. Stephens	1968-1976	(8)
Robert White	1968-1974	(6)
David Lanier	1974-	( )
Robert D. Crick	1974-	( )
French L. Arrington	1974-	( )
Walter Barwick	1976-	( )
H. Allen Gross	1976-	( )
Harold Stephens	1976-	( )
William T. George	1976-	( )

Appointed by Executive Committee.

───────────────────

Table 17

GRADUATE SCHOOL OF CHRISTIAN MINISTRIES

BOARD OF DIRECTORS

R. H. Sumner	1975-	( )
Donald S. Aultman	1975-	( )
Walter P. Atkinson	1975-1976	(1)
J. Herbert Walker, Jr.	1975-1976	(1)
Robert A. Blackwood	1975-	( )
Richard Dillingham	1976-	( )
Philemon Roberts	1976-	( )

Appointed by Executive Committee.

──────────────── *EVANGELISM* ────────────────

Table 18

EVANGELISM AND HOME MISSIONS BOARD[1]

C. Raymond Spain	1956-1958	(2)
Doyle Stanfield	1956-1960	(4)
Ray H. Hughes	1956-1960	(4)
G. W. Lane[2]	1956-1963	(7)
W. Edwin Tull[2]	1956-1960	(4)
C. S. Grogan[2]	1956-1960	(4)
L. Luther Turner	1958-1960	(2)

Ralph E. Williams	1960-1964	(4)
Walter R. Pettitt	1960-1963	(3)
A: M. Phillips[3]	1962	
W. H. Compton	1962-1968	(6)
John D. Smith	1964-1968	(4)
J. Frank Culpepper	1964-1966	(2)
Gene D. Rice	1964-1966; 1972-1976	(6)
John D. Nichols	1964-1970	(6)
Curtis Hill	1966-1968	(2)
Mark G. Summers	1966-1968	(2)
B. E. Ellis	1968-1976	(8)
Carl H. Richardson	1968-1972	(4)
Harvey L. Rose	1968-1976	(8)
Bennie S. Triplett	1968-1976	(8)
Aubrey D. Maye	1970-	( )
William E. Winters	1972-1976	(4)
Ray H. Sanders	1972-	( )
V. R. Mitchell	1976-	( )
Robert E. Blazier	1976-	( )
W. E. Dowdy	1976-	( )
J. D. Golden	1976-	( )
Bill J. Webb	1976-	( )

[1]Called National Evangelism Committee, 1956-1960; National Evangelism and Music Committee, 1960-1964.

[2]Member of National Music Committee before the two committees were combined in 1960.

[3]Died in office, December 24, 1962.

Appointed by Executive Committee.

———————————

Table 19

EVANGELISM AND HOME MISSIONS DIRECTORS

Walter R. Pettitt	1963-1968	(5)
Cecil B. Knight	1968-1970	(2)
C. Raymond Spain	1970-1974	(4)
John D. Nichols	1974-	( )

1963, appointed by Executive Committee.
Since 1964, nominated by General Council, elected by General Assembly.

Table 20

ARCHITECTURAL COMMITTEE

Walter R. Pettitt	1964-1968	(4)
Lowell T. Shoemaker[1]	1964-	( )
M. Fred Taylor[1]	1964-1976	(12)
Cecil B. Knight	1968-1970	(2)
Gene D. Rice	1968-1972	(4)
William E. Winters	1968-1972	(4)
C. Raymond Spain	1970-1974	(4)
L. E. Heil	1972-	( )
L. D. Hudson	1972-	( )
John D. Nichols	1974-	( )
James Ezell[1]	1976-	( )

[1]Advisor to the committee.
Appointed by Executive Committee.

———————————

Table 21

LAYMEN'S BOARD

Lynwood Maddox	1966-1968	(2)
Charles R. Beach	1966-1974	(8)
Arthur Hodge	1966-1968; 1976-	( )
H. A. Madden	1966-1970	(4)
J. D. Silver	1966-1976	(10)
Farrell R. Cornutt	1968-1976	(8)
Lee Watson	1968-1972	(4)
Robert D. Annis	1970-1974	(4)
Al Taylor	1972-1976	(4)
John Shambach	1974-	( )
Wilson Kilgore	1974-	( )
J. C. Childers	1976-	( )
Robert Gaines	1976-	( )

Appointed by Executive Committee.

———————— *BENEVOLENCES* ————————

Table 22

DEPARTMENT OF BENEVOLENCES DIRECTORS[1]

F. R. Harrawood	1943-1944	(1)
J. A. Muncy	1944-1948	(4)
William F. Dych	1948-1953	(5)
R. R. Walker	1953-1956	(3)

Cecil Bridges	1956-1964	(8)
P. H. McCarn	1964-1970	(6)
E. K. Waldrop	1970-1972	(2)
B. A. Brown	1972-1976	(4)
W. J. Brown	1976-	( )

[1]Called Orphanage Superintendents 1943-1954; Home for Children Superintendents 1954-1974.

Appointed by Executive Committee.

———————————

Table 23

DEPARTMENT OF BENEVOLENCES BOARD[1]

J. B. Ellis	c. 1920-1924	(4)
J. S. Llewellyn	c. 1920-1927	(7)
T. L. McLain	c. 1920-1927; 1929-1931	(9)
F. J. Lee	1924-1928	(4)
S. W. Latimer[2]	1927-1935	(8)
I. C. Barrett[2]	1927-1935	(8)
E. J. Boehmer	1931-1935; 1943-1944	(5)
R. R. Walker[3]	1935-1939; 1946-1953	(11)
Zeno C. Tharp	1935-1939	(4)
M. P. Cross	1935-1936	(1)
W. J. Milligan	1936-1938	(2)
D. B. Yow	1938-1941	(3)
E. L. Simmons	1939-1941	(2)
John C. Jernigan	1939-1941	(2)
J. D. Bright	1941-1942	(1)
Russell Huff	1941-1943	(2)
F. R. Harrawood	1941-1943	(2)
Robert E. Blackwood	1942-1943	(1)
L. H. Aultman	1943-1944	(1)
U. D. Tidwell	1943-1946	(3)
E. M. Ellis	1944-1945	(1)
T. A. Richard	1944-1945	(1)
James A. Cross	1945-1950	(5)
John D. Smith	1945-1950	(5)
E. C. Clark	1946-1948	(2)
J. M. Baldree	1948-1954	(6)
J. Frank Spivey	1950-1954	(4)
Houston R. Morehead	1950-1952	(2)
William F. Dych	1950-1952	(2)
John E. Douglas	1952-1954	(2)
H. L. Chesser	1952-1954	(2)
C. B. Godsey	1953-1954	(1)
Howard Russell	1954-1956	(2)
Cleo Watts	1954-1956	(2)

C. H. Webb	1954-1960	(6)
H. D. Williams	1954-1958	(4)
B. L. Alford	1954-1956	(2)
Lloyd L. Jones	1956-1964	(8)
Floyd J. Timmerman	1956-1958	(2)
Claude E. Yates	1956-1958	(2)
A. M. Phillips	1958-1962	(4)
T. W. Day	1958-1960	(2)
L. G. Alford	1958-1960	(2)
E. K. Waldrop	1960-1964	(4)
R. Leonard Carroll	1960-1964	(4)
C. J. Hindmon	1960-1962	(2)
C. Raymond Spain	1962-1964	(2)
Charles E. Tilley	1962-1968	(6)
W. Doyle Stanfield	1964-1970	(6)
Earl F. Causey	1964-1970	(6)
James H. Kear	1964-1966; 1968-1974	(8)
Sylvia Norman Britt[4]	1964-	( )
Garland Griffis	1964-1968	(4)
Lucille Walker	1964-1966	(2)
Anna Mae Carroll	1966-1972	(6)
Marshall E. Roberson	1966-1972	(6)
Earl T. Golden	1968-1974	(6)
James A. Stephens	1970-1976	(6)
B. J. Moffett	1970-1972	(2)
Mildred Lowery	1970-1974	(4)
Otis Clyburn	1972-	( )
Mrs. T. A. Perkins	1972-	( )
Warren Beavers	1972-	( )
Jeffrey F. Simpson	1974-	( )
Mrs. O. L. May	1974-	( )
Jewel L. Travis	1974-	( )
Aubrey C. Lowery	1976-	( )
P. F. Taylor	1976-	( )

[1]Called Orphanage Board, 1920-1956; Home for Children Board 1956-1974.
[2]Appointed by General Overseer between Assemblies, ratified by Assembly of 1928.
[3]Since 1946, the General Secretary-Treasurer has been an automatic member.
[4]Advisor since 1970.

1920-1942, appointed by General Overseer.
Since 1943, appointed by Executive Committee.

————————— PUBLICATIONS —————————

Table 24

EDITORS IN CHIEF[1]

A. J. Tomlinson	1910-1922	(12)
J. S. Llewellyn	1922-1927	(5)

S. W. Latimer	1927-1928; 1935-1939	(5)
M. W. Letsinger	1928-1931	(3)
R. P. Johnson[2]	1931-1932	(1)
E. C. Clark[3]	1932-1935; 1942-1946	(7)
E. L. Simmons	1939-1942	(3)
J. H. Walker, Sr.	1946-1948	(2)
J. D. Bright	1948-1952	(4)
Charles W. Conn	1952-1962	(10)
Lewis J. Willis	1962-1970	(8)
O. W. Polen	1970-	( )

[1]Called Editor and Publisher, 1910-1944; Managing Editor, 1944-1946.
[2]Served concurrently as Assistant General Overseer.
[3]Served concurrently as Assistant General Overseer, 1933-1934.

1910-1921, elected by General Assembly.
1922-1925, nominated by Council of Twelve, elected by General Assembly.
1926-1929, selected by Publishing Committee.
1930-1954, nominated by General Council, elected by General Assembly.
Since 1956, appointed by Executive Council and Editorial and Publications Board.

————————————

Table 25

PUBLISHERS[1]

E. C. Clark	1946-1948	(2)
A. M. Phillips	1948-1950	(2)
Cecil Bridges	1950-1955	(5)
E. C. Thomas	1955-1970	(15)
F. W. Goff	1970-	( )

[1]Editor and Publisher served as Business Manager until 1946.
Called Publishing House Business Managers 1946-1960.

Appointed by Executive Council and Editorial and Publications Board.

————————————

Table 26

EDITORS OF THE LIGHTED PATHWAY

Alda B. Harrison	1929-1948	(19)
Charles W. Conn	1948-1952	(4)
Lewis J. Willis	1952-1962	(10)
Clyne W. Buxton	1962-	( )

Privately published through 1936.
1937-1950, selected by Editorial and Publications Board.
1952-1954, appointed by Executive Council.
Since 1956, selected by Editorial and Publications Board.

Table 27

MUSIC EDITORS

Otis L. McCoy	1934-1945; 1947-1952; 1958-1961	(19)
V. B. (Vep) Ellis	1945-1946;[1] 1952-1956	(5)
A. C. Burroughs	1956-1958	(2)
Connor B. Hall	1961-	( )

[1]Office vacant from September 1, 1946, until January 1, 1947.

1934-1937, nominated by General Council, elected by General Assembly.
1938-1944, selected by Editor and Publisher and Editorial and Publications Board.
Since 1945, selected by Editor in Chief, Editorial and Publications Board, and Publisher.

————————————

Table 28

EDITORIAL AND PUBLICATIONS BOARD[1]

A. J. Tomlinson		1910-1916	(6)
T. L. McLain		1910-1916; 1926-1930	(10)
F. J. Lee		1910-1922	(12)
M. S. Lemons		1910-1916; 1919-1922	(9)
Sam C. Perry		1910-1916	(6)
A. J. Lawson		1910-1922	(12)
George T. Brouayer		1910-1922	(12)
R. M. Singleton	*c.*	1913-1916	(3)
J. L. Scott	*c.*	1913-1919	(6)
T. S. Payne		1916-1922	(6)
Louis Purcell		1926-1927	(1)
E. C. Clark		1926-1927	(1)
W. S. Wilemon		1926-1927	(1)
J. W. Culpepper		1926-1927	(1)
E. M. Ellis		1927-1930	(3)
George D. Lemons		1927-1930	(3)
W. D. Childers		1927-1930	(3)
I. C. Barrett		1927-1930	(3)
Zeno C. Tharp		1935-1941; 1956-1962	(12)
R. R. Walker		1935-1937	(2)
M. P. Cross		1935-1938	(3)
R. P. Johnson		1937-1939	(2)
E. L. Simmons		1938-1939; 1950-1956	(7)
John C. Jernigan		1939-1941	(2)
Earl P. Paulk, Sr.		1939-1942	(3)
J. D. Bright		1941-1942	(1)
Robert E. Blackwood		1941-1942	(1)
A. V. Beaube		1942-1944	(2)
Linwood Jacobs		1942-1943	(1)

W. E. Johnson	1942-1944	(2)
A. H. Batts	1943-1946	(3)
L. W. McIntyre	1944-1945	(1)
J. A. Bixler	1944-1950	(6)
J. D. Free	1945-1946	(1)
James L. Slay	1946-1950	(4)
D. C. Boatwright	1946-1948	(2)
T. W. Godwin	1946-1952	(6)
S. Whitt Denson	1946-1952	(6)
V. D. Combs	1948-1954	(6)
W. P. Stallings	1950-1956	(6)
H. D. Williams	1952-1954	(2)
W. J. (Bill) Brown	1952-1968	(16)
J. Frank Spivey	1954-1966	(12)
Marshall E. Roberson	1954-1960	(6)
H. T. Statum	1954-1958	(4)
E. O. Byington	1954-1958	(4)
W. C. Byrd	1956-1964	(8)
E. O. Kerce	1958-1962	(4)
Ralph W. Tedder	1958-1972	(14)
William H. Pratt	1960-1964	(4)
G. Frank Dempsey	1962-1972	(10)
P. H. McSwain	1962-1972	(10)
F. W. Goff	1964-1970	(6)
H. L. Rose	1964-1966	(2)
Robert J. Johnson	1966-1968	(2)
Walter C. Mauldin	1966-1974	(8)
Paul J. Eure	1968-1976	(8)
O. W. Polen	1968-1970	(2)
Elmer E. Golden	1970-1976	(6)
O. C. McCane	1970-	( )
B. G. Hamon	1972-1976	(4)
J. Newby Thompson	1972-	( )
W. W. Thomas	1972-	( )
James D. Jenkins	1974-	( )
Owen McManus	1976-	( )
John Gilbert	1976-	( )
Leon Phillips	1976-	( )

[1]Called Publishing Committee until 1930; Publishing Interest Committee, 1935-1946. The Publishing Committee was discontinued in 1922, and reactivated in 1926; it was discontinued in 1930, and reactivated as Publishing Interest Committee in 1935.

1910-1922, elected by General Assembly.

1926, the General Overseer selected the first man, the Council of Twelve selected the second man, and the Council of Seventy selected the third. These three board members then selected the remaining two men.

1927-1930; 1935-1942, appointed by General Overseer.

Since 1943, appointed by the Executive Committee.

_____*WORLD MISSIONS*_____

Table 29

EXECUTIVE SECRETARIES OF WORLD MISSIONS

M. P. Cross	1942-1946	(4)
J. Stewart Brinsfield	1946-1948	(2)
J. H. Walker, Sr.	1948-1952	(4)
Paul H. Walker	1952-1958	(6)
L. H. Aultman	1958-1964	(6)
Vessie D. Hargrave[1]	1964-1968	(4)
James L. Slay	1968-1970	(2)
W. E. Johnson[2]	1970-1973	(3)
T. L. Forester	1973-1976	(3)
Robert White	1976-	( )

[1]Called General Foreign Missions Director, 1964-1968.
[2]Resigned April, 1973, due to illness.

Appointed by Executive Committee.

_____

Table 30

FOREIGN MISSIONS FIELD REPRESENTATIVES

J. H. Ingram	1935-1938; 1939-1947	(11)
Paul H. Walker	1938-1939	(1)
Wade H. Horton	1952-1958	(6)
C. Raymond Spain	1958-1962	(4)
James L. Slay	1962-1968	(6)
T. L. Forester[1]	1968-1973	(5)
Jim O. McClain	1974-	( )

[1]Elevated to Executive Secretary of World Missions, May, 1973.

Appointed by Executive Committee.

_____

Table 31

WORLD MISSIONS BOARD

R. P. Johnson	1926-1930	(4)
E. L. Simmons	1926-1930	(4)
E. M. Ellis	1926-1932	(6)
M. W. Letsinger	1926-1929	(3)
M. P. Cross	1926-1942; 1946-1952	(22)
J. P. Hughes	1929-1936	(7)

424 Like a Mighty Army

E. W. Williams	1930-1941	(11)
Zeno C. Tharp	1930-1945	(15)
E. C. Clark	1932-1944	(12)
T. M. McClendon	1936-1939; 1945-1948	(6)
E. E. Winters	1939-1941	(2)
Earl P. Paulk, Sr.	1941-1943; 1952-1956	(6)
H. L. Chesser	1941-1944	(3)
J. Stewart Brinsfield	1942-1946	(4)
John C. Jernigan	1943-1944	(1)
Carl Hughes	1944-1945	(1)
George D. Lemons	1944-1950	(6)
J. L. Goins	1944-1946	(2)
Paul H. Walker	1945-1952	(7)
A. M. Phillips	1946-1958	(12)
Wade H. Horton	1948-1953	(5)
J. H. Hughes	1950-1952	(2)
T. Raymond Morse	1950-1958	(8)
W. E. Johnson	1950-1968	(18)
J. H. Walker, Sr.	1952-1958	(6)
S. E. Jennings	1952-1964	(12)
D. A. Biggs	1953-1970	(17)
T. L. Forester	1956-1968	(12)
L. H. Aultman	1957-1958	(1)
John D. Smith	1958-1960	(2)
Houston R. Morehead	1958-1962	(4)
J. D. Bright	1958-1962	(4)
H. B. Ramsey	1960-1966	(6)
P. H. McCarn	1962-1964	(2)
Wayne Heil	1962-1966	(4)
Estel D. Moore	1964-1972	(8)
Herschel L. Diffie	1964-1968	(4)
Antonio Collazo	1966-1974	(8)
John C. McClenden	1966-1970	(4)
A. W. Brummett	1968-1974	(6)
W. E. Dowdy	1968-1970	(2)
Walter R. Pettitt	1968-1976	(8)
James A. Cross	1970-	( )
Billy P. Bennett	1970-1976	(6)
G. M. Gilbert	1970-1976	(6)
W. Edwin Tull	1972-	( )
M. H. Kennedy	1974-	( )
Bob E. Lyons	1974-	( )
Russell Brinson	1976-	( )
Thomas Grassano	1976-	( )
Lamar McDaniel	1976-	( )

1926, the General Overseer selected the first man, Council of Twelve the second, Council of Seventy the third, then the three board members selected the remaining two men.

1927-1942, appointed by General Overseer.

Since 1943, appointed by Executive Committee.

——————————— *YOUTH AND CHRISTIAN EDUCATION* ———————————

Table 32

NATIONAL YOUTH AND CHRISTIAN EDUCATION DIRECTORS[1]

Ralph E. Williams	1946-1950	(4)
Lewis J. Willis	1950-1952	(2)
Ray H. Hughes	1952-1956	(4)
O. W. Polen	1956-1960	(4)
Cecil B. Knight	1960-1964	(4)
Donald S. Aultman	1964-1968	(4)
Paul F. Henson	1968-1972	(4)
Cecil R. Guiles	1972-1976	(4)
Floyd D. Carey, Jr.	1976-	( )

[1]Called National Youth Director, 1946-1952; General Sunday School and Youth Director, 1952-1954, 1968-1970; National Sunday School and Youth Director, 1954-1968.

1946, appointed by Executive Committee.
1948, nominated by General Council, elected by General Assembly.
1950, appointed by Supreme Council.
Since 1952, nominated by General Council, elected by General Assembly.

— — — — — — — — — —

Table 33

ASSISTANT YOUTH AND CHRISTIAN EDUCATION DIRECTORS

O. W. Polen	1954-1956	(2)
Cecil B. Knight	1956-1960	(4)
Donald S. Aultman	1960-1964	(4)
Paul F. Henson	1964-1968	(4)
Cecil R. Guiles	1968-1972	(4)
Floyd D. Carey, Jr.	1972-1976	(4)
Lamar Vest	1976-	( )

1954-1960, appointed by Youth and Christian Education Board.
Since 1962, nominated by General Council, elected by General Assembly.

— — — — — — — — — —

Table 34

GENERAL YOUTH AND CHRISTIAN EDUCATION BOARD[1]

Ralph E. Williams	1946-1952	(6)
Paul Stallings	1946-1950	(4)
Robert Johnson	1946-1948	(2)

E. T. Stacy	1946-1948	(2)
Manuel F. Campbell[2]	1946	
Brady Dennis	1947-1952	(5)
Lewis J. Willis	1948-1954	(6)
Ray H. Hughes	1948-1956	(8)
L. E. Painter	1950-1952	(2)
J. Newby Thompson	1952-1956	(4)
O. W. Polen	1952-1954; 1956-1960	(6)
Earl P. Paulk, Jr.	1952-1958	(6)
Earl T. Golden	1954-1960	(6)
Fred Jernigan	1954-1956	(2)
Ralph E. Day	1956-1962	(6)
Donald S. Aultman	1956-1960	(4)
Hollis Green	1958-1962	(4)
Wallace C. Swilley, Jr.	1960-1962	(2)
Paul Henson	1960-1964	(4)
Clyne W. Buxton	1960-1962	(2)
L. W. McIntyre	1962-1966	(4)
Paul L. Walker	1962-1966	(4)
Thomas Grassano	1962-1974	(12)
Haskell C. Jenkins	1962-1968	(6)
Cecil R. Guiles	1964-1968	(4)
James A. Madison	1966-1970	(4)
Leonard S. Townley[3]	1966-1970	(4)
James F. Byrd	1968-	( )
Floyd D. Carey, Jr.	1968-1972	(4)
Bill F. Sheeks	1968-1976	(8)
Lamar Vest	1968-1972	(4)
Gale A. Barnett	1970-	( )
Elisha Parris	1972-1976	(4)
Travis D. Henderson[4]	1972-1973	(1)
W. A. Davis	1972-	( )
Emerson M. Abbott	1974-1976	(2)
Bill D. Wooten	1974-	( )
Lawrence Leonhardt	1976-	( )
Orville Hagan	1976-	( )
Robert P. Herrin	1976-	( )

[1]Called National Youth Board, 1946-1952; National Sunday School and Youth Board, 1954-1968; General Sunday School and Youth Board, 1952-1954; 1968-1970.

[2]Served less than one year.

[3]Died December 3, 1970.

[4]Served less than one year.

Appointed by Executive Committee.

———————————*RADIO AND TELEVISION*———————————

Table 35

NATIONAL RADIO MINISTERS

Earl P. Paulk, Jr.	1958-1960	(2)
Ray H. Hughes	1960-1963	(3)
G. W. Lane	1963-1966	(3)
Floyd J. Timmerman	1966-1972	(6)
Carl Richardson	1972-	( )

Appointed by the Executive Council and Radio and Television Board.

———————————————————

Table 36

RADIO AND TELEVISION BOARD[1]

H. D. Williams	1958-1962	(4)
Ray H. Hughes	1958-1960	(2)
Earl P. Paulk, Jr.	1958-1960	(2)
Roy C. Miller	1960-1962	(2)
W. Edwin Tull	1960-1964	(4)
Marshall E. Roberson	1960-1966	(6)
Clifford V. Bridges	1960-1968	(8)
Charles W. Conn	1962-1964	(2)
Edward L. Williams	1962-1968	(6)
Harold F. Douglas	1964-1966	(2)
Jim O. McClain	1964-1966	(2)
John E. Black	1966-1970	(4)
William E. Lawson	1966-1968	(2)
E. H. Miles	1966-1972	(6)
Charles Mullinax	1966-1974	(8)
Don W. Rhein	1966-1972	(6)
Raymond E. Crowley	1968-1974	(6)
Arthur W. Hodge	1968-1976	(8)
A. V. Howell	1968-1970	(2)
A. M. Dorman	1970-1976	(6)
W. J. Brown	1970-1976	(6)
James R. Hockensmith	1972-	( )
F. L. Braddock	1972-	( )
Don Medlin	1974-	( )
Paul Jones	1974-	( )
Paul F. Henson	1976-	( )
Herbert Benton	1976-	( )
A. A. Ledford	1976-	( )

[1]Called National Radio Commission, 1958-1962; National Radio and Television Commission, 1962-1966.

Appointed by Executive Committee.

─────────────── LADIES AUXILIARY ───────────────

Table 37

LADIES AUXILIARY PRESIDENTS[1]

Mrs. Wade H. Horton	1964-1966; 1974-1976	(4)
Mrs. Charles W. Conn	1966-1970	(4)
Mrs. R. Leonard Carroll	1970-1972	(2)
Mrs. Ray H. Hughes	1972-1974	(2)
Mrs. Cecil B. Knight	1976-	( )

[1]Until 1970 the organization was known as The Ladies Willing Workers Band. It was formally organized nationally in 1964.

The wife of the General Overseer is *ex officio* president.

────────────────

Table 38

EXECUTIVE SECRETARIES OF LADIES AUXILIARY[1]

Ellen B. French	1964-1968	(4)
Willie Lee Darter	1968-	( )

[1]Called Ladies Willing Worker Band until 1970.

Appointed by Executive Committee.

────────────────

Table 39

LADIES AUXILIARY BOARD OF DIRECTORS

Mrs. Wade H. Horton[1]	1964-1966; 1968-1976	(10)
Mrs. Charles W. Conn[1]	1964-1970	(6)
Mrs. C. Raymond Spain[1]	1964-1970	(6)
Mrs. R. Leonard Carroll[1]	1964-1972	(8)
Mrs. Ralph E. Williams[1]	1964-1968	(4)
Mrs. Vessie D. Hargrave[1]	1964-1968	(4)
Mrs. G. R. Watson	1964-1966	(2)
Mrs. Willie Lee Darter	1964-1968	(4)
Mrs. W. H. Pratt	1964-1968	(4)
Mrs. Ray H. Hughes[1]	1966-1974; 1976-	( )
Mrs. S. E. Jennings	1966-1974	(8)
Mrs. J. D. Bright	1966-1972	(6)
Mrs. Max Atkins	1968-1970	(2)
Mrs. T. W. Day	1968-1970	(2)
Mrs. Cecil B. Knight[1]	1970-	( )
Mrs. G. W. Lane[1]	1970-1974	(4)

Mrs. Wayne S. Proctor	1970-1976	(6)
Mrs. H. G. Poitier	1970-1976	(6)
Mrs. W. C. Byrd[1]	1972-1974	(2)
Mrs. J. Frank Culpepper[1]	1972-	( )
Mrs. T. L. Lowery[1]	1974-	( )
Mrs. Floyd J. Timmerman[1]	1974-	( )
Mrs. C. E. Landreth	1974-	( )
Mrs. P. H. McSwain	1974-	( )
Mrs. Janet Spencer	1976-	( )
Mrs. Neigel Scarborough	1976-	( )

[1]*Ex Officio member;* wife of Executive Committee member.

Appointed by Executive Committee.

──────────────── STATISTICAL ────────────────

Table 40

GENERAL ASSEMBLIES

1.	January 26-27, 1906	Cherokee County, North Carolina
2.	January 9-13, 1907	Bradley County, Tennessee
3.	January 8-12, 1908	Cleveland, Tennessee
4.	January 6-9, 1909	Cleveland, Tennessee
5.	January 10-16, 1910	Cleveland, Tennessee
6.	January 3-8, 1911	Cleveland, Tennessee
7.	January 9-14, 1912	Cleveland, Tennessee
8.	January 7-12, 1913	Cleveland, Tennessee
9.	November 4-9, 1913	Cleveland, Tennessee
10.	November 2-8, 1914	Cleveland, Tennessee
11.	November 1-7, 1915	Cleveland, Tennessee
12.	November 1-7, 1916	Harriman, Tennessee
13.	November 1-6, 1917	Harriman, Tennessee

No Assembly in 1918 due to an Influenza epidemic.

14.	October 29-November 4, 1919	Cleveland, Tennessee
15.	November 3-9, 1920	Cleveland, Tennessee
16.	November 2-8, 1921	Cleveland, Tennessee
17.	November 1-7, 1922	Cleveland, Tennessee
18.	November 1-7, 1923	Cleveland, Tennessee
19.	October 29-November 4, 1924	Cleveland, Tennessee
20.	October 19-25, 1925	Cleveland, Tennessee
21.	October 18-24, 1926	Cleveland, Tennessee
22.	October 24-30, 1927	Cleveland, Tennessee
23.	October 22-28, 1928	Cleveland, Tennessee
24.	October 21-27, 1929	Cleveland, Tennessee
25.	October 20-26, 1930	Cleveland, Tennessee
26.	October 10-16, 1931	Cleveland, Tennessee
27.	October 8-14, 1932	Cleveland, Tennessee
28.	October 7-13, 1933	Cleveland, Tennessee
29.	October 6-12, 1934	Chattanooga, Tennessee
30.	October 5-11, 1935	Chattanooga, Tennessee

31.	October 2-8, 1936	Chattanooga, Tennessee
32.	October 8-14, 1937	Chattanooga, Tennessee
33.	August 30-September 4, 1938	Chattanooga, Tennessee
34.	October 11-15, 1939	Atlanta, Georgia
35.	October 1-6, 1940	Chattanooga, Tennessee
36.	September 2-3, 1941	Chattanooga, Tennessee
37.	September 1-6, 1942	Birmingham, Alabama
38.	August 27-29, 1943	Birmingham, Alabama
39.	August 28-September 1, 1944	Columbus, Ohio
40.	September 2-3, 1945	Sevierville, Tennessee
41.	August 29-September 1, 1946	Birmingham, Alabama
42.	August 28-31, 1948	Birmingham, Alabama
43.	August 24-27, 1950	Birmingham, Alabama
44.	August 14-17, 1952	Indianapolis, Indiana
45.	August 17-22, 1954	Memphis, Tennessee
46.	August 14-18, 1956	Memphis, Tennessee
47.	August 19-23, 1958	Memphis, Tennessee
48.	August 16-20, 1960	Memphis, Tennessee
49.	August 14-18, 1962	Memphis, Tennessee
50.	August 11-15, 1964	Dallas, Texas
51.	August 10-15, 1966	Memphis, Tennessee
52.	August 14-19, 1968	Dallas, Texas
53.	August 25-31, 1970	St. Louis, Missouri
54.	August 15-21, 1972	Dallas, Texas
55.	August 6-12, 1974	Dallas, Texas
56.	August 17-23, 1976	Dallas, Texas

Table 41

CHURCH OF GOD MEMBERSHIP

Year	U. S. & Canada	Worldwide
1886*	8	8
1896	c. 130	c. 130
1902	c. 20	c. 20
1903	c. 25	c. 25
1904	c. 39	c. 39
1910	1,005	1,005
1911	1,855	1,855
1912	2,294	2,323†
1913	3,056	3,116
1914	4,339	4,568
1915	6,159	6,503
1916	7,690	8,059
1917	10,076	10,566
1919	12,341	12,768
1920	14,606	15,051
1921	18,564	18,998
1922	21,076	21,673

1923	22,394	23,008
1924	23,560	24,220
1925	24,871	25,231
1926	25,000	25,410
1927	25,340	25,819
1928	24,332	24,902
1929	24,891	25,853
1930	25,901	27,149
1931	29,354	30,840
1932	41,680	43,439
1933	46,735	48,638
1934	46,923	49,310
1935	49,644	52,913
1936	57,417	64,614
1937	63,229	75,223
1938	55,424	64,215
1939	58,823	70,423
1940	63,216	83,552
1941	61,660	80,022
1942	61,762	81,508
1943	62,487	83,670
1944	67,137	91,078
1945	72,096	101,441
1946	77,926	115,978
1947	84,598	125,921
1948	93,315	135,452
1949	100,439	160,924
1950	115,425	174,960
1951	122,156	220,780
1952	127,151	229,836
1953	132,343	247,297
1954	138,349	263,676
1955	143,609	278,753
1956	147,929	288,737
1957	150,834	290,995
1958	155,541	304,271
1959	162,589	324,163
1960	170,088	335,297
1961	179,651	351,095
1962‡	190,776	368,795**
1964	206,141	396,227
1966	221,156	449,519
1968	244,261	511,034
1970	263,299	536,236
1972	276,598	600,024
1974	325,727	729,911
1976	361,099	828,643

*No accurate records were kept or statistical reports made until 1910.

†In 1911 the Church of God gained its first members outside the U.S.A. These were reported in 1912.

‡After 1962 membership statistics were compiled biennially.

**These figures do not include the missions work of the Full Gospel Church of God in Southern Africa.

Table 42

GENERAL CHURCH RECEIPTS*

Year	Tithe of Tithes†	Foreign Missions
1911		21.05
1912		22.55
1913		
1914	149.12	91.48
1915	206.82	196.58
1916	484.86	141.96
1917	491.19	1,815.72
1919	10,210.09	2,890.18
1920	16,330.23	1,926.19
1921‡	7,955.76	1,155.83
1922	10,612.66	975.88
1923	13,358.13	3,121.79
1924	11,597.17	2,966.13
1925	15,203.40	1,817.14
1926	16,312.27	1,747.64
1927	17,008.94	4,925.17
1928	19,366.28	2,205.95
1929	22,163.97	2,843.21
1930	22,308.74	2,476.18
1931	19,250.58	2,270.63
1932	16,550.32	3,308.59
1933	16,840.86	3,682.36
1934	25,767.49	6,533.37
1935	29,351.80	7,259.55
1936	37,862.22	14,719.85
1937	47,117.73	27,299.29
1938	43,049.64	28,429.74
1939	60,795.68	38,713.99
1940	63,526.34	53,963.30
1941	79,544.40	83,101.89
1942	117,549.29	106,665.19
1943	154,938.68	54,277.21
1944	208,452.79	170,229.61
1945	249,740.42	214,453.21
1946	269.248.92	340,848.54
1947	299,635.81	195,425.33
1948	346,467.43	295,778.36
1949	380,238.69	263,682.30
1950	386,540.01	264,216.98

1951	510,893.04	348,916.21
1952	521,902.20	311,232.42
1953	642,148.81	440,162.85
1954	649,254.26	535,171.07
1955	468,542.11	542,747.24
1956	623,669.42	590,432.03
1957	578,021.15	622,139.06
1958	597,033.77	577,448.71
1959	781,058.56	614,732.40
1960	625,594.92	665,721.99
1961	583,489.94	764,676.69
1962	780,318.81	787,852.55
1963	819,942.40	847,908.36
1964	948,023.47	1,017,341.51
1965	1,039,879.88	1,106,070.35
1966	1,308,373.17	1,317,223.33
1967	2,222,394.43	2,120,772.02
1968	2,162,804.75	1,656,220.57
1969	2,430,723.82	2,093,751.00
1970	2,688,210.81	1,925,260.87
1971	3,061,627.82	2,103,648.23
1972	3,245,818.09	1,938,466.06
1973	4,198,695.04	2,774,018.66
1974	4,565,426.00	4,293,428.30
1975	4,807,171.71	4,258,879.23
1976	5,615,569.05	4,426,696.79

*This table lists the tithes and contributions from the constituency of the Church only not the total receipts.

†Tithe of tithes is a term designating the one-tenth of local church tithes sent to the General Church Headquarters.

‡From January, 1921, to July, 1922, all local tithes were sent to Headquarters and distributed among the preachers. The tithe of tithes listed here is 10% of total tithes received during this period, plus the customary receipts after the system was changed in 1922.

———————————————

Table 43

POPULATION OF CHURCH LOCATIONS
U. S. & Canada
(1976)

Population	No. Churches	Percentage
Country Churches	573	12.42
Towns less than 1,000	672	14.56
Towns 1,000 to 5,000	1,075	23.29
Towns 5,000 to 25,000	1,048	22.71
Cities 25,000 to 100,000	612	13.26
Cities 100,000 to 250,000	234	5.07
Cities 250,000 to 500,000	142	3.08
Cities above 500,000	259	5.61
Total	4,615	100.00

Table 44 — STATE OVERSEERS

State	1911-1912	1912-1913	Jan.-Nov. 1913	1913-1914	1914-1915
Alabama	V. W. Kennedy	Geo. C. Barron	J. B. Ellis	Geo. T. Brouayer	W. S. Gentry
Arizona			R. M. Singleton		
Arkansas					
California			R. M. Singleton	R. M. Singleton	
Colorado		R. M. Singleton*	R. M. Singleton	R. M. Singleton	R. M. Singleton
Connecticut					
Delaware					
District of Columbia					
Florida	J. A. Giddens	M. S. Lemons	T. L. McLain	W. S. Caruthers	W. S. Caruthers
Georgia	H. W. McArthur	Geo. T. Brouayer	Geo. C. Barron	C. M. Padgett	W. R. Anderson
Idaho					
Illinois					
Indiana					
Iowa					
Kansas					
Kentucky	Sam C. Perry	Sam C. Perry	J. S. Llewellyn		W. F. Bryant
Louisiana					W. A. Capshaw**
Maine					
Maryland					
Massachusetts					
Michigan					
Minnesota					
Mississippi		Roy C. Miller	Z. D. Simpson	M. S. Lemons	M. S. Lemons
Missouri					
Montana					

Nebraska				
Nevada				
New Hampshire				
New Jersey				
New Mexico	R. M. Singleton*	R. M. Singleton	R. M. Singleton	R. M. Singleton
New York				
North Carolina	C. R. Curtis; R. C. Spurling*	Geo. T. Brouayer	A. H. Bryans	J. A. Davis
North Dakota				
Ohio				
Oklahoma				
Oregon				
Pennsylvania				
Rhode Island				
South Carolina		H. B. Simmons		J. C. Underwood
South Dakota				
Tennessee	W. F. Bryant; T. L. McLain	F. J. Lee	F. J. Lee	Geo. T. Brouayer
Texas				
Utah				
Vermont				
Virginia	J. J. Lowman; J. J. Lowman	J. J. Lowman	J. J. Lowman	H. L. Trim
Washington				
West Virginia		W. H. Rogers		W. M. Rumler**
Wisconsin				
Wyoming				
Central Canada††				
Eastern Canada‡				
Western Canada‡‡				

STATE OVERSEERS — (Continued)

State	1915-1916	1916-1917	1917-1918	1918-1919	1919-1920
Alabama	W. S. Gentry	T. S. Payne	J. B. Ellis	J. B. Ellis	Z. D. Simpson
Arizona			R. M. Singleton	R. M. Singleton	
Arkansas			E. J. Boehmer	John Burk	D. R. Holcomb
California		W. C. Hockett	W. C. Hockett	W. C. Hockett	
Colorado				O. R. Rouse	O. R. Rouse
Connecticut					
Delaware					
District of Columbia					
Florida	W. S. Caruthers	Sam C. Perry	Sam C. Perry	F. J. Lee	F. J. Lee
Georgia	J. S. Llewellyn	M. S. Lemons	M. S. Lemons	M. S. Lemons	S. W. Latimer
Idaho					
Illinois		D. P. Barnett	D. P. Barnett	D. P. Barnett	T. S. Payne
Indiana		W. H. Martin			S. O. Gillaspie
Iowa					
Kansas					
Kentucky	W. F. Bryant	W. F. Bryant	W. F. Bryant	Geo. T. Brouayer	Geo. T. Brouayer
Louisiana	A. B. Adams	M. S. Haynes	M. S. Haynes	M. S. Haynes	M. S. Haynes
Maine					
Maryland		John W. Pitcher	John W. Pitcher	J. W. Pitcher	
Massachusetts					
Michigan					
Minnesota					
Mississippi	M. S. Havnes	J. A. Davis	I. A. Davis	E. B. Culpepper	E. B. Culpepper
Missouri			Rov L. Cotnam	Roy L. Cotnam	E. L. Pinkley
Montana					

Nebraska					
Nevada					
New Hampshire					
New Jersey					
New Mexico	R. M. Singleton		O. R. Rouse	O. R. Rouse	O. R. Rouse
New York					
North Carolina	J. A. Davis	W. A. Capshaw	W. A. Capshaw	S. W. Latimer	J. A. Davis
North Dakota					
Ohio	Efford Haynes	Efford Haynes	Efford Haynes	Efford Haynes	Efford Haynes
Oklahoma	Roy L. Cotnam	Roy L. Cotnam		Roy L. Cotnam	John Burk
Oregon					
Pennsylvania					
Rhode Island					
South Carolina	J. C. Underwood	W. A. Walker	W. H. Cross	W. H. Cross	W. H. Cross
South Dakota					
Tennessee	Geo. T. Brouayer	F. J. Lee	F. J. Lee	J. S. Llewellyn	J. S. Llewellyn
Texas		Geo. T. Brouayer	Geo. T. Brouayer	H. N. Scoggins	H. N. Scoggins
Utah					
Vermont					
Virginia	H. L. Trim	T. L. McLain	T. L. McLain	J. A. Davis	F. W. Gammon
Washington					
West Virginia	W. M. Rumler	W. M. Rumler	W. M. Rumler	W. M. Rumler	W. M. Rumler
Wisconsin					
Wyoming					
Central Canada†					
Eastern Canada‡					
Western Canada‡					

State	1920-1921	1921-1922	1922-1923	1923-1924	1924-1925
Alabama	Z. D. Simpson	W. S. Wilemon	G. C. Dunn	G. C. Dunn	T. L. McLain
Arizona				J. A. Brown	J. A. Brown
Arkansas	John Burk	John Burk	E. C. Scarbrough	E. C. Scarbrough	J. M. Viney
California				J. A. Brown	J. A. Brown
Colorado		O. R. Rouse	O. R. Rouse	O. R. Rouse	O. R. Rouse
Connecticut					
Delaware					H. W. Poteat
District of Columbia					
Florida	F. J. Lee	F. J. Lee	John L. Stephens	John L. Stephens	J. A. Self
Georgia	S. W. Latimer	S. W. Latimer	S. W. Latimer	S. W. Latimer	John L. Stephens
Idaho					
Illinois	T. S. Payne	S. O. Gillaspie	S. O. Gillaspie 1 D. P. Barnett†	W. G. Rembert	G. A. Fore
Indiana	S. O. Gillaspie	F. W. Gammon	J. N. Hurley	W. G. Rembert	J. C. Coats
Iowa					
Kansas			J. M. Viney*	John Burk	J. C. Coats
Kentucky	F. W. Gammon	C. H. Randall	C. H. Randall 1 J. B. Ellis†	G. A. Fore	G. A. Fore
Louisiana	M. S. Haynes	H. B. Simmons	T. A. Richard 2 T. S. Payne†	T. A. Richard	G. C. Dunn
Maine					H. W. Poteat
Maryland	Paul H. Walker	Paul H. Walker	Paul H. Walker	H. W. Poteat	H. W. Poteat
Massachusetts					
Michigan		Efford Haynes	Efford Haynes	Efford Haynes	M. P. Cross
Minnesota				Paul H. Walker	Paul H. Walker
Mississippi	H. A. Pressgrove	H. A. Pressgrove	E. C. Rider 2 Efford Haynes†	Z. D. Simpson 3 E. B. Culpepper†	E. B. Culpepper
Missouri	E. L. Pinkley	E. L. Pinkley	J. M. Viney	John Burk	J. C. Coats
Montana					

Nebraska					
Nevada					
New Hampshire					
New Jersey		T. S. Payne			H. W. Poteat
New Mexico	O. R. Rouse	J. A. Davis	O. R. Rouse	O. R. Rouse	O. R. Rouse
New York					
North Carolina	W. M. Stallings	Geo. T. Brouayer	Geo. T. Brouayer [1] / S. W. Latimer†	T. L. McLain	S. W. Latimer [5] / E. C. Gault†
North Dakota	J. W. Barker	J. W. Barker	John Attey	Paul H. Walker	Paul H. Walker
Ohio	Efford Haynes	W. G. Rembert	W. G. Rembert	D. P. Barnett [4] / Efford Haynes†	Efford Haynes
Oklahoma	B. H. Doss	B. H. Doss	John Burk	J. M. Viney	A. L. Jenkins
Oregon					
Pennsylvania		W. M. Rumler	H. W. Poteat	H. W. Poteat	H. W. Poteat
Rhode Island					
South Carolina	W. H. Cross	J. W. Culpepper	J. W. Culpeper	J. W. Culpepper	E. M. Ellis
South Dakota					
Tennessee	M. W. Letsinger	M. W. Letsinger	M. W. Letsinger	M. W. Letsinger	E. L. Simmons
Texas	Geo. T. Brouayer	H. N. Scoggins	H. N. Scoggins	H. N. Scoggins	R. P. Johnson
Utah					
Vermont					
Virginia	J. A. Davis	F. J. Crowder	J. A. Davis [2] / H. B. Simmons†	H. B. Simmons	W. B. Davis
Washington					
West Virginia	W. M. Rumler	E. L. Simmons	E. L. Simmons	E. L. Simmons	H. N. Scoggins
Wisconsin					
Wyoming					
Central Canada††					
Eastern Canada‡					
Western Canada‡‡					

STATE OVERSEERS — (Continued)

State	1925-1926	1926-1927	1927-1928	1928-1929	1929-1930
Alabama	J. B. Ellis	E. M. Ellis	S. J. Heath	T. L. McLain	J. C. Padgett
Arizona	A. F. Sutter	C. W. Clelland	C. W. Clelland	C. W. Clelland	J. H. Ingram
Arkansas	J. M. Viney	Jesse Danehower	Jesse Danehower	Jesse Danehower	J. C. Coats [6] S. F. Beard[†]
California	A. F. Sutter	C. W. Clelland	C. W. Clelland	C. W. Clelland	J. H. Ingram
Colorado	O. R. Rouse	O. R. Rouse	O. R. Rouse	O. R. Rouse	M. E. Drake
Connecticut					
Delaware	H. W. Poteat	H. W. Poteat	H. W. Poteat	H. W. Poteat	H. W. Poteat
District of Columbia					
Florida	J. A. Self	J. A. Self	J. A. Self	R. P. Johnson	R. P. Johnson
Georgia	John L. Stephens [6] J. W. Culpepper[†]	J. W. Culpepper	J. W. Culpepper	J. W. Culpepper	T. L. McLain
Idaho					
Illinois	M. W. Letsinger	M. W. Letsinger	M. W. Letsinger	E. L. Simmons	E. L. Simmons
Indiana	E. C. Clark	J. L. Goins	J. L. Goins	J. L. Goins	C. H. Standifer
Iowa					
Kansas	E. C. Clark	D. R. Moreland	D. R. Moreland [7] F. R. Harrawood[†]	F. R. Harrawood	W. J. Milligan
Kentucky	G. A. Fore	G. A. Fore	R. H. Bell	G. A. Fore	R. H. Bell
Louisiana	J. C. Coats	J. C. Coats	G. C. Dunn	G. C. Dunn	E. E. Simmons
Maine	H. W. Poteat	H. W. Poteat	H. W. Poteat	H. W. Poteat	H. W. Poteat
Maryland	H. W. Poteat	H. W. Poteat	M. S. Lemons	M. S. Lemons [8] F. B. Marine[†]	F. B. Marine
Massachusetts					
Michigan	M. P. Cross	M. P. Cross	M. P. Cross	M. P. Cross	M. P. Cross
Minnesota	Paul H. Walker	M. L. Lowe	M. L. Lowe	M. L. Lowe	M. L. Lowe [3] Paul H. Walker[†]
Mississippi	G. C. Dunn	C. G. Edwards	C. G. Edwards	E. B. Culpepper	S. J. Heath
Missouri	E. C. Clark	D. R. Moreland	D. R. Moreland [7] F. R. Harrawood[†]	F. R. Harrawood	W. J. Milligan
Montana	Paul H. Walker	M. L. Lowe	M. L. Lowe	M. L. Lowe	M. L. Lowe

Nebraska				
Nevada				
New Hampshire	H. W. Poteat			
New Jersey				
New Mexico	O. R. Rouse	O. R. Rouse	O. R. Rouse	M. E. Drake
New York				
North Carolina	Roy E. Blackwood	Roy E. Blackwood	Roy E. Blackwood	John L. Stephens
North Dakota	Paul H. Walker	Paul H. Walker	Paul H. Walker	Paul H. Walker
Ohio	Efford Haynes	Efford Haynes	Efford Haynes	Efford Haynes
Oklahoma	A. L. Jenkins	E. W. Williams	B. L. Hicks	L. L. Vaught
Oregon				
Pennsylvania	H. W. Poteat	H. W. Poteat	H. W. Poteat	H. W. Poteat
Rhode Island				
South Carolina	E. M. Ellis	W. E. Raney	W. E. Raney	W. E. Raney
South Dakota			Paul H. Walker	Paul H. Walker
Tennessee	T. L. McLain	T. L. McLain	H. N. Scoggins	H. N. Scoggins
Texas	R. P. Johnson	R. P. Johnson	E. W. Williams	S. J. Wood
Utah				
Vermont				
Virginia	W. B. Davis & John C. Jernigan†	John C. Jernigan	John C. Jernigan	H. B. Simmons
Washington				
West Virginia	H. N. Scoggins	H. N. Scoggins	T. L. McLain	B. L. Hicks
Wisconsin			E. C. Clark	E. C. Clark
Wyoming				
Central Canada††				
Eastern Canada‡				
Western Canada‡‡				

STATE OVERSEERS — (Continued)

State	1930-1931	1931-1932	1932-1933	1933-1934	1934-1935
Alabama	B. L. Hicks	B. L. Hicks	W. W. Harmon	W. W. Harmon	G. C. Dunn
Arizona	J. H. Ingram	J. H. Ingram	J. H. Ingram	J. H. Ingram	Simmie Tapley
Arkansas	J. A. McCullar	J. A. McCullar	J. A. McCullar	L. G. Rouse	S. J. Wood
California	J. H. Ingram	J. H. Ingram	J. H. Ingram	J. H. Ingram	W. G. Webb
Colorado	M. E. Drake	M. E. Drake	M. E. Drake	M. E. Drake	John E. Douglas
Connecticut					
Delaware	H. W. Poteat	F. B. Marine	D. G. Phillips	F. B. Marine	F. B. Marine
District of Columbia				F. B. Marine*	F. B. Marine
Florida	R. P. Johnson	E. W. Williams	E. W. Williams	E. W. Williams	E. W. Williams
Georgia	J. W. Culpepper	J. W. Culpepper	R. P. Johnson	J. W. Culpepper	J. P. Hughes
Idaho					
Illinois	H. N. Scoggins	H. N. Scoggins	M. P. Cross	T. L. McLain	J. L. Goins
Indiana	C. H. Standifer	C. H. Standifer	C. H. Standifer	C. H. Standifer	C. H. Standifer
Iowa					
Kansas	W. J. Milligan	W. J. Milligan	W. J. Milligan	D. K. Murphy	John E. Douglas
Kentucky	John C. Jernigan	John C. Jernigan	John C. Jernigan	John C. Jernigan	John C. Jernigan
Louisiana	E. E. Simmons	E. E. Simmons	J. B. Cole	J. B. Cole	Robt. E. Blackwood
Maine	H. W. Poteat	H. W. Poteat	H. W. Poteat	H. W. Poteat	H. W. Poteat
Maryland	F. B. Marine	F. B. Marine	D. G. Phillips	F. B. Marine	F. B. Marine
Massachusetts					
Michigan	M. P. Cross	M. P. Cross	Earl P. Paulk	D. G. Phillips	D. G. Phillips
Minnesota	Paul H. Walker	Paul H. Walker	D. C. Boatwright	D. C. Boatwright	Paul H. Walker
Mississippi	S. J. Heath 4 G. G. Williams†	G. G. Williams	T. M. McClendon	T. M. McClendon	T. M. McClendon
Missouri	W. J. Milligan	W. J. Milligan	W. J. Milligan	W. J. Milligan	W. J. Milligan
Montana	M. L. Lowe	Leslie Cook	Robert Seyda	Robert Seyda	Paul H. Walker

				Sidney Pearson	Reuben H. Martin
Nebraska					
Nevada					
New Hampshire				H. W. Poteat	H. W. Poteat
New Jersey			J. A. Muncy	J. A. Muncy	C. H. Blankenship
New Mexico	M. E. Drake		M. E. Drake	M. E. Drake	M. E. Drake
New York			W. M. Morrow	H. W. Poteat	H. W. Poteat
North Carolina	John L. Stephens		John L. Stephens	John L. Stephens	John L. Stephens
North Dakota	Paul H. Walker		Paul H. Walker	Paul H. Walker	Paul H. Walker
Ohio	Efford Haynes		Efford Haynes	Efford Haynes	Efford Haynes
Oklahoma	Graham Oglesby		Graham Oglesby	S. J. Wood	S. J. Wood
Oregon					
Pennsylvania	H. W. Poteat		H. W. Poteat	H. W. Poteat	C. H. Blankenship
Rhode Island					
South Carolina	H. L. Whittington		H. L. Whittington	H. L. Whittington	Earl P. Paulk
South Dakota	Paul H. Walker		Paul H. Walker	Paul H. Walker	Paul H. Walker
Tennessee	Alonzo Gann		T. S. Payne	T. S. Payne	M. P. Cross
Texas	S. J. Wood		J. C. Coats	J. C. Coats 9 R. P. Johnson†	R. P. Johnson
Utah				J. H. Ingram*	John E. Douglas
Vermont					
Virginia	L. L. Vaught		L. L. Vaught	L. L. Vaught	I. H. Brabson
Washington					
West Virginia	E. C. Clark		H. N. Scoggins	H. N. Scoggins	H. N. Scoggins
Wisconsin					
Wyoming			Robert Seyda*	Sidney Pearson	Sidney Pearson
Central Canada††					
Eastern Canada‡					
Western Canada‡‡	Paul H. Walker		Paul H. Walker	Paul H. Walker	Paul H. Walker

STATE OVERSEERS — (Continued)

State	1935-1936	1936-1937	1937-1938	1938-1939	1939-1940
Alabama	G. C. Dunn	G. C. Dunn	H. L. Whittington	H. L. Whittington	H. L. Chesser
Arizona	W. G. Webb	E. M. Ellis	John E. Douglas	I. L. Benge	I. L. Benge
Arkansas	J. A. McCullar	Odis Smith	Odis Smith	W. H. Henry	W. H. Henry
California	W. G. Webb	E. M. Ellis	John E. Douglas	I. L. Benge	I. L. Benge
Colorado	John E. Douglas	John E. Douglas	S. J. Wood	S. J. Wood	H. E. Ramsey
Connecticut		H. G. Flowers	H. G. Flowers	Ralph Koshewitz	Paul H. Walker
Delaware	W. Carl Milligan	W. Carl Milligan	J. A. Muncy	W. E. Raney	W. J. Milligan
District of Columbia	W. Carl Milligan	C. H. Standifer 6 W. E. Raney†	W. E. Raney	W. E. Raney	W. J. Milligan
Florida	E. W. Williams	E. W. Williams	E. M. Ellis	E. M. Ellis	E. M. Ellis
Georgia	J. P. Hughes	John C. Jernigan	John C. Jernigan	John C. Jernigan	Earl P. Paulk
Idaho		J. B. Camp	J. B. Camp	J. B. Camp	J. B. Camp
Illinois	J. L. Goins	J. R. Thomas	J. R. Thomas	J. R. Thomas	H. O. Harris
Indiana	C. H. Standifer	W. M. Morrow	C. H. Standifer	Roy J. Staats	Roy J. Staats
Iowa	J. M. Snyder*	J. L. Goins	J. L. Goins	J. L. Goins	J. L. Goins
Kansas	J. M. Snyder	J. B. Raney	J. T. Campbell	J. T. Campbell	S. J. Wood
Kentucky	John C. Jernigan	T. M. McClendon	T. M. McClendon	B. L. Hicks	B. L. Hiicks
Louisiana	Robt. E. Blackwood	Robt. E. Blackwood	Clyde C. Cox	Clyde C. Cox	Clyde C. Cox
Maine	H. W. Poteat	G. M. Bloomingdale	M. J. Headley	Ralph Koshewitz	G. M. Bloomingdale
Maryland	W. Carl Milligan	W. Carl Milligan	(E.) J. A. Muncy (W.) W. E. Raney	W. E. Raney	W. J. Milligan
Massachusetts	H. W. Poteat*	H. G. Flowers	H. G. Flowers	Ralph Koshewitz	G. M. Bloomingdale 10 Paul H. Walker†
Michigan	D. G. Phillips	Paul H. Walker	Paul H. Walker	C. H. Standifer	E. O. Kerce
Minnesota	Paul H. Walker	H. E. Ramsey	H. E. Ramsey	H. E. Ramsey	J. J. Kisser
Mississippi	T. M. McClendon	H. J. Headley	T. W. Godwin	T. W. Godwin	J. L. Dorman
Missouri	W. J. Milligan	H. N. Scoggins	H. L. Marcum	H. L. Marcum	Houston R. Morehead
Montana	Paul H. Walker	H. W. Poteat	M. L. Lowe	M. L. Lowe	M. L. Lowe

Nebraska	J. M. Snyder	James A. Cross	James A. Cross	James A. Cross	J. L. Goins	J. L. Goins
Nevada	H. W. Poteat	E. M. Ellis	John E. Douglas	John E. Douglas	I. L. Benge	I. L. Benge
New Hampshire	C. H. Blankenship	G. M. Bloomingdale	M. J. Headley	M. J. Headley	Ralph Koshewitz	G. M. Bloomingdale
New Jersey	John E. Douglas	C. H. Blankenship	Roy J. Staats	Roy J. Staats	T. S. Payne	Paul H. Walker
New Mexico	John E. Douglas	John E. Douglas	S. J. Wood	S. J. Wood	S. J. Wood	H. E. Ramsey
New York	H. W. Poteat	D. R. Moreland				Paul H. Walker
North Carolina	John L. Stephens	John L. Stephens	E. W. Williams	E. W. Williams	E. W. Williams	E. W. Williams
North Dakota	Paul H. Walker	Frank W. Lemons	Frank W. Lemons	Frank W. Lemons	D. C. Boatwright	D. C. Boatwright
Ohio	Efford Haynes	D. G. Phillips	John L. Stephens	John L. Stephens	E. C. Clark	E. C. Clark
Oklahoma	S. J. Wood	S. J. Wood	G. M. Bloomingdale	G. M. Bloomingdale	G. M. Bloomingdale	S. J. Wood
Oregon		L. L. Milam	L. L. Milam	L. L. Milam	J. B. Camp	J. B. Camp
Pennsylvania	C. H. Blankenship	C. H. Blankenship	Roy J. Staats	Roy J. Staats	T. S. Payne	Paul H. Walker
Rhode Island		H. G. Flowers	H. G. Flowers	H. G. Flowers	Ralph Koshewitz	Paul H. Walker
South Carolina	R. P. Johnson	R. P. Johnson	A. V. Beaube	A. V. Beaube	A. V. Beaube	J. D. Bright
South Dakota	Paul H. Walker	D. C. Boatwright	D. C. Boatwright	D. C. Boatwright	D. C. Boatwright	D. C. Boatwright
Tennessee	M. P. Cross	M. P. Cross	M. P. Cross	M. P. Cross	E. L. Simmons	John C. Jernigan
Texas	T. S. Payne	T. S. Payne	T. S. Payne	(N.) H. N. Scoggins (S.) T. S. Payne	H. N. Scoggins	H. N. Scoggins
Utah	John E. Douglas	John E. Douglas	John E. Douglas	S. J. Wood	S. J. Wood	H. E. Ramsey
Vermont		G. M. Bloomingdale	G. M. Bloomingdale	M. J. Headley	M. J. Headley	G. M. Bloomingdale
Virginia	J. L. Dorman	J. L. Dorman	J. L. Dorman	J. L. Dorman	J. L. Dorman	W. E. Johnson
Washington		J. B. Camp	J. B. Camp	J. B. Camp	J. B. Camp	J. B. Camp
West Virginia	E. C. Clark	E. C. Clark	E. C. Clark	E. C. Clark	M. P. Cross	M. P. Cross
Wisconsin		H. E. Ramsey	H. E. Ramsey	H. E. Ramsey	H. E. Ramsey	H. E. Ramsey & J. J. Kissert†
Wyoming	Paul H. Walker	D. C. Boatwright	D. C. Boatwright	D. C. Boatwright	D. C. Boatwright	D. C. Boatwright
Central Canada†					C. H. Standifer	E. O. Keree
Eastern Canada‡	H. W. Poteat	Paul H. Walker	Paul H. Walker	Paul H. Walker		G. M. Bloomingdale
Western Canada‡‡	Paul H. Walker	Charles Bowen	Max Brandt	Max Brandt	Max Brandt	M. L. Lowe

STATE OVERSEERS — (Continued)

State	1940-1941	1941-1942	1942-1943	1943-1944	1944-1945
Alabama	H. L. Chesser	H. L. Chesser	E. M. Ellis	E. M. Ellis	J. T. Roberts
Arizona	I. L. Benge	C. C. Rains	C. C. Rains	O. C. Crank	O. C. Crank
Arkansas	A. C. Burroughs	A. C. Burroughs	A. L. Burroughs	A. L. Burroughs	M. B. Norris
California	I. L. Benge	James L. Slay	James L. Slay	John E. Douglas	John E. Douglas
Colorado	H. E. Ramsey	H. E. Ramsey	S. J. Wood	D. A. Biggs	D. A. Biggs
Connecticut	T. C. Messer	G. W. Lane	Wm. F. Morris	J. H. Davis	F. J. Thibodeau
Delaware	W. J. Milligan	D. C. Boatwright	D. C. Boatwright	D. C. Boatwright	C. C. McAfee
District of Columbia	W. J. Milligan	Wade H. Horton	Wade H. Horton	Wade H. Horton	C. C. McAfee
Florida	E. M. Ellis	John C. Jernigan	John C. Jernigan	John C. Jernigan	W. E. Johnson
Georgia	A. V. Beaube	A. V. Beaube	A. V. Beaube	A. V. Beaube	L. W. McIntyre
Idaho	John E. Douglas	John E. Douglas	John E. Douglas	Ray T. Hill	Ray T. Hill
Illinois	H. O. Harris	H. O. Harris	E. O. Kerce	E. O. Kerce	E. O. Kerce
Indiana	Clyde C. Cox	H. R. Corley	C. M. Jenkerson	C. M. Jenkerson	G. W. Lane
Iowa	J. L. Goins	J. L. Goins	J. L. Goins	J. L. Goins	W. H. Henry
Kansas	W. H. Henry	W. H. Henry	W. H. Henry	W. H. Henry	A. R. Pedigo
Kentucky	B. L. Hicks	W. J. Milligan	W. J. Milligan	W. J. Milligan	W. J. Milligan
Louisiana	A. H. Batts	Woodrow C. Byrd	Woodrow C. Byrd	Woodrow C. Byrd	C. M. Jenkerson
Maine	J. Stewart Brinsfield	J. Stewart Brinsfield	Wm. F. Morris	Wm. F. Morris	Wm. F. Morris
Maryland	W. J. Milligan	D. C. Boatwright	D. C. Boatwright	D. C. Boatwright	C. C. McAfee
Massachusetts	J. Stewart Brinsfield	J. Stewart Brinsfield	Wm. F. Morris	Wm. F. Morris	Wm. F. Morris
Michigan	E. O. Kerce	E. O. Kerce	Paul H. Walker	Paul H. Walker	Houston R. Morehead
Minnesota	D. L. Lemons	D. L. Lemons 11 H. A. Bobert	Lemuel Johnson	Lemuel Johnson	Lemuel Johnson
Mississippi	J. L. Dorman	Clyde C. Cox	Clyde C. Cox	Clyde C. Cox	Wm. M. Stallings
Missouri	Houston R. Morehead	Houston R. Morehead	G. R. Watson	G. R. Watson	G. R. Watson
Montana	John Sharp	John Sharp	Ray T. Hill	Alvin Thompson	W. H. Godwin

Nebraska	J. L. Goins	W. H. Henry	W. H. Henry	W. H. Henry	W. E. Dowdy
Nevada	I. L. Benge	James L. Slay	James L. Slay	John E. Douglas	John E. Douglas
New Hampshire	J. Stewart Brinsfield	J. Stewart Brinsfield	Wm. F. Morris	Wm. F. Morris	Wm. F. Morris
New Jersey	T. C. Messer	G. W. Lane	G. W. Lane	G. W. Lane	W. E. Tull
New Mexico	H. E. Ramsey	H. E. Ramsey	V. B. Rains	V. B. Rains	L. H. Aultman
New York	T. C. Messer	G. W. Lane	Roland Verrico	J. B. Camp	J. B. Camp
North Carolina	Earl P. Paulk	E. M. Ellis	H. L. Chesser	H. L. Chesser	R. P. Johnson
North Dakota	D. C. Boatwright	Glyndon Logsdon	Glyndon Logsdon	Glyndon Logsdon	Glyndon Logsdon
Ohio	E. C. Clark	E. C. Clark	E. W. Williams	E. W. Williams	J. H. Hughes
Oklahoma	S. J. Wood	H. D. Williams	H. D. Williams	J. L. Dorman	L. L. Hughes
Oregon	John E. Douglas	John E. Douglas	John E. Douglas	C. C. Rains	C. C. Rains
Pennsylvania	Paul H. Walker	Paul H. Walker	J. Stewart Brinsfield	J. Stewart Brinsfield	J. Stewart Brinsfield
Rhode Island	T. C. Messer	G. W. Lane	Wm. F. Morris	J. H. Davis	F. J. Thibodeau
South Carolina	J. D. Bright	M. P. Cross	L. W. McIntyre	L. W. McIntyre	Zeno C. Tharp
South Dakota	D. C. Boatwright	Glyndon Logsdon	Glyndon Logsdon	Glyndon Logsdon	Glyndon Logsdon
Tennessee	John C. Jernigan	J. D. Bright	J. D. Bright	J. D. Bright	U. D. Tidwell
Texas	T. W. Godwin	T. W. Godwin	T. W. Godwin	T. W. Godwin	V. B. Rains
Utah	H. E. Ramsey	H. E. Ramsey	S. J. Wood	D. A. Biggs	D. A. Biggs
Vermont	J. Stewart Brinsfield	J. Stewart Brinsfield	Wm. F. Morris	Wm. F. Morris	Wm. F. Morris
Virginia	W. E. Johnson	W. E. Johnson	W. E. Johnson	W. E. Johnson	D. C. Boatwright
Washington	John E. Douglas	John E. Douglas	John E. Douglas	C. C. Rains	C. C. Rains
West Virginia	M. P. Cross	B. L. Hicks	B. L. Hicks	E. L. Simmons	J. L. Goins
Wisconsin	D. L. Lemons	D. L. Lemons 11 / H. A. Bober†	Lemuel Johnson	Lemuel Johnson	Lemuel Johnson
Wyoming	D. C. Boatwright	John Sharp	R. H. Klaudt	R. H. Klaudt	W. H. Godwin
Central Canada†	M. L. Lowe	M. L. Lowe	M. L. Lowe	Harry Lane	Glenn C. Pettyjohn
Eastern Canada‡	J. Stewart Brinsfield	J. Stewart Brinsfield	Wm. F. Morris	Wm. F. Morris	Wm. F. Morris
Western Canada‡‡	John Sharp	John Sharp 6 / Wm. Pospisil†	Wm. Pospisil	Wm. Pospisil	Wm. Pospisil

STATE OVERSEERS — (Continued)

State	1945-1946	1946-1947	1947-1948	1948-1949	1949-1950
Alabama	J. T. Roberts	J. T. Roberts	J. T. Roberts	W. E. Johnson	W. E. Johnson
Arizona	O. C. Crank	John E. Douglas	John E. Douglas	John E. Douglas	John E. Douglas
Arkansas	M. B. Norris	M. B. Norris	M. B. Norris	L. L. Hughes	L. L. Hughes
California	John E. Douglas	J. H. Hughes	J. H. Hughes	J. H. Hughes	J. H. Hughes
Colorado	R. C. Muncy	R. C. Muncy	R. C. Muncy	W. J. Cothern	W. J. Cothern
Connecticut	J. B. Camp	J. B. Camp	J. B. Camp	J. B. Camp	J. B. Camp
Delaware	Paul H. Walker	O. C. Crank	O. C. Crank	O. C. Crank 8 G. W. Lane†	G. W. Lane
District of Columbia	Paul H. Walker	O. C. Crank	O. C. Crank	O. C. Crank 8 G. W. Lane†	G. W. Lane
Florida	W. E. Johnson	W. E. Johnson	W. E. Johnson	J. T. Roberts	J. T. Roberts
Georgia	A V. Beaube	A. V. Beaube	A. V. Beaube	E. L. Simmons	E. L. Simmons
Idaho	Howard D. Statum	Howard D. Statum	Howard D. Statum	R. C. Muncy	R. C. Muncy
Illinois	E. O. Kerce	M. P. Cross	M. P. Cross	M. P. Cross	M. P. Cross
Indiana	G. W. Lane	C. C. Rains	C. C. Rains	C. C. Rains	C. C. Rains
Iowa	W. H. Henry	H. O. Harris	H. O. Harris	Carl Cox	Carl Cox
Kansas	A. R. Pedigo	A. R. Pedigo	A. R. Pedigo	W. E. Dowdy	W. E. Dowdy
Kentucky	E. W. Williams	L. H. Aultman	L. H. Aultman	L. H. Aultman	L. H. Aultman
Louisiana	John L. Byrd	John L. Byrd	John L. Byrd	T. M. McClendon	T. M. McClendon
Maine	J. B. Camp	J. B. Camp	J. B. Camp	J. B. Camp	J. B. Camp
Maryland	Paul H. Walker	O. C. Crank	O. C. Crank	O. C. Crank 8 G. W. Lane†	G. W. Lane
Massachusetts	J. B. Camp	J. B. Camp	J. B. Camp	J. B. Camp	J. B. Camp
Michigan	Houston R. Morehead	Houston R. Morehead	Houston R. Morehead	D. C. Boatwright	D. C. Boatwright
Minnesota	Lemuel Johnson	W. H. Godwin	W. H. Godwin	Y. W. Kidd	Y. W. Kidd
Mississippi	Wm. M. Stallings	Wm. M. Stallings	Wm. M. Stallings	John L. Byrd	John L. Byrd
Missouri	G. R. Watson	W. H. Henry	W. H. Henry	W. H. Henry	W. H. Henry
Montana	W. H. Godwin	Wm. Pospisil	Wm. Pospisil	Wm. Pospisil	Wm. Pospisil

Nebraska	W. E. Dowdy	W. E. Dowdy	W. E. Dowdy	Carl Cox	Carl Cox
Nevada	Howard D. Statum	Howard D. Statum	Howard D. Statum	J. H. Hughes	J. H. Hughes
New Hampshire	J. B. Camp	J. B. Camp	J. B. Camp	J. B. Camp	J. B. Camp
New Jersey	C. H. Blankenship	C. H. Blankenship	C. H. Blankenship	John Adair	John Adair
New Mexico	L. H. Aultman	Bascom Stanley	Bascom Stanley	Bascom Stanley	Bascom Stanley
New York	C. H. Blankenship	C. H. Blankenship	C. H. Blankenship	John Adair	John Adair
North Carolina	R. P. Johnson	E. W. Williams	E. W. Williams	E. W. Williams	E. W. Williams
North Dakota	C. C. McAfee	C. C. McAfee	C. C. McAfee 8 T. M. McClendon†	Glenn C. Pettyjohn	Glenn C. Pettyjohn
Ohio	J. H. Hughes	J. L. Goins	J. L. Goins	E. C. Clark	E. C. Clark
Oklahoma	L. L. Hughes	L. L. Hughes	L. L. Hughes	C. J. Hindmon	C. J. Hindmon
Oregon	C. C. Rains	Lemuel Johnson	Lemuel Johnson	R. C. Muncy	R. C. Muncy
Pennsylvania	J. Stewart Brinsfield	Glyndon Logsdon	Glyndon Logsdon	Glyndon Logsdon	Glyndon Logsdon
Rhode Island	J. B. Camp	J. B. Camp	J. B. Camp	J. B. Camp	J. B. Camp
South Carolina	Zeno C. Tharp	Zeno C. Tharp	Zeno C. Tharp	Houston R. Morehead	Houston R. Morehead
South Dakota	C. C. McAfee	C. C. McAfee	C. C. McAfee 8 T. M. McClendon†	Glenn C. Pettyjohn	Glenn C. Pettyjohn
Tennessee	U. D. Tidwell	U. D. Tidwell	U. D. Tidwell	A. V. Beaube	A. V. Beaube
Texas	V. B. Rains	E. O. Kerce	E. O. Kerce	E. O. Kerce	E. O. Kerce
Utah	R. C. Muncy	R. C. Muncy	R. C. Muncy	W. J. Cothern	W. J. Cothern
Vermont	J. B. Camp	J. B. Camp	J. B. Camp	J. B. Camp	J. B. Camp
Virginia	D. C. Boatwright	D. C. Boatwright	D. C. Boatwright	John C. Jernigan	John C. Jernigan
Washington	C. C. Rains	Lemuel Johnson	Lemuel Johnson	R. C. Muncy	R. C. Muncy
West Virginia	J. L. Goins	Paul H. Walker	Paul H. Walker	Paul H. Walker	Paul H. Walker
Wisconsin	Lemuel Johnson	Lemuel Johnson	Lemuel Johnson	Y. W. Kidd	Y. W. Kidd
Wyoming	W. H. Godwin	W. H. Godwin	W. H. Godwin	Wm. Pospisil	Wm. Pospisil
Central Canada††	Glenn C. Pettyjohn	Glenn C. Pettyjohn	Glenn C. Pettyjohn	Darrell L. Lindsay	Darrell L. Lindsay
Eastern Canada‡	J. B. Camp	J. B. Camp	J. B. Camp	J. B. Camp	J. B. Camp
Western Canada‡‡	Wm. Pospisil	J. B. Reesor	J. B. Reesor	J. A. Rafferty	J. A. Rafferty

STATE OVERSEERS — (Concluded)

State	1950-1951	1951-1952	1952-1953	1953-1954	1954-1955
Alabama	E. W. Williams 4 H. D. Williams†	(N.) H. D. Williams (S.) H. T. Statum†	(N.) H. D. Williams (S.) H. T. Statum	(N.) H. D. Williams (S.) H. T. Statum	G. W. Lane 14 John L. Byrd†
Arizona	Y. W. Kidd	Y. W. Kidd	C. W. Collins	C. W. Collins	C. W. Collins
Arkansas	L. L. Hughes	L. L. Hughes	G. W. Hodges	G. W. Hodges	G. W. Hodges
California	H. B. Ramsey	H. B. Ramsey	H. B. Ramsey	H. B. Ramsey	Ralph E. Williams
Colorado	W. J. Cothern	W. J. Cothern	A. G. Thompson	A. G. Thompson	A. G. Thompson
Connecticut	D. G. Homner	D. G. Homner	D. G. Homner	D. G. Homner	V. D. Combs
Delaware	G. W. Lane	G. W. Lane	Woodrow C. Byrd	Woodrow C. Byrd	Woodrow C. Byrd
District of Columbia	G. W. Lane	G. W. Lane	Woodrow C. Byrd	Woodrow C. Byrd	Woodrow C. Byrd
Florida	J. T. Roberts	J. T. Roberts	E. L. Simmons	E. L. Simmons	Earl P. Paulk
Georgia	E. L. Simmons	E. L. Simmons	D. C. Boatwright	D. C. Boatwright	D. C. Boatwright
Idaho	F. W. Goff	F. W. Goff	Charles E. Tilley	Charles E. Tilley	Charles E. Tilley
Illinois	James L. Slay	James L. Slay 12 Floyd Timmerman†	Floyd Timmerman	Floyd Timmerman	F. W. Goff
Indiana	C. R. Spain	C. R. Spain	C. R. Spain	C. R. Spain	James A. Stephens
Iowa	Carl Cox	Carl Cox	Joseph L. McCoy	Joseph L. McCoy	Joseph L. McCoy
Kansas	W. E. Dowdy	W. E. Dowdy	Doyle Stanfield	Doyle Stanfield	Doyle Stanfield
Kentucky	R. R. Walker	R. R. Walker	R. R. Walker 15 A. M. Phillips†	A. M. Phillips	A. M. Phillips
Louisiana	T. M. McClendon	T. M. McClendon	Y. W. Kidd	Y. W. Kidd	Y. W. Kidd
Maine	D. G. Homner	D. G. Homner	D. G. Homner	D. G. Homner	V. D. Combs
Maryland	G. W. Lane	G. W. Lane	Woodrow C. Byrd	Woodrow C. Byrd	Woodrow C. Byrd
Massachusetts	D. G. Homner	D. G. Homner	D. G. Homner	D. G. Homner	V. D. Combs
Michigan	M. P. Cross	M. P. Cross	M. P. Cross	M. P. Cross	C. R. Spain
Minnesota	W. A. Nicholson	W. A. Nicholson 8 Estel D. Moore†	Estel D. Moore	Estel D. Moore	G. L. Waters
Mississippi	G. C. Hamby	G. C. Hamby	G. C. Hamby	G. C. Hamby	H. T. Statum
Missouri	Glyndon Logsdon	Glyndon Logsdon	Glyndon Logsdon	Glyndon Logsdon 1; B. E. Ellis†	B. E. Ellis
Montana	Doyle Stanfield	Doyle Stanfield	Manuel F. Campbell	Manuel F. Campbell	A. E. Erickson

Nebraska	W. R. Collins	W. R. Collins	W. R. Collins	W. R. Collins	Frank Bradley
Nevada	H. B. Ramsey	H. B. Ramsey	H. B. Ramsey	H. B. Ramsey	Ralph E. Williams
New Hampshire	D. G. Homner	D. G. Homner	D. G. Homner	D. G. Homner	V. D. Combs
New Jersey	Walter Pettitt	Walter Pettitt	H. R. Appling	H. R. Appling	H. C. Stoppe
New Mexico	J. L. Summers	J. L. Summers	Brady Dennis	Brady Dennis	Brady Dennis
New York	Walter Pettitt	Walter Pettitt 10 / M. W. Sindle†	M. W. Sindle	M. W. Sindle	M. W. Sindle
North Carolina	Earl P. Paulk	Earl P. Paulk	Earl P. Paulk	Earl P. Paulk	L. H. Aultman
North Dakota	T. L. Forrester	T. L. Forrester	L. E. Painter	L. E. Painter	L. E. Painter
Ohio	Paul H. Walker	Paul H. Walker	J. H. Walker	J. H. Walker	J. H. Walker
Oklahoma	C. J. Hindmon	C. J. Hindmon	T. A. Perkins	T. A. Perkins	T. A. Perkins
Oregon	F. W. Goff	F. W. Goff	F. W. Goff	F. W. Goff	D. G. Homner
Pennsylvania	James A. Cross	James A. Cross	C. J. Hindmon	C. J. Hindmon	C. J. Hindmon
Rhode Island	D. G. Homner	D. G. Homner	D. G. Homner	D. G. Homner	V. D. Combs
South Carolina	John L. Byrd	John L. Byrd	James A. Cross	James A. Cross	H. B. Ramsey
South Dakota	T. L. Forrester	T. L. Forrester	L. E. Painter	L. E. Painter	L. E. Painter
Tennessee	A. V. Beaube	A. V. Beaube	W. E. Johnson	W. E. Johnson	W. E. Johnson
Texas	L. H. Aultman	L. H. Aultman	J. D. Bright	J. D. Bright	J. D. Bright
Utah	W. J. Cothern	W. J. Cohern	A. G. Thompson	A. G. Thompson	A. G. Thompson
Vermont	D. G. Homner	D. G. Homner	D. G. Homner	D. G. Homner	V. D. Combs
Virginia	John C. Jernigan 13 / T. W. Godwin†	T. W. Godwin	T. W. Godwin 9 / George D. Lemons†	George D. Lemons	George D. Lemons
Washington	F. W. Goff	F. W. Goff	F. W. Goff	F. W. Goff	D. G. Homner
West Virginia	J. H. Hughes	J. H. Hughes	G. W. Lane	G. W. Lane	G. C. Hamby
Wisconsin	Estel D. Moore	Estel D. Moore	Estel D. Moore	Estel D. Moore	Estel D. Moore
Wyoming	Doyle Stanfield	Doyle Stanfield	Manuel F. Campbell	Manuel F. Campbell	A. E. Erickson
Central Canada††	Darrell L. Lindsay	Darrell L. Lindsay	Wm. F. Sullivan	Wm. F. Sullivan	Wm. F. Sullivan / George W. Ayers†
Eastern Canada‡	D. G. Homner	D. G. Homner	D. G. Homner	D. G. Homner	V. D. Combs
Western Canada‡‡	J. A. Rafferty	J. A. Rafferty 14 / James A. Stephens†	James A. Stephens	James A. Stephens	Wm. H. Pratt

State	1955-1956	1956-1958***	1958-1960	1960-1962	1962-1964	1964-1966
Alabama	John L. Byrd	John L. Byrd	D. A. Biggs	D. A. Biggs	Houston R. Morehead	Houston R. Morehead
Alaska				Millard L. Cowdell	L. L. Hughes	L. L. Hughes
Arizona	C. W. Collins	David L. Lemons	David L. Lemons	J. H. Hughes	J. H. Hughes	O. C. McCane
Arkansas	G. W. Hodges	Brady Dennis	Brady Dennis	Harvey Rose	H. L. Rose	T. F. Harper
California	Ralph E. Williams	Ralph E. Williams	L. W. McIntyre	L. W. McIntyre	Floyd J. Timmerman	Floyd J. Timmerman
Colorado	E. W. Carden	E. W. Carden	James R. Ray	James R. Ray	Ray T. Hill	Ray T. Hill
Connecticut	V. D. Combs	George W. Ayers	George W. Ayers	O. C. McCane	O. C. McCane	P. H. McSwain
Delaware	W. C. Byrd	Ray H. Hughes	Ray H. Hughes	W. J. Brown	W. J. Brown	T. W. Day
Florida	Earl P. Paulk, Sr.	A. M. Phillips	Houston R. Morehead	Houston R. Morehead	James A. Cross	James A. Cross
Georgia	D. C. Boatwright	W. E. Johnson	W. E. Johnson	H. B. Ramsey	H. B. Ramsey	John D. Smith
Hawaii				Ronnie Helton	Z. E. Cagle	Z. E. Cagle
Idaho	Charles E. Tilley	Charles E. Tilley	A. G. Thompson	Howard L. Helms	George W. Broome	George W. Broome
Illinois	F. W. Goff	F. W. Goff	H. T. Statum	C. M. Jinkerson	C. M. Jinkerson	H. L. Rose
Indiana	James A. Stephens	James A. Stephens	L. E. Painter	David L. Lemons	David L. Lemons	Cecil B. Knight
Iowa	Joseph L. McCoy	Grady L. Waters	Grady L. Waters	Grady L. Waters	R. D. Harris	R. D. Harris
Kansas	Doyle Stanfield	L. E. Painter	Charles E. Tilley	Charles E. Tilley	H. D. Sustar	H. D. Sustar
Kentucky	A. M. Phillips	T. A. Perkins	T. A. Perkins	T. L. Forester	T. L. Forester	Earl P. Paulk, Sr.
Louisiana	Y. W. Kidd	V. D. Combs	J. H. Walker, Sr.	A. V. Beaube	A. V. Beaube	A. G. Thompson
Maine	V. D. Combs	George W. Ayers	George W. Ayers	O. C. McCane	O. C. McCane	P. H. McSwain
Maryland	W. C. Byrd	Ray H. Hughes	Ray H. Hughes	W. J. Brown	W. J. Brown	T. W. Day
Massachusetts	V. D. Combs	George W. Ayers	George W. Ayers	O. C. McCane	O. C. McCane	P. H. McSwain
Michigan	C. Raymond Spain	C. Raymond Spain	Floyd J. Timmerman	Floyd J. Timmerman	L. W. McIntyre	L. W. McIntyre
Minnesota	Grady L. Waters	W. J. Brown	W. J. Brown	T. W. Day	T. W. Day	Bert F. Ford
Mississippi	H. T. Statum	H. T. Statum	Wade H. Horton	John D. Smith	John D. Smith	T. L. Forester
Missouri	B. E. Ellis	B. E. Ellis	W. Paul Stallings	W. Paul Stallings	Paul T. Stover	Paul T. Stover
Montana	A. E. Erickson	A. E. Erickson	A. S. Yorkman	J. E. DeVore	J. E. DeVore	Robert White

Nebraska	Frank Bradley	James R. Ray	Ray T. Hill	Ray T. Hill	W. L. Edgar	W. L. Edgar
Nevada	Ralph E. Williams	Ralph E. Williams	L. W. McIntyre	L. W. McIntyre	Floyd J. Timmerman	Floyd J. Timmerman
New Hampshire	V. D. Combs	George W. Ayers	George W. Ayers	O. C. McCane	O. C. McCane	P. H. McSwain
New Jersey	Henry C. Stoppe	Henry C. Stoppe	Henry C. Stoppe	Henry C. Stoppe	Wayne S. Proctor	Wayne S. Proctor
New Mexico	Brady Dennis	D. G. Homner	D. G. Homner	W. M. Horton	W. M. Horton	W. M. Horton
New York	M. W. Sindle	M. W. Sindle	C. E. Yates	C. E. Yates	C. E. Yates	C. E. Yates
North Carolina	L. H. Aultman	L. H. Aultman	John L. Byrd	John L. Byrd	H. D. Williams	H. D. Williams
North Dakota	L. E. Painter	W. Paul Stallings	Paul H. Walker	Paul H. Walker	Paul H. Walker	John D. Nichols
Ohio	J. H. Walker, Sr.	D. C. Boatwright	D. C. Boatwright	F. W. Goff	F. W. Goff	H. B. Ramsey
Oklahoma	T. A. Perkins	G. W. Hodges	G. W. Hodges	A. G. Thompson	A. G. Thompson	Frank L. Muller
Oregon	D. G. Homner	Estel D. Moore	Estel D. Moore	John D. Nichols	John D. Nichols	J. Frank Culpepper
Pennsylvania	C. J. Hindmon	George D. Lemons	George D. Lemons	James A. Stephens	Walter R. Pettitt	Estel D. Moore
Rhode Island	V. D. Combs	George W. Ayers	George W. Ayers	O. C. McCane	O. C. McCane	P. H. McSwain
South Carolina	H. B. Ramsey	H. B. Ramsey	B. E. Ellis	B. E. Ellis	D. A. Biggs	D. A. Biggs
South Dakota	L. E. Painter	W. Paul Stallings	Paul H. Walker	Paul H. Walker	Paul H. Walker	John D. Nichols
Tennessee	W. E. Johnson	W. C. Byrd	W. C. Byrd	Earl P. Paulk, Sr.	Earl P. Paulk, Sr.	L. H. Aultman
Texas	J. D. Bright	(N) C. W. Collins (S) J. H. Walker, Sr.	(N) P. H. McCarn (S) C. W. Collins	P. H. McCarn	W. Paul Stallings	C. M. Jinkerson
Utah	E. W. Carden	E. W. Carden	James R. Ray	James R. Ray	Ray T. Hill	Ray T. Hill
Vermont	V. D. Combs	George W. Ayers	George W. Ayers	O. C. McCane	O. C. McCane	P. H. McSwain
Virginia	George D. Lemons	J. D. Bright	J. D. Bright	James L. Slay	James A. Stephens	James A. Stephens
Washington	D. G. Homner	Estel D. Moore	Estel D. Moore	T. F. Harper	T. F. Harper	M. H. Kennedy
West Virginia	G. C. Hamby	G. C. Hamby	Ralph E. Williams	Ralph E. Williams	P. H. McCarn	F. W. Goff
Wisconsin	Estel D. Moore	W. J. Brown	W. J. Brown	T. W. Day	T. W. Day	J. E. DeVore
Wyoming	A. E. Erickson	A. E. Erickson	C. W. Batson	C. W. Batson	P. F. Taylor	Robert White
Canada	(C) George W. Ayers (E) V. D. Combs (W) W. H. Pratt	(C) C. Raymond Spain (E) George W. Ayers (W) W. H. Pratt	(C) Floyd J. Timmerman (E) George W. Ayers (W) Darrell L. Lindsey			

State	1966-1968	1968-1970	1970-1972	1972-1974	1974-1976	1976-1978
Alabama	G. W. Lane	G. W. Lane	James A. Cross	James A. Cross	E. C. Thomas	C. Raymond Spain
Alaska	L. L. Hughes	L. L. Hughes	Russell A. Brinson	Russell A. Brinson	Bill Rayburn	Bill Rayburn
Arizona	O. C. McCane	Robert White	Robert White	J. Frank Spivey	John E. Black	John E. Black
Arkansas	T. F. Harper	Frank L. Muller	Travis Henderson	Travis Henderson 6 / C. E. Landreth†	C. E. Landreth	Billy P. Bennett
California	Wayne S. Proctor	(N) L. W. McIntyre / (S) Wayne S. Proctor	(N) L. W. McIntyre / (S) B. G. Hamon	(N) Donald S. Aultman / (S) B. G. Hamon	(N) Manuel F. Campbell 14 / (S) W. D. Watkins	(N) James A. Stephens† / (S) Cecil R. Guiles
Colorado	Ray T. Hill	Clifford V. Bridges	Clifford V. Bridges	B. J. Moffett	B. J. Moffett	George W. Alford
Connecticut	P. H. McSwain	Earl P. King	Earl P. King	Earl P. King	R. H. Sumner	R. H. Sumner
Delaware	T. W. Day	O. W. Polen	A. W. Brummett	A. W. Brummett	Robert E. Fisher	B. J. Moffett
Florida	James A. Stephens	D. A. Biggs	D. A. Biggs	(T) Ralph E. Williams / (J) H. G. Poitier	(T) Ralph E. Williams / (J) W. C. Menendez	(T) Bennie S. Triplett / (J) W. C. Menendez
Georgia	John D. Smith	W. C. Byrd	W. C. Byrd 16 / Floyd J. Timmerman†	Floyd J. Timmerman	Ray H. Hughes	(N) Paul F. Henson / (S) Robert J. Hart
Hawaii	Z. E. Cagle 6 / C. E. Allred†	Robert E. Fisher	Robert E. Fisher	Robert E. Fisher	Bill F. Sheeks	Bill F. Sheeks
Idaho	George W. Broome	H. B. Thompson	H. B. Thompson	H. B. Thompson	Jessie M. Boyd	Jessie M. Boyd
Illinois	H. L. Rose	John D. Nichols	Wayne S. Proctor	Wayne S. Proctor	H. B. Thompson	H. B. Thompson
Indiana	Cecil B. Knight	P. H. McSwain	P. H. McSwain	Bennie S. Triplett	Bennie S. Triplett	A. A. Ledford
Iowa	W. M. Horton	Charles E. Tilley	A. A. Ledford	A. A. Ledford	A. A. Ledford	David Lanier
Kansas	W. L. Edgar	Bert F. Ford	Bert F. Ford	Rex Hudson	Rex Hudson	W. A. Bingham
Kentucky	W. C. Byrd	W. J. Brown	W. J. Brown	P. H. McSwain	P. H. McSwain	Clifford V. Bridges
Louisiana	A. G. Thompson	J. E. DeVore	J. E. DeVore	Clifford V. Bridges	Clifford V. Bridges	Terrell Taylor
Maine	Rex Hudson	Rex Hudson	Rex Hudson	E. M. Abbott	E. M. Abbott	A. S. Yorkman
Maryland	T. W. Day	O. W. Polen	A. W. Brummett	A. W. Brummett	Robert E. Fisher	B. J. Moffett
Massachusetts	P. H. McSwain	Earl P. King	Earl P. King	Earl P. King	R. H. Sumner	R. H. Sumner
Michigan	Estel D. Moore	Estel D. Moore	Lewis J. Willis	Walter R. Pettitt	Walter R. Pettitt	O. C. McCane
Minnesota	Bert F. Ford	Terrell Taylor	Terrell Taylor	James E. Allen	Ray H. Sanders	Ray H. Sanders
Mississippi	T. L. Forester	J. Frank Culpepper	H. D. Sustar	H. D. Sustar	B. G. Hamon	W. C. Ratchford
Missouri	A. W. Brummett	A. W. Brummett	R. D. Harris	R. D. Harris	Vessie D. Hargrave	E. M. Abbott
Montana	Robert White	J. Frank Spivey	J. Frank Spivey	Cheslie N. Collins	Cheslie N. Collins	W. G. Abney

Nebraska	Gene D. Rice	Gene D. Rice	W. C. Ratchford	W. C. Ratchford	W. C. Ratchford	W. C. Ratchford	Paul F. Barker
Nevada	Wayne S. Proctor	(N) L. W. McIntyre (S) Wayne S. Proctor	(N) L. W. McIntyre (S) B. G. Hamon	(N) L. W. McIntyre (S) B. G. Hamon	(N) Donald S. Aultman (S) B. G. Hamon	(N) Manuel F. Campbell 14 (S) W. D. Watkins	(N) James A. Stephens† (S) Cecil R. Guiles
New Hampshire	Rex Hudson	Rex Hudson	Rex Hudson	E. M. Abbott	E. M. Abbott	E. M. Abbott	A. S. Yorkman
New Jersey	Travis Henderson	Travis Henderson	Paul J. Eure	Paul J. Eure	Paul J. Eure	F. L. Braddock	Wayne Taylor
New Mexico	Mark G. Summers 14 B. G. Hamon†	B. G. Hamon	Thomas H. Ashley	Thomas H. Ashley	Thomas H. Ashley	J. Newby Thompson	J. Newby Thompson
New York	R. D. Harris	R. D. Harris	Manuel F. Campbell	Manuel F. Campbell (NYC) J. D. Golden	Manuel F. Campbell (NYC) J. D. Golden	John E. Lemons (NYC) J. D. Golden	John E. Lemons (NYC) J. D. Golden
North Carolina	David L. Lemons	David L. Lemons	P. H. McCarn	P. H. McCarn	P. H. McCarn	C. Raymond Spain	E. C. Thomas
North Dakota	John D. Nichols	Bennie S. Triplett	Bennie S. Triplett	Robert J. Hart	Robert J. Hart	Robert J. Hart	Delbert D. Rose
Ohio	H. B. Ramsey	(N) Raymond E. Crowley* (S) L. H. Aultman	(N) Raymond E. Crowley (S) L. H. Aultman	(N) Raymond E. Crowley (S) W. J. Brown	(N) Raymond E. Crowley (S) W. J. Brown	(N) Billy P. Bennett (S) W. J. Brown	(N) B. A. Brown (S) W. D. Watkins
Oklahoma	Frank L. Muller	O. C. McCane	O. C. McCane	O. C. McCane	Paul F. Henson	Paul F. Henson	F. L. Braddock
Oregon	J. Frank Culpepper	B. A. Brown	B. A. Brown	Terrell Taylor	Terrell Taylor	Terrell Taylor	B. L. Kelley
Pennsylvania	Paul T. Stover	Paul T. Stover	Gene D. Rice	Gene D. Rice	Gene D. Rice	Earl P. King	Earl P. King
Rhode Island	P. H. McSwain	Earl P. King	Earl P. King	Earl P. King	Earl P. King	R. H. Sumner	R. H. Sumner
South Carolina	Wade H. Horton	Vessie D. Hargrave	J. Frank Culpepper	J. Frank Culpepper	J. Frank Culpepper	P. H. McCarn	P. H. McCarn
South Dakota	John D. Nichols	Bennie S. Triplett	Bennie S. Triplett	Bennie S. Triplett	Robert J. Hart	Robert J. Hart	Delbert D. Rose
Tennessee	L. H. Aultman	Ralph E. Williams	Ralph E. Williams	Ralph E. Williams	D. A. Biggs	D. A. Biggs	Gene D. Rice
Texas	C. M. Jinkerson	M. H. Kennedy	M. H. Kennedy	L. W. McIntyre	L. W. McIntyre	Gene D. Rice	C. E. Landreth
Utah	Ray T. Hill	John D. Nichols	H. B. Thompson	H. B. Thompson	H. B. Thompson	Jessie M. Boyd	Jessie M. Boyd
Vermont	Rex Hudson	Rex Hudson	Rex Hudson	Rex Hudson	E. M. Abbott	E. M. Abbott	A. S. Yorkman
Virginia	H. D. Sustar	H. D. Sustar	E. C. Thomas	E. C. Thomas	E. C. Thomas	E. C. Thomas	M. H. Kennedy
Washington	M. H. Kennedy	George W. Broome	W. D. Watkins	W. D. Watkins	W. D. Watkins	Russell A. Brinson	Russell A. Brinson
West Virginia	F. W. Goff	Walter R. Pettitt	Walter R. Pettitt	Robert White	Robert White	Paul J. Eure	Paul J. Eure
Wisconsin	J. E. DeVore	Billy P. Bennett	Billy P. Bennett	Billy P. Bennett	Billy P. Bennett	Billy P. Bennett	Jack H. Adams
Wyoming	Robert White	Clifford V. Bridges	Clifford V. Bridges	B. J. Moffett	B. J. Moffett	B. J. Moffett	George W. Alford
Canada							

NOTES TO STATE OVERSEERS' TABLE

*Appointed between Assemblies.

**Not officially appointed, but supervised the state work.

***Beginning in 1956 the listings are biennial rather than annual.

†Replaced former overseer between Assemblies.

††Central Canada refers to Ontario.

‡Eastern Canada refers to Nova Scotia.

‡‡Western Canada refers to Saskatchewan, Alberta and Manitoba.

1 Removed from office because of betrayal of trust concerning the impeachment of A. J. Tomlinson.

2 Removed from office because of indecision during Tomlinson impeachment; later proved loyalty to the church.

3 Replaced because of failure to move permanently to the state.

4 Resigned because of ill health.

5 Resigned to become pastor of North Cleveland, Tennessee, church.

6 Resigned for personal reasons.

7 Resigned to do evangelistic work.

8 Removed from office.

9 Died in office.

10 Resigned to devote full time to oversight of other states.

11 Resigned because of illness in family.

12 Resigned to do missionary-evangelistic work in South Africa.

13 Resigned to accept presidency of Lee College.

14 Resigned to accept local pastorate.

15 Resigned to become Superintendent of Home for Children.

16 Elected Third Assistant General Overseer April 15, 1972.

C—Central

E—East

J—Jacksonville

N—North

S—South

T—Tampa

W—West

BIBLIOGRAPHY

ARCHIVES

Archives of the Church of God, Cleveland, Tennessee.
> The official files of the Church of God, correspondence, records, reports and minutes of most boards and committees, are housed in the General Offices of the Church of God.

Lee College Pentecostal Research Center, Cleveland, Tennessee.
> This is the most extensive collection of Pentecostal materials in the Church of God, and one of the finest in the Pentecostal world. It houses all known published works and numerous unpublished manuscripts.

Church of God Publishing House Research Library, Cleveland, Tennessee.
> This library specializes in materials relating to the publishing interests of the Church of God.

Archives of Church of God World Missions, Cleveland, Tennessee.
> Files on all countries outside the United States and Canada where the Church of God operates were made available.

Archives of the European Church of God, Urbach, Germany.
> Official files of the Church of God in the European countries are housed here. This was very helpful in this area of research.

Latin American Official Files, San Antonio, Texas.
> The collection of materials here covers all areas of the Church of God in Latin America. It was an invaluable source for major portions of my research.

PRIMARY AND OFFICIAL SOURCES

Admatha, Annual of the International Preparatory Institute, San Antonio, Texas, 1952.

Alford, Denton L. *Music in the Pentecostal Church.* Cleveland, Tennessee: Pathway Press, 1967.

Book of Doctrines, The. A symposium. Cleveland, Tennessee: Church of God Publishing House, c. 1920.

Buckalew, J. W. *Incidents in the Life of J. W. Buckalew.* Cleveland, Tennessee: Church of God Publishing House, c. 1920.

Church of God Evangel. Volumes 1-67, Cleveland, Tennessee: Church of God Publishing House, 1910-1976.

Clark, E. C. *Marvelous Healings God Wrought Among Us.* Cleveland, Tennessee: Church of God Publishing House, c. 1946.

Conn, Charles Paul. *The Music Makers.* Cleveland, Tennessee: Pathway Press, 1958.

Conn, Charles W. *Pillars of Pentecost.* Cleveland, Tennessee: Pathway Press, 1956.

—— *The Evangel Reader.* Cleveland, Tennessee: Pathway Press, 1958.

—— *Where the Saints Have Trod.* Cleveland, Tennessee: Pathway Press, 1959.

—— *Journal.* 21 volumes, 1955-1976. Unpublished.

Cook, Robert F. *A Quarter Century of Divine Leading in India.* Ootacamund, South India: Ootacamund & Nilgiri Press, *c.* 1939.

—— *Half a Century of Divine Leading.* Cleveland, Tennessee: Church of God Missions Department, 1955.

Cross, J. A. *Healing in the Church.* Cleveland, Tennessee: Pathway Press, 1962.

Echols, Evaline, editor. *Lee College Faculty Handbook.* Cleveland, Tennessee: Lee College, 1976.

Ellis, J. B. *Blazing the Gospel Trail.* Cleveland, Tennessee: Church of God Publishing House, *c.* 1941. (Reprint edition: Plainfield, New Jersey: Logos International, 1976.)

El Evangelio de la Iglesia de Dios, Volumes 1-14. Cleveland, Tennessee: Church of God Publishing House; San Antonio, Texas: Editorial Evangélica, 1945-1959.

Furman, Charles T. *Guatemala and the Story of Chuce.* Cleveland, Tennessee: Church of God Publishing House, 1940.

Gause, R. H. *Church of God Polity.* Cleveland, Tennessee: Pathway Press, 1973.

Hargrave, Vessie D. *Evangelical Social Work in Latin America.* San Antonio, Texas: Trinity University, 1951. An unpublished Master of Science thesis.

——, *South of the Rio Bravo.* Cleveland, Tennessee: Church of God Missions Department, 1952.

Harrison, Alda B. *Mountain Peaks of Experience.* Cleveland, Tennessee: Church of God Publishing House, n.d.

Horton, E. Gene. *A History of Lee Junior College.* Vermillion, South Dakota: University of South Dakota, 1953. An unpublished Master of Education thesis.

Horton, Wade H., editor. *The Glossalalia Phenomenon.* Cleveland, Tenn.; Pathway Press, 1966.

Ingram, J. H. *Around the World With the Gospel Light.* Cleveland, Tennessee: Church of God Publishing House, 1938.

Juillerat, L. Howard, editor. *Book of Minutes.* Annual Assembly Minutes, 1-13, 1906-1917, Cleveland, Tennessee: Church of God Publishing House, 1922.

Knight, Cecil B. *An Historical Study of Distinctions Among the Divergent Groupings of American Pentecostalism.* Indianapolis, Indiana: Butler University, 1968. An unpublished Master of Arts thesis.

Lauster, Herman. *The Hand of God and the Gestapo.* Cleveland, Tennessee: Church of God Missions Department, 1952.

Lee, F. J. *Diary.* 4 volumes, 1914-1926. Unpublished.

——, *Book of General Instructions for the Ministry and Membership.* Cleveland, Tennessee: Church of God Publishing House, 1927.

Lee, Mrs. F. J. *Life Sketch and Sermons of F. J. Lee.* Cleveland, Tennessee: Church of God Publishing House, *c.* 1929.

Lemons, F. W. *Our Pentecostal Heritage.* Cleveland, Tennessee: Pathway Press, 1963.

Lighted Pathway, The. Volumes 1-47. Cleveland, Tennessee: Church of God Publishing House, 1929-1976.

Macedonian Call, The. Volumes 1-4. Cleveland, Tennessee: Church of God Publishing House, 1945-1950.

McBrayer, Terrell. *Lee College, Pioneer in Pentecostal Education.* Cleveland, Tennessee: Pathway Press, 1968.

McCracken, Horace, editor. *History of Church of God Missions.* Cleveland, Tennessee: Church of God Missions Department, 1943.

McLain, T. L. *Diary.* Unpublished.

Memorabilia. Annual of International Bible College, Estevan, Saskatchewan, 1947-1948.

Minutes of the General Assembly of the Church of God. Volumes 1-56. 1906-1976. Cleveland, Tennessee: Church of God Publishing House.

O Evangelho da Igreja de Deus. Volume 5. Rio de Janerio, 1957.

On Guard, Volumes 1-15. Cleveland, Tennessee: Church of God Servicemen's Department, April 1961—December 1976.

Paulk, Earl P., Jr. *Your Pentecostal Neighbor.* Cleveland, Tennessee: Pathway Press, 1958.

Pullin, Alice. *In the Morning, Sow.* Cleveland, Tennessee: Church of God Missions Department.

Pulse. Vol. 1. Cleveland, Tennessee: Church of God Department of Education, 1976.

Simmons, E. L. *History of the Church of God.* Cleveland, Tennessee: Church of God Publishing House, 1938. Also, the manuscript of an unpublished Revised Edition.

Slay, James L., *This We Believe.* Cleveland, Tennessee: Pathway Press, 1963.

Sow. Volumes 1-15. Cleveland, Tennessee: Church of God World Missions Department, 1961-1976.

Tomlinson, A. J. *Answering the Call of God.* Cleveland, Tennessee: The White Wing Publishing House, n.d.

——, *Journal of Happenings.* 5 volumes, 1901-1923. Original manuscripts.

Vindagua. Annual of Lee College, Cleveland, Tennessee, Vol. 1-36, 1941-1977.

Walker, J. H. Jr., *L'Eglise de Dieu, Ensignments et Organiations.* Port-au-Prince: privately published, 1949.

Walker, John Herbert, Jr., and Walker, Lucille. *Haiti.* Cleveland, Tennessee: Church of God Publishing House, 1950.

Walker, Paul H. *Paths of a Pioneer.* Cleveland, Tennessee: Pathway Press, 1971.

Walker, R. R. *My Testimony.* Cleveland, Tennessee: Church of God Publishing House, c. 1942.

COLLATERAL SOURCES

Bartleman, Frank. *How "Pentecost" Came to Los Angeles.* Los Angeles: F. Bartleman, 1925.

Brumback, Carl. *"What Meaneth This?"* Springfield, Missouri: The Gospel Publishing House, 1947.

Campbell, Joseph E. *The Pentecostal Holiness Church, 1898-1948.* Franklin Springs, Georgia: The Publishing House of the Pentecostal Holiness Church, 1951.

Clark, Elmer T. *The Small Sects in America.* Nashville, Tennessee: Abingdon-Cokesbury, 1937. Revised Edition, 1949.

Frodsham, Stanley H. *With Signs Following.* Revised Edition. Springfield, Missouri: Gospel Publishing House, 1941.

Gee, Donald. *The Pentecostal Movement.* London: Elim Publishing Co.,

Hollenweger, Walter J. *The Pentecostals.* Minneapolis: Augsburg Publishing House, 1972.

Miller, Elmer C. *Pentecost Examined.* Springfield, Missouri: Gospel Publishing House, 1936.

Nichol, John Thomas. *Pentecostalism.* New York: Harper & Rowe, Publishers, 1966.

BACKGROUND SOURCES

Bainton, Roland, *Here I Stand.* Nashville, Tennessee: Abingdon-Cokesbury, 1950.

Callahan, North. *Smoky Mountain Country.* New York: Duell, Sloan, and Pearce, 1952.

Cannon, William R. *The Theology of John Wesley.* Nashville, Tennessee: Abingdon-Cokesbury, 1946.

Drummond, Andrew Landale. *Story of American Protestantism.* Boston: The Beacon Press, 1950.

Durant, Will. *The Story of Civilization:* Caesar and Christ. New York: Simon and Schuster, 1944.

Evangelical Action! A symposium. Boston: United Action Press, 1942.

Hamer, Philip M. *Tennessee—A History, 1673-1932.* New York: The American Historical Society, Inc., 1933.

Hyma, Albert. *World History—A Christian Interpretation.* Revised Edition. Grand Rapids, Michigan: Wm. B. Eerdmans Publishing House, 1952.

Kuiper, B. K. *The Church in History.* Grand Rapids, Michigan: Wm. B. Eerdmans Publishing Company, 1951.

Latourette, Kenneth Scott. *A History of Christianity.* New York: Harper and Brothers Publishers, 1953.

Lindsell, Harold, *Park Street Prophet.* Wheaton, Illinois: Van Kampen Press, 1951.

Luccock, Halford E.; Hutchinson, Paul; Goodloe, Robert W. *The Story of Methodism.* New York: Abingdon-Cokesbury, 1949.

Mead, Frank S. *The March of Eleven Men.* New York: The Bobbs-Merrill Company, 1932.

Miller, Perry; Calhoun, Robert L.; Pusey, Nathan M.; and Niebuhr, Reinhold. *Religion and Freedom of Thought.* New York: Doubleday and Company, Inc., 1954.

Morris, Richard B. *Encyclopedia of American History.* New York: Harper and Brothers, 1953.

Schaff, Philip. *History of the Christian Church.* Volumes 1-8. New York: Charles Scribner's Sons, 1910.

Smith, W. Earle. *Foundations for Freedom.* Philadelphia: The Judson Press, 1952.

Stuber, Stanley I. *How We Got Our Denominations.* New York: Association Press, 1951.

Sweet, William Warren. *Revivalism in America.* New York: Charles Scribner's Sons, 1944.

PERSONAL INTERVIEWS

Part One
THE PENTECOSTAL AWAKENING
1886-1905

Agnes Bryant Benton
Julius Bryant
Nettie Bryant
W. F. Bryant

W. M. Coleman
Tom Elrod
F. W. Lemons
M. S. Lemons

Ella Bryant Robinson
Richard G. Spurling, III

Part Two
THE PENTECOSTAL FRONTIER
1905-1920

D. P. Barnett
Agnes Bryant Benton
E. J. Boehmer
Nettie Bryant
W. F. Bryant
Nora I. Chambers
M. P. Cross
J. B. Ellis
W. V. Eneas

Ella Fry
J. R. Kinser
Mrs. F. J. Lee
F. W. Lemons
M. S. Lemons
Alora Lee McLain
Lillie Lee Million
Carl M. Padgett
T. S. Payne

Sam C. Perry
Mrs. L. A. Richard
Ella Robinson
F. L. Ryder
E. L. Simmons
Zeno C. Tharp
Milton A. Tomlinson
G. R. Watson
John O. Yates

Part Three
TRIAL BY DISILLUSION
1920-1923

E. J. Boehmer
Nettie Bryant
W. F. Bryant
M. P. Cross
J. B. Ellis

J. R. Kinser
Mrs. F. J. Lee
F. W. Lemons
M. S. Lemons
T. S. Payne

E. L. Simmons
Zeno C. Tharp
Milton A. Tomlinson
Paul H. Walker
V. C. Weech

Part Four
THE DEEPENING YEARS
1923-1935

E. J. Boehmer
M. P. Cross
Mrs. M. P. Cross
Alda B. Harrison
John C. Jernigan
R. P. Johnson

Barbara King
S. W. Latimer
F. W. Lemons
Sallie Bell McCune
Houston R. Morehead
Alice Pullin

Thomas Pullin
E. L. Simmons
Zeno C. Tharp
Paul H. Walker
G. R. Watson
Ethel Zaukelius

Part Five
THE FLOWERING OF PENTECOST
1936-1956

Maria W. Atkinson
A. V. Beaube
E. J. Boehmer
Cecil B. Bridges
J. Stewart Brinsfield
A. W. Brummett
R. Leonard Carroll
H. R. Carter
Margarette Catha
H. L. Chesser
E. C. Clark
Robert F. Cook
James A. Cross
David duPlessis
V. B. (Vep) Ellis
C. E. French
Ellen B. French
Margaret Gaines
R. H. Gause

Vessie D. Hargrave
D. B. Hatfield
Wade H. Horton
Ray H. Hughes
J. H. Ingram
H. G. Jenkins
John C. Jernigan
John P. Kluzit
Boutros Labib
Herman Lauster
Lydia Lauster
F. W. Lemons
Marcos Mazzucco
Mario Mazzucco
Wayne C. McAfee
Otis L. McCoy
M. G. McLuhan
Houston R. Morehead
Edmund Outhouse

Johnny M. Owens
Earl P. Paulk, Sr.
George Savchenko
E. L. Simmons
Pearl M. Stark
Hanna K. Suleiman
Peter Swanepoel
E. M. Tapley
Alex Thompson
T. M. Varughese
Irene Wales
J. H. Walker, Sr.
Paul H. Walker
R. R. Walker
Albert J. Widmer
H. D. Williams
Ralph E. Williams
Lewis J. Willis
Dorothy Wooderson

Part Six
THE THRESHOLD OF GREATNESS
1956-1976

Delton L. Alford
W. D. Alton
J. Don Amison
Donald S. Aultman
L. H. Aultman
Charles R. Beach
Antonino Bonilla
Clifford V. Bridges
A. W. Brummett
Stanley Butler
R. Leonard Carroll
Lovell R. Cary
Virginia Cary
Margarette Catha
James A. Cross
Lambert DeLong
Mary Lauster DeLong
Evaline Echols
R. P. Fields
C. E. French
Ellen B. French
Margaret Gaines

R. H. Gause
Yung-Chul Han
Vessie D. Hargrave
Edward Hasmatali
L. E. Heil
Ho L. Senduk
Wade H. Horton
Ray H. Hughes
Khoe Soe Liem
Cecil B. Knight
Bobbie Lauster
Herman Lauster
Walter Lauster
David L. Lemons
James E. Lewis
Andre Marcelin
Millard Maynard
T. D. Mooneyham
Odine Morse
Ong Ling Kok.
Earl P. Paulk, Jr.
Earl P. Paulk, Sr.

A. M. Phillips
H. G. Poitier
O. W. Polen
Alejandro Portugal
Carl Richardson
J. T. Roberts
Heinrich Scherz
C. Raymond Spain
Roy Stricklin
Luke R. Summers
G. A. Swanson
E. C. Thomas
Bennie S. Triplett
Laud O. Vaught
J. H. Walker, Jr.
Lucille Walker
Paul H. Walker
Horace Ward, Jr.
Andre Weber
H. D. Williams
Ralph E. Williams
Lewis J. Willis

INDEX

INDEX TO SCRIPTURAL REFERENCES

DATE DUE

AG 27 '85		
Sept. 10		
JE 26 '86		
AG 19 '86		
MY 14 '87		
MR 31 88		
NOV 2 4		
MY 9 '91		
FEB 28 '94		
MAY 4 '98		
JUL 2 0		

HIGHSMITH 45-102   PRINTED IN U.S.A.